A CORNISHMAN ABROAD

Books by A. L. Rowse

Literature

A CORNISH CHILDHOOD
A CORNISHMAN AT OXFORD

POEMS OF A DECADE
POEMS CHIEFLY CORNISH
POEMS OF DELIVERANCE
POEMS PARTLY AMERICAN
POEMS OF CORNWALL AND AMERICA
STRANGE ENCOUNTER: POEMS

SHAKESPEARE THE MAN
WILLIAM SHAKESPEARE: A BIOGRAPHY
SHAKESPEARE'S SONNETS: A MODERN
    EDITION WITH NOTES
SHAKESPEARE'S SOUTHAMPTON
CHRISTOPHER MARLOWE: A BIOGRAPHY
SIMON FORMAN: SEX AND SOCIETY IN
    SHAKESPEARE'S AGE

JONATHAN SWIFT: MAJOR PROPHET
TIMES, PERSONS, PLACES
THE ENGLISH SPIRIT: ESSAYS IN
    HISTORY AND LITERATURE
DISCOVERIES AND REVIEWS FROM
    RENAISSANCE TO RESTORATION
MATTHEW ARNOLD: POET AND
    PROPHET

CORNISH STORIES
PETER, THE WHITE CAT OF TRENARREN
A CORNISH ANTHOLOGY
BROWN BUCK: A CALIFORNIAN
    FANTASY

History

SIR RICHARD GRENVILLE OF THE
    REVENGE
TUDOR CORNWALL
THE CORNISH IN AMERICA

THE ENGLAND OF ELIZABETH I
THE EXPANSION OF ELIZABETHAN
    ENGLAND
THE ELIZABETHAN RENAISSANCE:
    (I) THE LIFE OF THE SOCIETY
    (II) THE CULTURAL ACHIEVEMENT

RALEGH AND THE THROCKMORTONS
THE ELIZABETHANS AND AMERICA

THE EARLY CHURCHILLS
THE LATER CHURCHILLS

THE SPIRIT OF ENGLISH HISTORY
BOSWORTH FIELD
THE TOWER OF LONDON IN THE
    HISTORY OF THE NATION
WINDSOR CASTLE IN THE HISTORY OF
    ENGLAND
OXFORD IN THE HISTORY OF THE
    NATION

ALL SOULS AND APPEASEMENT
THE END OF AN EPOCH

ST AUSTELL: CHURCH, TOWN, PARISH
VICTORIAN AND EDWARDIAN CORN-
WALL FROM OLD PHOTOGRAPHS
(with Sir John Betjeman)

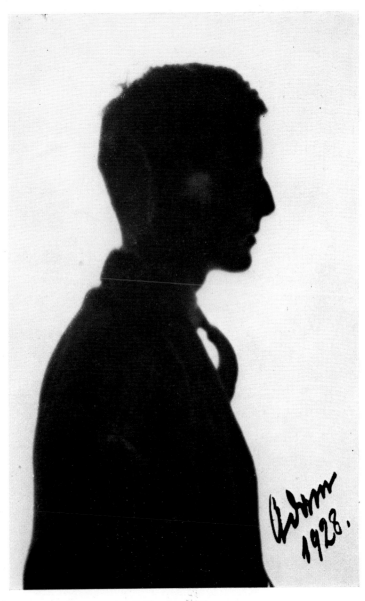

Adam von Trott

A Cornishman Abroad

A. L. Rowse

JONATHAN CAPE

THIRTY BEDFORD SQUARE LONDON

FIRST PUBLISHED 1976
© 1976 BY A. L. ROWSE
JONATHAN CAPE LTD, 30 BEDFORD SQUARE, LONDON WCI
ISBN 0 224 01244 4

To Noreen
my old schoolfriend
with love over the years

Printed in Great Britain by
Cox & Wyman Ltd,
London, Fakenham and Reading

ACKNOWLEDGMENTS

I am indebted to Lord David Cecil, Mrs T. S. Eliot, Graham Greene, and Sir Penderel Moon for kind permission to quote passages from original letters addressed to me.

A.L.R.

Contents

The great advantage of being a writer is that one can say exactly what one thinks.

Voltaire

A man of the people ... a free spirit who could let his powers develop to the full, without having to keep glancing nervously over his shoulder.

John Gross

Prologue: Summer in Cornwall

O the sense of the beauty of life, in this sixtieth year of my age. (Picasso: 'At sixty we are young, but it is too late.') But not too late—never have I felt it more acutely, more intensely, pressing in upon me at every moment as if this were to be my last! Never have I known a more beautiful summer (except the fatal summers of 1914 and 1940), or Trenarren in greater beauty. The last two days—last of August and first of September 1964—there have been hot sun and a high south-easterly gale. At this moment the heat-hazy blue bay is running white horses in full career, hurrying along, crested manes flowing, breaking at the Point. Not a boat out in these sizzling summer seas, though frequently I have looked up from work this August to see Shelley-white sails spreading wings across the crystalline-blue bay. Or I have come down the narrow neck of lane from Lobb's Shop (who was Lobb? a common enough Cornish name—evidently a blacksmith with smithy annexed: neither shop nor smithy now) to see the inset of the bay from Silvermine and Gwendra to Porthpean[1] and beyond. At this moment a whole crew of seagulls are making their difficult way inland in high wind across the valley. I watch the frantic spiralling upwards of a leaf caught in the summer gale; a moment later, a superb Red Admiral borne along the terrace.

Hardly ever have I been in such a press of work, such a tight schedule to get *Shakespeare's Southampton* finished, the proofs of *A Cornishman at Oxford* done and various urgent articles, before leaving for America. And all the while there was the summer campaign in the garden—a subtropical jungle when I came

[1] Gwendra means 'white place'; I suspect it may have been Gwendreath, meaning 'white sand'. Porthpean means 'little beach'.

down in July—having to work with each of the men in turn to get it cleared and in some order before I leave. Yet, tired out every night, limbs aching, never have I had such a sense of enjoyment.

At my homecoming there was all the hay on more than an acre of steep bank and paddock, which had been cut, to rake up and burn. I started the very evening I arrived, having driven down from Oxford. Too hurried properly to savour them, yet there were the scents and sounds in the air, the forms and shapes of Trenarren just round the corner of one's eye as one worked. Someone asked Miss Jekyll once whether she got much pleasure out of working so hard in her garden. Perhaps not, the great gardener allowed—and then, on reflection, sometimes on leaving after a hard day's work she turned round and looked, and it caught her by the throat. Evidently one of those 'Tintern Abbey' moments of illumination such as I experience again and again on looking up, in the midst of working like a galley-slave. The sibilance of all the trees in the ocean of sound above one; the melancholy beauty of the waiting house on the terrace, the more exquisite for its strange, not unfriendly, melancholy—merely withdrawn, as if waiting, listening, looking; those well-proportioned Georgian windows with the faint purple sheen in the glass. There is a strangeness in my relation to the house, which is not mine: I used to long to live here so ardently as boy and youth, yet now that I am its occupant, it is still its fate to be deserted, when I am so much at Oxford and in America. I might be described as its visitant, almost a *revenant*.

No one could have got more into, or out of, a summer than I have this year 1964—Shakespeare Year. Not only the Shakespeare campaign I embarked on on my return from the Huntington Library, which I deliberately undertook to deal with the fatuous critics. Even some of that I enjoyed, though a chore that should not have been necessary in the least; then my four or five days in Paris in May, lecturing at the Sorbonne, very much taken under the wing of Princess Bibesco (she once described Colette to me with a curious word, 'un peu couveuse'—it rather described her solicitous kindness to me: she introduced me to Proust's Faubourg, I was even taken to lunch with a Grammont—that made me feel still closer to Proust. Behind the dining-table was a portrait of

Louis XV, and beneath this the young son of the house descended from him.)

Still more, there were the Birthday Celebrations at Stratford—not that they asked me as a guest among the 'official' representatives from all over the world. What did *he* mean to all those pomposities, and who will remember them the day after they are gone? It was all the more poignant to go to the church alone when all was over, and, with nobody watching, to throw my flower over the communion rail upon the grave. It was a little sprig of flowering currant I picked from the ground he owned outside, coming round the corner to the church-way he often came along. It meant far more than the grand official wreaths piled up from all over the world by the grand official guests, of whom I was not one. But all alone in the evening, the church now empty, I could not refrain from tears, remembering him and all that he meant to me.

My unofficial visits to Stratford yielded far more secret pleasure—swishing along the Warwickshire lanes, long grasses and all the flourish of May and June, up the long hill he knew well that drops down to Alcester; passing by Oversley, which Sir George Throckmorton had an eye on and grudged to Thomas Cromwell, as I remembered from when researching thereabouts for *Ralegh and the Throckmortons*. And so on to their Coughton, and all those tombs in the church, myself among them holding forth that golden summer afternoon to the congregation crowded in the pews. Or that other afternoon, hot and fragrant, to the grandeur of Ragley, the splendid Gibbs entrance hall, Adam stables a semicircle at the back, and the charming *châtelaine* to show me round. Or exploring up lanes and byroads to other vanished Throckmorton places, eating my picnic lunch in the cool, shadowed by beeches and chestnuts at Haseley, of the Puritan Clement Throckmorton, who got it from his Catholic uncle Michael, confidant in exile of Cardinal Pole. Or up into bare wolds to a lonely church where lie the Petos, of that old family—not a house now—and a splendid classic monument, black and white marble, by Nicholas Stone, hidden away in that secret spot.

Most of all I have enjoyed my West Country forays into Devon and Somerset—the week-end at Dunster, worn out with pulling and dragging and hooking and raking, sitting quietly alone all

Sunday morning on the terrace looking across to the Quantocks and the Bristol Channel; all the scents of roses, magnolias, lilies, box, around me, and over the great Castle mound the bells of Dunster church ringing to morning service. Thence on across Somerset to the Mendips, and a day with the Waldegraves seeing their treasures, talking of Duchess Sarah and her daughters, looking at letters and manuscripts, of which they have thousands in that scholarly house—a miniature Public Record Office for the eighteenth century.

On my way back, hot and dusty with archives and driving, a few miles down valley from Tiverton I happened upon a paradise of a tea-garden—beside the Exe, unspoiled Elizabethan bridge, deep salmon-pools on either side, the noise of water over the weir loud and refreshing, drowning any other noise. Where was I? It must be Bickleigh I decided, mounting the hill to the church, for there was the Carew girl from the Castle, who married a Cornish Erisey from the Lizard and died in childbirth. There she is on her tomb—I had remembered her from thirty years before—the years bearing their rich burden, like the fruits, golden and ruddy, in an orchard.—As it might be the orchard at the bottom of the garden where I have been pruning the apple trees and feeding them with ash from the fires, with Jack and George; old Mr Julyan attending to the kitchen-garden up over the ferny steps under the thick fig trees.

The dear Hartleys have been here paying their summer visit to the magic valley they adore—and they know how to make the most of it: days on the headland, all day on the little beaches, the tiny coves with few about. It is like their own discovered paradise, with Apollo, the splendid Labrador, swimming about in the sea after Harold, apprehensive for him. And the charm of their cottage, with the fresh colour washes George put on, primrose and cherry-pink, the astonishing decoration Joan made from wild flowers growing in the hedges, with what imagination; and the scrumptious meal she cooked, Cornish duck and Californian avocado stuffed with shrimp, our own cream from the farm with the delicious sweet.

One even more beautiful day we went across county to St Breock and picnicked above the church, in a field looking over to haunted Trevorder: I told them the saga of wicked Jan Tregagle.

After tea, down the steep hill to the church deep in the lush ferny valley, the saint's stream running fresh by the porch-door; inside, the coloured slate monument to Vyells and Arundells—the little *hirondelles* disporting themselves on the many coats of arms. Grey slabs to the Tregagles behind the altar in the side-aisle—though none to the Evil One: no one knows where in the church he is buried.

The rectory above the church is one of my several Naboth's Vineyards in Cornwall, along with Luxulyan and St Winnow vicarages. Now up for sale, it was doubly inviting; we trespassed into the garden: green lawns under beech and ilex, and out to a long walk backed by a fruit-wall, sideways along the edge of the secret valley. Buoying ourselves up with the thought of inspecting for possible purchase, we penetrated into the back of the roomy, rambling house, vast stone-floored kitchen at the back. In front there was the long low Queen Anne panelled drawing-room, with three windows on to the terrace. The whole place has a strongly nostalgic atmosphere—and there is a story.

It is said to be haunted. One day the Rector's wife, sitting in that room, was conscious of a presence, but invisible. At that moment there was a ring at the front door. She went out—and the lady at the door said, 'Is this house haunted?' (As I write the word there is a flicker behind me in my own open-windowed study here at Trenarren, for this house is no less atmospherical: all authentic Cornish houses have an aura.)

Trenarren, after all, is far more beautiful, for here is the sea, with this rare optical illusion the old Princess always notices: the V-shaped valley makes a chalice, in which the sea, from the terrace, seems to be above one. (I hadn't noticed it, until she drew my attention to it; she notices everything, clever old friend of Proust. When I visited her in her apartment in the house on the Île St Louis, with wide window like a ship's bridge looking up the Seine, white lilies were arranged, each in a separate big scent-bottle, like a procession of nuns making their devotions to Nôtre Dame.) Here there are all the varied greens of the trees, different sorts of rhododendron, the beeches of the jungle behind, paler green of pittosporum, more delicate shade of Chinese bamboo, the dark coarse green of yew, puffs of green of the further pine (like the pines of the Pincio)—all held in the cup of the magic valley, with the sound of the sea upon the coast, and wind and sea together in the tossing trees, ebbing and flowing.

No: there is nowhere more beautiful to live in Cornwall. And yet, the day after tomorrow, early in September, I leave it, as every year, for America. Never have I been so reluctant to leave; the sadness of impending departure has added to the poignancy of the pleasure.

A kind of farewell party took place at my neighbours' at Porthpean, where the old Princess made herself, quite naturally, instinctively, the centre of the party, surrounded by her court. We sat ourselves on the two garden seats, front stalls for that familiar childhood view (seen, in those days, from down below on the beach).[1] Gull Rock on the left, where I used to climb with some trepidation above the pool one might easily fall into, and in at the mouth of the mine-adit that went in and in to the dark interior of the headland above. Beyond, the Gribbin pensinsula, glimpsed at sea-level; on the west, enclosing the bay, Black Head and the neck of Trenarren. As evening wore on, the scene became hopelessly beautiful, for how can one evoke the perfection of such a scene?—the bay still as a mill-pool, with the iridescent sheen of mother-of-pearl, milky white-grey-blue, set off by a foreground of brilliant plots of scarlet geranium, and a pink-and-lavender screen of sweet peas hanging over the evening sea.

And so home again to the secrecy of Trenarren, where there will never be such a party. I prefer it infinitely alone: breakfasting alone on the terrace; or exchanging a few words in the cool of the morning with Farmer Bovey bringing the milk; or visited by Peter, the white cat, rousing himself from some warm nest among the montbretias, or under the abelia, now in full flower (beloved of the rare hawk-moth with long proboscis), himself dazed and drunk with sleep and sun and summer. Or, turning in after the day's last task, watering my new plants, to catch that strange northern sunlight on the big black gate, so disturbing, coming from the north-west late on summer evenings. Or looking back at the immense ravaged column of the ancient insignis pine, now drawing towards its end, which I have seen ash-coloured in early

[1] Cf. *A Cornish Childhood.*

16

morning moonlight, or with the pale green of verdigris—standing like a solitary monolith of some vanished Greek temple: An Ozymandias among trees, the recognizable monument of Trenarren through the years, known all my life—with no long future now before it falls.

1964

1

The Autumn of 1926

A Cornishman at Oxford concludes with a concatenation of crises which knocked me out for that summer. At the end of May 1926 there was the rejection by my old college, Christ Church, which—however one may look at it—made a lifelong mark on my mind and set the pattern for many future rejections. A normal, ordinary public-school type would not have made such heavy weather of it, and would not have taken it so much to heart. I think that in my account of it in that previous volume I saw it fairly enough, for I said that, on the evidence, I would have made the same choice as they did. They chose an older man, a better scholar, with more experience and the right background—father a professor, the son a Wykehamist: what could be more right?

The paradox was that I was more reasonable about it at the time than I became subsequently: I *allowed* it to gnaw at my vitals. It is interesting to watch psychologically how, if one allows a crevice to open, the poison seeps into the wound and the damage spreads through the system. There was no one to warn, and I should have been too proud to listen. It is only too obvious that I was not the ordinary public-school boy who took such rebuffs in his stride, but an over-sensitive Celt, with a consciousness of genius, and the stigmata—the daemonic mental energy, the one skin too few.

It was intolerable to be rejected by a lot of second-rate dons, whose existence I knew even then would hardly be recorded except in these pages.

Then there was the General Strike, which posed a searching problem for an ingenuous young don, still hardly more than an undergraduate, of Labour convictions. Some of my pupils wrote an apologetic note to say that they were going down to help the government. Ought I not to down tools, drop my tutorials, and go down to help the strikers? The Manciple of the day, a grizzled, ill-tempered old Scot, who had been trained at Balmoral and detested the Junior Fellows, said to me outright that I should be helping the government—though it was not his place, as a servant, to say so.

The dilemma was resolved by my being rushed off to the Acland for an emergency operation for peritonitis. When I next saw him, *he* was apologetic, gruffly kindly: he was too late, his sympathy coldly received. In mid-August I struggled home feebly to recuperate, too young and innocent to realise that I was taking too much out of myself—for years always on the stretch, making my own way to Oxford, in those days when it was excruciatingly difficult. And all the rest of it—having to get a First in the History School, when I intended English Literature; then working flat out to get a prize Fellowship at All Souls. It had all been accomplished, but here was the consequence: a permanent ulcer gnawing at my vitals.

That I did not understand. I thought that the operation had dealt with it, and the doctors didn't enlighten me. I did not know that it had been so much touch and go, to save my life, that there was no dealing with the ulcer. It was still there, doing its nefarious work.

The reader must forgive these distasteful details—there will have to be more of them—for this illness was the condition of my life and work for many years. I don't know if this book may have any use in the medical profession in providing a case-history of a duodenal type. My own doctor, young at the time, had never had to deal with it, and didn't even recognize the Hippocratic look on my face as I was passing out into unconsciousness—that fell to a clever young Fellow of All Souls, Reggie Harris, to whom I owed my life. Nor were the doctors candid after the rescue-operation: they told me nothing, hoping for the best, I suppose, and I had no idea of the true state of affairs. I went on as before.

What I should have had was a long, long rest, a careful diet for months, with no worries, until the ulcer was cured and healed. But I could not have done it. My mind was teeming with ideas, mental energy drove me on relentlessly, reading and writing, 'thinking out my position', endless notes, for poems, stories, arguments, books, even a play about Swift, which possessed my mind and turns up again and again in various forms. (I have only just got it off my chest, fifty years later, in the form of a straight biography.) I was driven by a daemon.

André Billy concludes his biography of Balzac with the words: 'Il est mort. Il a cinquante-deux ans. Il était assassiné par son démon.'

But Balzac had written the *Comédie humaine*. What had I to show for my efforts?

So far there was only, or essentially, the Diary: I had kept it going since I was a schoolboy; I was now up to vol. 21, the first half-dozen volumes having been destroyed.

And now at home that summer I was doubtful. What was the point of keeping it up?

I have no irresistible feeling in favour of its continuance. Perhaps on balance it may in future be of more use to me than harm. If I don't keep it up as a record of thoughts and feelings, I may continue it as a scrap-book, to collect the things, outside of my proper work, that attract and excite me. Which reminds me: the misplaced relative in the line above is a sign that I shall never learn to write except by writing.

So there was one prime purpose the Diary served; then I was assailed by doubt whether this form of extempore composition might not be a worse influence upon one's writing. 'That chronic state of indecision is characteristic of everything I am about nowadays. Perhaps it only means that I have not yet recovered strength from my illness. Let's hope it's only that.'

No one to talk to, no one to confide in, let alone ask advice of, in an ignorant working-class home, poor souls — it is only now that it comes clear to me, at the end of my life, that the Diary fulfilled that function. I sought to think things out for myself in it, I argued with myself, it became my counsellor and my lifelong companion.

Not until September did I begin to wake up and breathe again, after my nasty experience in the Acland; and to resume my usual round. I did my best for myself with walks around the country-side, ever faithful to Carn Grey — scene of my early intense experiences alone—a whole day on the beach at Porthpean, a long tramp with the older sister of a schoolfriend, who was very kind and attentive. She was, apparently, too much with me: 'That, though pleasant and good for my health, has not been exhilarating in mind. I am afraid too much company does no good—and I am a good deal sought after nowadays: flattering, but not at bottom satisfying.' Illness was driving me further in upon myself, reinforcing the loneliness that I hugged as yielding the intensest experiences while at the same time resenting being cut off from 'life'. Here was the tension; tension is the necessary condition of creative achievement, but I was driving myself too hard. Here—psychologists take note—were the makings of a prize duodenal mentality.

The walks spoke to me more than the woman. One day we walked down by the river from Truro to romantic Malpas—the ferry-crossing where, in the medieval French romances, Tristram found his Iseult waiting for him on the opposite bank (not for me!)—then up through the lovely woods of Lamorran to St Michael Penkivel of the Boscawens, the church full of their family monuments, and round by Ruan Lanihorne and Tregony.

Late at night we arrived at Grampound and, tired out, sat on the steps of the old broken cross half-way up the steep hill, waiting for the last bus to St Austell. *That* was the finest thing in my holiday: just like a scene from a Chekhov play. Groups of village people came downhill, in earnest talk about rights of way and hedging and the crops. One rheumatic old fellow was much in request for lawyerly advice: he was pressing a younger man to go into Truro to 'see about it'. Another group's talk was all about brass bands [a great feature of old Cornish life, among the miners in America too[1]]. All the while a woman in her bedroom window across the road sat there intently listening and watching [characteristic rural occupation] ...

I had a strange sensation on first entering the circle of light, that we were observed characters, like Michael Henchard and his woman tramping to the fair at the beginning of *The Mayor of Casterbridge*. A row of women were gossiping over

[1] Cf. *The Cornish in America*.

the hedge when we first arrived at the cross, when I had said, 'It's five-and-twenty to nine by this clock: my watch must be five minutes slow.'—As if saying something tremendously significant: for a moment I seemed to be watching myself from the outside, like a spectator following the first significant words of an actor in a play. Perhaps it was only an effect of tiredness, but it was enough to *fix* the scene in my mind: night and dark clouds, the village people going to bed, homelight in the windows of a house on the brow of the hill.

Actually, it was an example of something a little more strange: what I called, at the time, the *culte de sensations*. I cherished the idea—which intrigued Lionel Curtis at All Souls, though he disapproved—that illness sharpened my apprehensions and my mind, and I made a cult of the intense and marginal sensations illness gave me. I called them 'experiences'. I am afraid that there was a good deal of the Manichee in this young man, bent on denying the legitimate and natural demands of the flesh, especially those of sex, to sharpen the edge of his mind. Naturally, I suppose, the body suffered.

That night I read the Book of Revelation; I was reading Gogol's *Dead Souls* and Dostoievsky: *The Brothers Karamazov* with immense admiration, but I simply couldn't take *Crime and Punishment*. I was shocked by the gratuitous murder it begins with, and later had nothing but disapproval of Gide's *culte de l'acte gratuit*. Moralistic young man! The dual nature of my interests came out, more literary than historical; though I was reading Cheyney's continuation of Froude's great history to the end of Elizabeth's reign, in my period, and the erratic Charles Beard's *Economic Interpretation of the Constitution of the United States*. Beard was much the fashion at that time with Left intellectuals, like Harold Laski, always anxious to be *dans le mouvement* with no real depth of reflection. Though Beard did not really speak to me, this book corroborated my Marxist trend of thought; it was only later that his unbalanced bias was shown up, with his crazy book on Roosevelt's foreign policy, from which it transpired that the Japanese did not attack the Americans at Pearl Harbor, but rather that the Americans attacked the Japanese. See how we were misled! Or, rather, to be honest, how the cleverest of us misled ourselves.

Better, and more lasting, fodder for the mind was the folklore I was observing among my own simple folk. My mother could tell from the feel of the feather bed, when making it in the morning, that it was going to rain, for it was damp and heavy. When she shivered, it was somebody walking over her grave. One night there was a very fine moon, and I was led on to tell Mother and Father that, if we were living on the moon, the finest sight in the heavens would be the earth, shining brighter than the moon to us. They had never thought of this; Mother, much impressed: 'I don't understand it. It's all a mystery to me, from the beginnin' to the endin', and from the endin' to the beginnin'.' I don't suppose the astronomers have got much further.

There were local characters from the past my mother told me about—I had, from a child, longed to know about the past: an extension of knowledge, I suppose, the present I could find out about for myself, though this hadn't the same interest, the bloom of the inaccessible upon that. There was Penrice, the manor-house of the parish, lying hidden in the woods below—the village of Tregonissey belonged in part to the manor—to me mysterious and impenetrable. 'The Sawles have been the leading family here ever since Oliver Sawle, yeoman, bought the place, with King's Wood and a large shoulder of Pentewan Valley in 1651. That is, in the vast property ramp after the Civil Wars, when prudent Parliamentarians bought cheap land which had been the foundation of many an older Royalist family.' Actually, all this land in and around St Austell belonged to the Duchy manor of Tewington. I have never known how, when Royal lands were resumed at the Restoration, the Duchy manor of Tewington came not to be restored to the Crown. What was the explanation? Did some money pass to the Duchy officials? It can hardly have been a Crown decision to let its patrimony go; but it was the foundation of the fortunes of the leading family in the parish.

Not that it matters now, for the family has come to an end. 'The present baronet is blind and lives in London mostly, away from the estate; his son and heir was killed in the war, and now the second daughter has died, also without children. Mother remembered the grand old Sir Charles, the reigning squire from

1849 to 1903, coming to church with his Lady in carriage-and-pair every Sunday morning when in residence at Penrice. He would walk foremost; then came old Lady Graves-Sawle, on the arm of one of her maids, for she was gouty, hair white as snow.' This was the kind of thing I liked to hear about, something beyond my ken—Charles Beard I could deal with for myself.

Nor did I know then that this old lady was the niece of, and named for, Rose Aylmer, of Landor's most famous lyric:

> Ah, what avails the sceptred race,
>   Ah, what the form divine!
> What every virtue, every grace!
>   Rose Aylmer, all were thine.
>
> Rose Aylmer, whom these wakeful eyes
>   May weep, but never see,
> A night of memories and sighs
>   I consecrate to thee.

This perfect little poem, much admired by romantic Victorians, made the name very famous. The niece in turn became a great friend of Landor; I happen to possess the privately printed copy of her Diaries, which she presented to the widow of Richard Ford, of the famous *Handbook to Spain*. The second Rose—Lady Graves-Sawle—became in turn a friend of Landor in his last years in Florence. He wrote a poem to her, too, much less well-known. Her Diaries give a picture of an intelligent woman and of high Victorian culture: travels in Italy, visits to the galleries, friendship with Landor and Browning, an occasional highbrow visiting remote Penrice.

What a contrast with the granddaughter, the last heiress to live there, who never opened a book and had an acute sense of inferiority towards those who did! The old lady gave the Aylmer name to her son and heir, the next baronet, Francis Aylmer. I was surprised, when I was taken to inspect our college estate out at Padbury in Buckinghamshire, to see his name upon a memorial tablet there, where he died, without coming into residence at Penrice. In later years, when I went to live at the neighbouring place, Trenarren, I came to know Penrice and its haunted wood well. But the last occupant, who became my acquaintance, a

Philistine with a set against her family, knew nothing and cared less about these interesting associations. In 1926 I concluded sagely, 'One hardly knows whether to regret that the old ways and people have vanished, or to be glad that their rule is at an end.'

Here was another duality, another conflict: which inflexion would prevail with me? At any rate, with Rosemary's death the place has come to an end—and, with it, the mysterious way of life into which I had at last penetrated and, ironically, am almost alone here now in keeping up. The ambivalence of mind continues; for, with her attitude to the past and its riches of association —they were a naval family, at Bunker's Hill, Yorktown, the glorious First of June, Aboukir, Copenhagen (Luny painted sea-pieces of these that came to the house)—perhaps it deserved to come to an end, as she certainly intended that it should, with her. As for my sympathies, it is the historian in me who has won.

Then, all those years ago, the visual was no less strong, and I was learning by watching, insatiably. There were walks up over the hills to lovely Luxulyan and its secret Valley, 'though not alone', I added regretfully. Skies of Italian blue, like Della Robbia, for I had not been to Italy: 'skies like that are always the background when I day-dream about it.' In the bare granite house where we had tea the woman who served it was of the rough 'Higher Quarters' type: big-boned and massive, square head and high cheek-bones. 'But she seems to have too much to do, with five men in the house to do for.' I have no memory of the poor woman, but I still remember that autumn walk, the place by the stream where we sat to read aloud Keats's Ode, for I always carried a book in my pocket. We explored farther up the steep sides of the Valley, to reach the granite quarry I had always wanted to find: 'for it presents a cliff visible for miles around, which I have often watched from Carn Grey, when the westering sun beat full upon it, turning it to a rich gold.' There was a vein of ochre in it, from which came the splendid block of luxulyanite for Wellington's tomb in St Paul's.

At Carn Grey I could be alone, silver-grey shadowing the long stretches of moorland and farmland away to Brown Willy and Rowtor. 'Night, when it came on, was wonderful, so high up. The thick cap of cloud that overhung the Rock [Carn] passed over and left the sky over the moor blue and bare, until the stars came

out. What I did there so long I hardly know. There was a coil of
mist over Hensbarrow, and I remembered a walk up there when
snow came on, and green and pink lights played round the edges
of the horizon', evidently an *aurora borealis*. In my head I was
collecting phrases and lines:

> Where the dim lights of rainbow hue flicker
> And play a dubious game along the line
> Of earth and sky.

Phrases like 'nothing between the moon and me', or 'the white
moonstone on the moor', came into my mind while watching
'how the grey boulders caught what light there was and glim-
mered white out of the surrounding darkness. It came home to me
how the stone crosses upon the moorland ways served the old
people as guides to church and market and home through the
winter nights.'

'And reflections like these', I repined, 'are all that I have to show
for the mind's activity these months.'

There was one excitement before I went back to Oxford for
term: a more social occasion, a fire in the English China-Clays
offices in the town. The fire-bell ringing started everybody's
excitement, clouds of smoke drifting across the sky, the middle-
class housewives of New Road, 'the better-off quarter of Tregonissey, as excited as anybody else. When I got into town, High
Cross Street thronged and people quite festive as the fire was got
under. I watched from a corner of the old cemetery, where only
a few had gathered. Only a few! remembering the headstones and
the shadows, how many there were, and what an interest *they*
would have shown in a big fire down the street, if they were
alive.' This was the scene of one of my best poems later, 'The Old
Cemetery at St Austell'. At the moment the visual prevailed:
'Too late to see the roof cave in, there were other delights in
watching the flames break out behind the gable at the other end
of the long beams.' In such excitement I even chatted away with
an unknown young man from one of the china-clay offices.

And so, recovered, back to the excitements of my Oxford life,
redoubled now that I was a Fellow of All Souls; for there were all
my undergraduate friends whom I held on to, with the new and

grander acquaintance All Souls opened out to one. There was a certain cosiness in the life of the college in those last days of an elect society. Not so much in the physical sense, for we were behindhand in modern conveniences. Keynes once described the Spartan conditions prevailing—no doubt as against the luxury of King's, of which he was Bursar, and Cambridge dons did themselves well, far better than we did at Oxford. (One or two Cambridge dons, a Fellow of Trinity and a Fellow of St John's died simply of over-eating.) Cyril Radcliffe described our old-fashioned regimen as 'public splendour and private squalor', and he almost died of congestion of the lungs one winter. There was, for example, no bathroom or W.C. on my staircase, the probationers' rooms in the old quad; later in the 'thirties, when I became more and more ill and was often sick at night, I have had to descend in the dark, muffled up in dressing-gown and rug, to shuffle along to the draughty passage where the lavatories were, sometimes in snow, the spire of St Mary's looking glumly on.

It is difficult to describe the college atmosphere in those delicious days—doubly delicious to me, with my working-class background, for here the *train-de-vie* of the Victorian upper class went on undisturbed: this was what I had felt excluded from at home, almost as a natural birthright, for my tastes were much more in accordance with it than many of the Philistine types who had it at command, born to it. This I had always resented. Now, as a bonus, I missed out on middle-class life, and, in fact, have never caught up with it or with them.

It was not so much the public side of it that appealed to me, the ceremonial meals in hall, the silver, the candlelight, the portraits looking down on the scene—Archbishop Chichele to whom we owed it all, Christopher Wren and the great Blackstone, Edward Young the poet and Bishop Heber, bishops and Lord Chancellors, and more recent celebrities like Curzon and the Prime Minister Lord Salisbury (my friend David Cecil's grandfather)—nor the grand gatherings at week-ends, when the important figures in public life came down, but the kindly life in the week, when we were few. I think now, with affection, half a century after, of those winter tea-times around the fire in the smoking-room, the servants (old friends, not forgotten) answering the bell, the kindly talk, the friendliness of it all, the welcome to one's own young friends, darkness coming down in the garden, with Herbert Trench's Neapolitan statue of a nude youth, over the wall the lights coming on in the long line of Queen's, and later the bells of New College ringing to evensong.

Too much external life; I filled my empty Diary with someone else's poems, one O——, a pupil of Ernest Jacob, who put him on to me because he was lonely and knew no one in Oxford. 'As a matter of fact he knows one other man, a poet at Worcester, who wrote the epitaph:

> Here lies Sir Ebenezer Pott,
> Who had a house and seven cars;
> Among the things he had not got
> Were all the skies and all the stars.'

This was Denzil Batchelor, an interesting character who had a curious career, became an authority on pugilism and wrote on sport, but wrote no more poetry.

What became of the poet O—— I never knew. He rather alarmed me. When I took him up to my upper room to see the Charles I oak panelling with the dolphin hinges, his fancy was immediately taken with the beam upon which my predecessor had hanged himself and which gave me such palpitations at night. O—— knew nothing of the story, but at once commented that there was an easy way of ending the business when one was tired of life. 'It was a frightening experience'—and these were the 'experiences' that fascinated me.

Not suicide—anything but: I had had far too much of a struggle not to attach the utmost importance to holding on to life. Yet here were these young men with far easier backgrounds, who had had everything done for them and yet were ready to throw it all away —I simply could not understand it, and had no sympathy for them. For O—— was suicidal. He lived high up in an attic room in Peck which I knew well, from its previous occupant—in utter loneliness, knowing no one, the Mona Lisa in one corner:

> An upper room, that is a dream's tomb,

as he wrote. When I penetrated this remote attic, 'Can't you see I'm trembling all over?' he said; 'I've been like it the last three weeks.' He was much taller and stronger than I; unhappily I called to mind the remark of my friend Roger Makins, my 'twin' at All Souls, about homicidal mania giving a man superhuman strength. Whether O—— intuited my nervousness or not, he said, 'No, I'm really quite robust; and don't look as if you were going soon.' I went.

His poems were quite promising. 'It will be interesting to watch him, as indeed others I have known in the brief days here, and see what he and they make of their lives in the world.' I do not know what became of him. When he came to take Schools, he refused to answer any questions, but scribbled verses all over his papers—and so disappeared. I suppose he was mad.

While looking through old letters, I came upon one from Graham Greene from this time, in that beautiful finicking hand that has remained unchanged through the years. Patrick Monkhouse—another of my friends with a well-known parent to sponsor him, Alan Monkhouse of the *Manchester Guardian*—had asked me for a poem for the *Oxford Outlook*, which he was taking over from Graham, to whom I sent it. For he wrote,

> I like the poem very much indeed, more than anything else I've seen of yours. Alas! I have not put off Finals after all, and have been working here the whole vac. I am no longer tortured though; I have grown fatalistic. I have given up the *Outlook*, but have forwarded your poem to Monkhouse. I'm feeling quite excited at the moment with bringing out a book with Blackwell on May 1 and b. with efforts to wangle myself into the Asiatic Petroleum Co. which is my latest idea for a profession. I should simply love to be an oil magnate.

I have forgotten what this book was that Graham brought out with Blackwell. But this was very much what John Betjeman has described as the Basil Blackwell period at Oxford. Only the other day Sir Basil, in his ripe eighties, was telling me how tired he became of discovering these young talents, who, immediately after he had published their first books for them, popped off to a London publisher. My acquaintance of those days, Harold Acton, was another: we used to see the bright begonias of his book-jackets in Blackwell's shop window with *empressement* and some envy.

Why had I nothing to publish?—I forget: C. K. Ogden had

already published my little book, *On History*; I mean poems, a more personal, creative book.

It suggests a curious theme—that of the talented young men one has known, of far above average intelligence and gifts, who have inexplicably thrown their lives away, done away with themselves. Why ever? Why? Is too much intelligence something unnatural, a strain that some human beings cannot bear? There was a brilliant young classical scholar of Balliol, Bruce McFarlane's early friend, Stephen Kirby, dark and handsome, the world before him. Think what he might have achieved, if he had held on his course. There was a friend of Roger's at the House, a young Scottish aristocrat, with wildly romantic good looks—what was wrong with him? Or Quintin Hogg's half-brother, Eddie Marjoribanks, who was benevolent towards me at Christ Church, and already having great success in public life—what a career lay before him!

I think of it simply as a wicked waste, throwing the most precious gift of life away—perhaps they would value it the more if they had had a tough struggle to hold on to it.

Among my exact contemporaries, Evelyn Waugh and Graham Greene tell us in their autobiographies that each of them made such an attempt—the former's rather ludicrous, the latter's nastier. Brian Howard succeeded, and there were others among my contemporaries. Why ever? They all had good parents, solicitous for their welfare, looking after them; they had money or, at least, prospects. Were they just spoiled, things made *too* easy for them? With my hard background I am inclined to think so—young fools; and yet, think of the loss to literature if Evelyn or Graham had succeeded! These public-school boys—Etonians and Harrovians, Wykehamists and Rugbeians, even Berkhamstedians and Lancingites—were all years ahead of me, so much more sophisticated. What is more, they mucked in together, went to London to live the literary life; I remained on the side-lines: for years I could not bring myself to the exposure of publishing a volume of poems, until Eliot got it out of me and held my hand. By then, I had produced several books of history and politics; yet poetry had always come first. I still cannot explain it, or wholly understand the complex I had about it—perhaps too revealing. (Cecil Roberts: 'Too reticent'; Athenais Russell: 'Much too inhibited'.)

Here was a Sunday at the end of October—'a day wasted, in point of time and energy and real pleasure', i.e. evidently because it was not solitary, as I preferred, but social. 'Got up late and breakfasted almost alone with Evelyn Baring, who is going out to India because life there will be less easy for him than in England.' He was Roger's friend, a splendid fellow, whom I immensely admired; Lady Ottoline Morrell's daughter showed me a photograph the other day, of Roger, Evelyn and me between these over-six-footers, each bound for a grand public career, for the country and the Empire we were all proud of. And what will remain of it? And mine?

The morning slipped away, what with a long conversation with A. F. Pollard on University Reforms in London [what remains of that, on which he spent so much time and energy?], and a gathering of young men in Otis's[1] rooms in Oriel, himself and Auden (a poet who may achieve something, if his genius conquers his deficiencies of character).

How priggish that sounds, after all the years that have elapsed since I first knew him and the revolution in morals that has so recently come about! Who can have told me what was what about him?—the malicious Otis, I suppose: they were birds of a feather. The young poet, on his side, was anxious to pursue the acquaintance, for two days later I find in my engagement-book: 'Lunch with Thomson? Or Auden, Christ Church?' Mark Thomson was a friend from undergraduate days, to become an historian of considerable authority on the eighteenth century. There was the dichotomy: history? or poetry?

That same Sunday there was 'a grand and exhausting lunch at the Warden's [Pember], who is now Vice-Chancellor'. Among the guests was John Buchan, who fascinated me on a subject that greatly appealed to me—fear, which inspired several of my poems —and with a story of panic that came over him and a friend when climbing in the Breisgau. I remembered his story of the Old Man of the Cairngorms he had told me on a previous occasion, up at Elsfield. (All very well, but there *is* something ominous about the Cairngorms: Scrymgeour-Wedderburn's mother and sister were

[1] cf. *A Cornishman at Oxford.*

walking up there when a flash of lightning felled them, and one of them did not rise again.) John's wife was extraordinarily kind and 'friendly and likeable'—how good indeed they were to me through all the years that followed! John was a fellow-sufferer, another member of the duodenal club, over-work, over-tension, over-drive. When I was having my last operation—a dangerous short-circuiting one over which I nearly died—in 1938, he was on leave as Governor-General of Canada for a spell in a clinic at Ruthin, whence he wrote to cheer me up. Today Susan, his widow, is my oldest friend—appearing gallantly on television at over ninety, and still writing solicitously to inquire after *my* health!

Vincent Massey was present, whom I couldn't make out, except that he was going to the new Canadian Embassy in Washington. I came to know him later as a generous benefactor to Balliol, his college; and on my first visit to Canada, where he was Governor-General, he was in residence at the historic Citadel in Quebec and showed me all over the place. He told me many things that were of special interest to an historian. Not far away was an enclosed order of nuns, perhaps the famous Ursulines, whom not even the Archbishop of Quebec had the right to visit. The Governors-General of Canada had, in succeeding to the prerogatives of the Kings of France; and Vincent Massey acted on it by going reverently to tea, once a year during his period of residence, with the Reverend Mother Superior.

There, too, alone in his glory, all in purple, was one of the college bishops, the celebrated Hensley Henson, Bishop of Durham. I grew to be fond of him; but, at this moment of intolerant youth, I thought him a bit of a mountebank. There *was* something of a diminutive episcopal mountebank about him, too: it was part of his charm. The night before I had had to sit near Henson and Canon Streeter—also celebrated in his day as a very Modernist theologian—while Henson held forth, in his extraordinary affected creaking voice, about 'the callous system of terrorisation which kept the miners from returning to their duty and their work'. I thought that that was for my benefit: he knew that I was a young Labour man.

My narrow squeak that summer had given me something else to think about than the coal-miners' strike, which went on and on for months, obstinately, dismally, in the event tragically. Both coal-owners and coal-miners were an exceedingly obstinate set of men, the leadership of the Miners' Union hopeless, under such emotional types as Bob Smillie and A. J. Cook. What was needed was a strong non-party government, such as Lloyd George could have led, which would have banged the heads of both sides together and brought about an agreement in the interests of the country and of us all. As it was, there was never any leadership from the indolent Baldwin, who always took the line of least resistance. Rather a nice man personally, without reproach—unlike the naughty Celt of genius, L. G., 'the Goat'—Baldwin was a shrewd man. He had bought time earlier, to lay in large stocks of coal, and then allowed the miners to go on with their strike in the most disadvantageous conditions for months all through the summer. A small portion of the immense sums lost to industry and production would have given the miners a decent deal. Baldwin did nothing about it, but allowed the conflict to continue, the miners to be ground down. The long-term consequences—like the not-so-long-term consequences of Appeasement in the 'thirties—were disastrous. The coal-miners developed an inflamed sense of injustice, a mentality cut off from the rest of the community, a will to hold it to ransom if and when they could, from which we still suffer today.

Henson was in the front line as Bishop of Durham, where he described himself as 'like a whale stranded on the sea-coast of Patagonia'. He had a great gift for a phrase; what made this the funnier was that he was so diminutive, but thought of himself as the grand occupant of the Palatine Bishopric. His own fascinating autobiography, *Retrospect of an Unimportant Life* (he never at any time thought of himself as unimportant), has an unconscious humour. He despised his vapid Dean, fat Bishop Welldon, ex-headmaster of Harrow, who was always getting into trouble with the miners. Once at a miners' gala, upon which he intruded his unmistakable bulk, they kicked his tall top hat with strings into the river: it floated forlornly, without the Dean, down the Wear. It must have provided a ludicrous spectacle, one of the entertainments one would have enjoyed. Henson on Welldon: 'He can neither speak with effect nor hold his peace with dignity.'

Himself could always speak with effect, though not always the effect he intended. His unfortunate phrase 'the Protestant under-world' lost the Church the Revised Prayer Book in the unspeak-able assembly, the Tory House of Commons, so much keener on this nonsense-issue than on settling the coal-mines conflict. Once in college Henson was holding forth about the Palatine rights of his bishopric: 'If these were the Middle Ages, my wife would be a Princess Palatine.' E. L. Woodward,[1] always mean about the Church for which he had intended himself, but an historian, commented to me: 'If these were the Middle Ages, she would be nothing of the sort: no Princess Palatine, but a concubine.'

In short, Hensley Henson, who made so much noise in his day, was constantly in the headlines. Of him I was rather fond—he was such fun, unlike the pretentious Woodward, whom we called the Abbé, from his spell in Paris with the circle of the Abbé Loisy; but Henson *was* a bit of an ecclesiastical mountebank.

Such were the grandees whom this ingenuous young man had under observation, duly impressed, but privately not over-impressed. What did impress him from the first was their extra-ordinary kindness: he had never met anything like it before. That these busy public men should put themselves out to pay attention to an unknown youngster, very much an outsider among them, surprised me. Warden Pember, a conventional man, frequently asked me to his lunch-parties or dinner-parties, or would take me to the theatre for something of interest: Jack Westrup's first performance of Monteverdi's *Coronation of Poppaea*, for example (the Victorian Warden, with no ear for music, slept through most of it).

This did not apply to Woodward; but then he was not a grandee, and had a rather mean attitude towards those who were. He wanted to reduce everything to his own middle-class scale; year after year he would try to bring the Encaenia Luncheon, which the college gave to the university, to an end. A splendid spectacle in the long Codrington Library, with all the scarlet gowns, the college silver out, summer flowers and flowery ladies from the great world—it appeals to anyone with any aesthetic sense or taste. The Abbé had none. He once shocked me by describing the country gentry as the worst stratum in the whole social fabric. Taken aback by this, though a Labour man, I couldn't

[1] cf. *A Cornishman at Oxford.*

35

agree: in the country, for example, it was the gentry who had improved the landscape, planted the trees and woods, made the parks, built the country houses, played a responsible part in the local community, etc.

This exchange, which took me by surprise, was quite symptomatic sociologically. Woodward, the son of a civil servant in the Admiralty, had the characteristic middle-class envy of the upper class and patronizing attitude towards the working class. (Bruce McFarlane, also the son of an Admiralty civil servant, and Richard Pares, who should have known better, also had this middle-class inferiority complex.) In fact, the middle classes were riddled with envy of the old upper class, gentry and aristocracy alike. Middle-class people were mostly urban and suburban; I was a countryman —this was why I could appreciate what the gentry had done for the country, historically and aesthetically, was shocked by Woodward's dislike of them, and discounted Richard's and Bruce's anti-aristocratic complex.

All kinds of things were involved, symptomatically for the future of our society, in this clash and difference of inflexions. For one thing, as a working man, I was outside the conflict between middle and upper class; for another, as someone whose fundamental values were aesthetic, my sympathies were upper-class, though I did not belong. The middle class hated the aristocracy, as these despised the middle class (I knew well the attitude of the Cecils, curiously corroborated, Kenneth Rose tells me, in the correspondence of Lord Robert). But *the middle classes have done them in*: they have won, not the working class really, any more than in Communist Russia or Eastern Europe—as I know from what Visiting Fellows tell me from Communist countries. It is naturally not the proletariat or the peasants who rule—how could they? It is the lower-middle-class mentality that rules now, and by means of a vastly inflated and powerful bureaucracy. What really civilized man, let along a creative artist or aesthete, could have any liking for it?

In effect, the Woodwards have won—and what kind of a society is it? I find it contemptible, and prefer to opt out of the show. To think what this country once was, and as I knew it—a country of beautiful small villages and towns, of gracious country houses in their parks, beside their churches, a small country that was yet the first in the world (when one travelled abroad one was made aware of it), the centre of the greatest Empire in the world's history, that was on the whole a force for good. (How much better has the world shown up for its disappearance? The greatest imperialism today is that of Soviet Russia—far less humane and free, let alone civilized and kindly.) And now Britain today ...! falling apart at home, and with no respect whatever in the outside world.

No, the middle classes and their bureaucracy are nothing like so effective in holding society together as the old gentry were up and down the country—now largely gone, their houses destroyed, in ruins, or turned into flats—apart from the astonishing achievement they accomplished in the world in the past four centuries since the age of Elizabeth I and Shakespeare.

The middle-class mentality expects to patronize working people. The Abbé Woodward could not patronize me. He thought that I was presumptuous and uppish—no doubt rightly enough, where he was concerned. As Domestic Bursar, responsible for the internal arrangements of the College, he affected a shade of authority over the Junior Fellows and was brought most in contact with us. He could always take in and mesmerize dear, innocent Richard Pares; me, he thought to take the mickey out of, always trying to score off or take me down a peg or two. Quite the wrong policy with a sensitive Celt, with whom you can do anything if treated with warmth and affection, let alone a tensed-up type, overstrung and always on the edge of illness.

I responded in character: I watched him, I took down his dreadfully revealing sayings; I totted up his earnings and makings —an old soldier of the 1914–18 war, he was a past master at scrounging. It all added up to a pretty figure: I added it up—and imparted the information to Richard, who passed it on to the Abbé. He responded sheepishly, vulgarly as I thought: 'Can't a fellow turn an honest penny?' Something Dickensian about that. Richard: 'Turn an honest ten thousand!'

But Woodward had pretensions to write; we were treated to philosophizing and poeticizing prose-pieces in the *Spectator*, in one of which I counted forty-six 'I's. These proses were subsequently gathered together under the title, *The Twelve-Winded Sky*. Surreptitiously he wrote a couple of novels, too, which came to nothing. A predecessor as Domestic Bursar—Grant Robertson, a great bore but a great dear—had also written novels under the romantic name Wymond Carey; he never admitted to it, but he did at least get them published. One was called *Love, the Judge*—or was it *Love the Judge?*—one didn't know whether *Love* was a noun or a verb; or, if a verb, whether a query or an imperative. We naughty Junior Fellows had a great deal of fun; but the Abbé wasn't altogether fun for me.

What did his writing add up to? That was the root of the matter. Too ingenuous at first, I subsequently realized that he had the all too common envy of the uncreative for the creative. The jealousy of inferior people one has to put up with all the way along—see Francis Bacon on that subject; but it strikes me as particularly unattractive when a man of an older generation is jealousy of inferior people one has had to put up with all the way younger—as I received nothing but encouragement from Trevelyan and Neale and Eliot, and in America from Samuel Eliot Morison and Allan Nevins.

The truth was that, in these years, the Abbé did not add up to much. Honesty compels me to say that, in later life, he did much better and our relations improved. The Institute at Princeton offered him a very handsome *traitement*—and wasn't Oxford envious when he threw up everything there, the professorship he had at last attained, to accept it! There, in the last half of his life, he wrote his books, away from the discouraging atmosphere of university life, and good books they were. We ended on quite friendly terms—but I never forgot that he had not been good to me when I was young and ill, and needed it.

How many reflections that Sunday lunch at Warden Pember's hospitable table has given rise to—the dining-room with the red Morris wallpaper, the sad last portrait of Charles I, coming down from the faithful Warden Sheldon, I suppose, that room looking out on the shed gold leaves and chestnuts of autumn—though not so many reflections as Virginia Woolf's luncheon in King's inspired in *A Room of One's Own*.

After lunch, a walk round the Meadows with Otis, and tea with the Rawlinsons. He was always my friend, I thought; not until recently did I learn that he was strongly against me over the

Christ Church job. When he was defeated in a fair election to the Lady Margaret professorship by Nippie Williams, a better scholar, Rawlers went off to be an Archdeacon. Meeting the Abbé Woodward on Oxford station, he held forth against the Master of Balliol (then A. D. Lindsay) dressing like an undergraduate in flannel trousers. The Abbé did not fail to comment how absurd the Archdeacon looked, in gaiters and frock-coat, top hat with button and attached strings. (Perhaps the Diary served, too, the purpose of a novel.) 'For the good of my soul, and the betterment of my temper,' that entry ends, 'I'd better do a little reading in the *Communist Manifesto* before facing the barrage of conversation on a Sunday night in college.'

November 2nd, I kept my first All Souls' Day in college, 'not so badly', in spite of champagne and madeira at the Gaudy—bad for a duodenal type: I didn't like to declare myself a teetotaller, as I became later on, after more and more trouble. Two hours in Chapel, Matins, Sermon, Communion, conducted by another of the college bishops, Headlam—another strong personality, not so outrageous or charming as Henson; I became fond of him too, still more when, years later, we shared rooms and he, old and ill, the milk ration I was specially allowed. Modern-minded people were beginning to defect from Chapel; Cyril Radcliffe described one's slinking out of Chapel before the Communion, past the Warden's blenching look, as 'the most difficult walk in life'. It was, and the marble steps were exceedingly slippery. We still had services every morning and evening for the very few of us who lived in college. The *bien-pensants*, like Geoffrey Dawson, wanted to keep us at it: he 'liked the idea of vicarious prayer'—he would have done better to attend to what the Germans were up to. A shadow of a *quondam* (former Fellow) turned up, Sir Arthur Hardinge: apparently a brilliant Anglo-Indian, broken by his son's death, visibly failing. I could not keep my eyes off him, wandering about, forgetting himself in Chapel, and staying to the end at dessert in Common Room. As Junior Fellow, 'screw', at the bottom of the table, I led him out. Kenneth Bell (history tutor at Balliol, a *quondam*) played me a trick. He was left behind; since it was my duty to be last out of the room, I went back for him. He wasn't there! I looked behind the thick curtains and the splendid hammered-leather screen—nowhere to be found. I even looked under the tables, wondering whether I might not be a bit tight. But no; my head was my one strong organ, it was my stomach that failed me. I found him in the smoking-room; he had jumped out of the window. He was more than a little mad; when I first came into college I was afraid of the lash of his tongue—until I stood up to him, and for a time we became good friends, though he was never my type: too much of a Philistine.

I couldn't stand the atmosphere of the smoking-room, thick with cigar-fumes, cigarette-smoke, odious pipes, the aura of club-life, drink, gentlemen at ease. I circled round the outskirts watchfully, observing the menagerie. 'Gwyer, Wilkinson, Swinton, placidly on the sofa.' Sir Maurice Gwyer had made a constructive contribution to education in India, cleaning up and setting on foot an effective university. Spenser Wilkinson was an admirable military historian and colossal bore, with a sentimental heart. Dearle was another bore—like Wilkinson, not a Prize Fellow but a Research Fellow from outside the charmed circle. Hence Raymond Asquith's naughty lines, that began:

How pleasant to walk the Turl
With Spenser Wilkinson or Dearle!

General Swinton was Wilkinson's successor, nothing like so good a military historian, but a more amusing and gifted man. He had tasted success with his Kiplingesque stories as Ole-Luk-Oie, and was one of the chief inventors of the tank. Swinton was much in and out of the college, for he liked the life, though as Dean he could not impose the discipline of a mess on us. All Fellows were equal, the most junior with the grandest public figure. For all that he disapproved of my militant opinions, he was rather fond of me, in an avuncular manner—he once gave me a very sportive red tie, which I have duplicated years after in his memory. For my part, I had never met a militarist before, and could hardly believe my ears when he would tell the same story three times over, unblushing.

Kenneth Bell was now in evidence, holding forth on an arm of a chair on the virtues of Balliol, while Feiling, in origin a Balliol man, made up to him with the remark that the combination of Christ Church and Balliol wasn't a bad one. Old C. R. L. Fletcher, a Kiplingesque historian, had made a speech in praise of old days, especially with a greater menace before us than they had had to

face. I thought he was eyeing me, whom he regarded with disapproval, until he found out that I was partial to cats; after that,
he became partial to me.

Alington, Head Master of Eton, handsome as a grey-haired
Apollo, was holding the fire, saying Floreat Etona to an appreciative audience of Etonians. Alington was kind enough to ask me
several times over to stay with him at Eton; I would never go,
but did stay with him to explore the Deanery at Durham later. He
had a honey-pot of a wife, a Lyttelton, who told me a grand *mot*
of the dragon, Bishop Creighton's wife—so much of a German
dragoness that Queen Victoria would never make him Dean of
Windsor: 'To think of money is un-Christian; to talk of it is
middle-class.' What a secure upper-class world that reveals!

Into this fug there materialized—I did not see him enter—the
most remarkable and, then, the most famous man in the room:
Lawrence of Arabia. It was the night on which he ceased to be a
Fellow. A legend in college, as throughout the world, he stood out
the more remarkably for his appearance. Into the room over-
crowded with people in dinner-jackets, *quondams* in tails, bishops
in purple, there turned up a corporal in the R.A.F., in air-force
blue uniform. More remarkable still, he had succeeded, with his
slight figure, and lower-class hair-cut in making himself look like
an anonymous boy of nineteen; what betrayed him were the
blazing eyes of genius, and the tortured mouth.

Lionel Curtis, ever avuncularly kind and protective, wanted to
introduce me to the great little Fellow; but he was surrounded by
a crowd of those who knew him, and I refused—too proud to butt
in. I already knew the story of Lawrence's life in college: withdrawn, remaining in his rooms all day subsisting on dried fruit and
biscuits while writing his book; refusing to descend to dine, but
coming into the smoking-room very late at night when he would
talk fascinatingly to a few; quarrelling with Curzon—Foreign
Secretary and a former Fellow—over Middle Eastern policy and
threatening to present two peacocks, to be called George and
Nathaniel, to strut about the quad. When he left college for the
R.A.F., he would occasionally dash back for a few hours in the
night, then off again before dawn on his motor-bike. Lionel
Curtis was his closest friend, to whom he wrote his most revealing
letters; in college we knew the strange family story, but did not

divulge it to the world. That was left to the caddish Richard Aldington, envious of Lawrence's fame. Later I was to meet his eldest and youngest brothers.

The real business of All Souls' tide is to elect the Prize Fellows on the basis of the examination in October. As Junior Fellow I had had to give out and collect the papers, and I was on tenterhooks to have Otis elected. He was a good historian, who had won a university prize; pimpled and unappetizing, he was yet my *protégé* and, I thought innocently, my disciple and friend. I saw the Abbé sitting by quietly, waiting for the opportunity to discuss Otis's election with Feiling—which I hoped was assured.

I was wrong, doubly wrong. Next day, at the college meeting, he was not elected. I was furiously disappointed, I had set so much store on having him to back me up in college; but I was wrong, the 'old men', as it turned out, were right not to elect him. Promising historian as he was, better educated and a better linguist than I—he knew German—his weakness was that he did not write very well; he wrote crabbedly and constipatedly, rather like a German, as appeared when he tried his hand at journalism. From this he disappeared into a second-rate career in Education. Instead, we elected A. H. M. Jones, a Labour Club acquaintance of mine, who went on to become the foremost, and most prolific, Roman historian in the country; and G. F. Hudson, a dark horse, strongly backed by Woodward, who became an intimate and lifelong friend of mine, one of the dearest to me. The longer one lives the more one sees how ironically things work out.

There is an angry note in the Diary that night: 'The moral is not to expect too much from men and institutions [still I continued to do so]. I have been so happy in college since I came back from my illness that I have been in danger of sinking myself in it. It's just as well to have an occasional jolt ... not to set too much store by its doings ... The things that I most care for I must keep to myself.'

However, with my temperament and sensibilities, I could not but care too much about everything. Trivialities upset me, though I knew they were 'not worth a rational man's thought'. My duties as 'screw', for example. As Junior Fellow I had to sit on and on till the Senior Fellows had finished their port—often up to 9 p.m. It was intolerable. Old Holdsworth was the worst offender, soaking up glass after glass of the college port; with the constitution of an ox, he would then go away and write solidly at his immense book till midnight. I used to think the *History of English Law* must be solidified All Souls port. But his sensibilities were such that he couldn't tell whether it was port or claret, or the two mixed. Once I decanted the claret into the port decanter, to be detected by the palate of old Sir Henry Sharp—made a member of Common Room while secretary of the University Commission. A scarecrow of an Anglo-Indian, parchment skin and totally without a sense of humour, he had a synthetic laugh on three descending notes. But hanging on in Common Room with mounting impatience and anger was not good for an ulcer. In the end, I began to go out; protests or no, my little revolt gradually brought this *corvée* to an end.

On this particular night, I went off to my rooms to console myself by translating into English verse Rimbaud's sonnet, which I then thought wonderful, but now think sentimental:

> Morts de quatre-vingt-douze et de quatre-vingt-treize
> Qui, pâles du baiser fort de la liberté ...

There were compensations and jokes to mitigate irritations. At some occasions of the medieval Church, Epiphany for one, the Manciple came round at dinner to distribute 'pie money', half a crown in a little envelope with the college crest of the mallard upon it—half a crown was quite a perquisite to a medieval Fellow. On Ascension Day St Mary's choirboys came into college 'beating the bounds' of the parish and scrambling for pennies on the lawn. According to a rota, one was steward of the week to choose the menus for dinner. One week I was challenged to produce lampreys, such a delicacy in the Middle Ages. Our London fish-shop hadn't heard of a lamprey for years; they had ceased to exist in the Thames, but there were still some in the Severn. On the last day of the week the lampreys arrived: horrid objects like fat worms with gills, suckers with which they attached themselves to their carrion. The chef assassinated them in the kitchen. The word went round, and one by one the Fellows took their names off from dining. So the lampreys were made into a *soufflé*, and served at the lunch at which Jones was entertaining his fiancée. They survived, and married happily.

In the middle of the lamprey crisis there were 'calls on the telephone from Lady Ottoline, whom I'd forgotten to reply to about lunch today, a hurried attempt to screw David Cecil up to walking to Garsington with me this afternoon, and a rush to the bus-office to make arrangements for transport'.

There were charms even in dining in Common Room on quiet Sunday evenings when Oman was there. It was fascinating to hear *his* reminiscences, they went back so far. He had been in Frankfurt and seen the state entry of old Emperor William I, Moltke and Bismarck riding abreast on their war-horses into the city, the soldiery cheering, the citizenry, having been recently annexed to Prussia, silent and in sulks. Most vivid was his memory of Napoleon III and the Empress Eugénie, sitting on a garden seat in the Tuileries watching their son, the Prince Imperial, drilling his little squad of cadets; the Emperor prematurely aged and crumpled up, the Empress straight as a dart in a crinoline with black and white zebra stripes. (I didn't know then of the Empress's remark to one of his numerous mistresses: 'Mademoiselle, vous tuez l'Empereur.')

For the rest, in spite of my preference for solitude expressed in the Diary, my Engagements Book records a very active social life: walks and talks with my undergraduate friends; dining at Christ Church with Masterman, Ryle and even Dundas, at Queen's with benevolent Streeter; walks with Bowra and having him to dine, though I was never one of his entourage—I had an entourage of my own. Lunching at Garsington with Ottoline, or having a hardly less exotic lady to lunch, Marie Beazley, who had taken me up at Christ Church. I couldn't really cope with her, any more than I could with Ottoline. Jacky Beazley's wife—*he* was a man of genius—was as tiresome as she was talented: a gifted pianist, she wouldn't play the piano any more; an exquisite cook, she preferred her philosophizing, which meant talking pretentious nonsense. With her dark and glittering Levantine appearance, her voluptuous figure and seductive way of waggling her hips, she mesmerized me a bit, Madame la Sorcière, as I privately called her. I called to mind the young man in Firbank's story who had a fixation on an old lady: 'He adored to distraction her little schoolboy moustache.' Mrs Beazley confessed to *un petit fixe* on All Souls, because she had met her Jacky there; had she a little *fixe*, innocent of course, on me? I could not do justice to her; she

told me once that only a young Greek girl could undermine my
defences. There is a more endearing portrait of her in Harold
Acton's delightful *Memoirs of an Aesthete*: he could talk to her in
her own language, I couldn't.

Not many concerts this term, perhaps because people had to
economize on fuel—we were having wood fires in college, no
hardship. But I did hear Paderewski in the flesh, evidently in
decline from what he had been before the war, since his period in
politics. Clemenceau's *mot* was justified in the event, on
Paderewski becoming President of Poland: 'Quelle chute!'

December 4th, 1926, was my twenty-third birthday, and 'no
such thing to show for it as Milton's Sonnet on his ... I may have
in the end to stand or fall by this Diary: if only all the complex
threads could be woven into one texture I should not be ashamed
of it as a picture of my life.'

There followed an entry to bear this out: another visit to Robert
Bridges, when he told me something historically interesting.
McFarlane and I walked up through Matthew Arnold's Hinksey—

> In the two Hinkseys nothing keeps the same;
>   The village street its haunted mansion lacks,
> And from the sign is gone Sybilla's name,
>   And from the roofs the twisted chimney-stacks.

The more hideous changes of our time were on the way:

> Along the ridge roads and crescents are being planned across
> the open fields ... Bridges not in his gruff bear's mood, but
> kindly and genuinely interested to talk. So unlike a Masefield
> affair [next door], where conversation is manufactured by Mrs
> Masefield before one's eyes. Chilswell, the house beautiful,
> in design and workmanship; Mrs Bridges presiding in no
> fussy lion-tamer's spirit, but with a quiet, ordered beauty in
> all her movements. Laurence Binyon's daughter, Nicolette,
> there: very pleasant walking back through country lanes
> with her and Bruce, trying to avoid the puddles.

Bridges talked away about Q, he admired his short stories, but
mainly about the war and his admiration for Sir Henry Wilson,
he was 'such a good fighter'. Most interesting was what he had to
say over the envenomed controversy with the Germans about Sir

Morrell Mackenzie's diagnosis and treatment of the Emperor Frederick's cancer of the throat—'if what he says can be regarded as true,' I added sagely. Bridges had been a doctor, and knew the inside gossip.

He said there could be no doubt that Sir Morrell Mackenzie was sent out to give a wrong diagnosis of the throat-trouble; but that this was a private matter between Victoria and her daughter [Vicky, Frederick's wife, and mother of Kaiser William]. But William II ought not to have minded that his father got the title for a few months. This was known to few people. But many in the profession knew Mackenzie to be unscrupulous enough to put through that sort of thing and often called him Sir Immorrell Mackenzie.

In the inflamed inferiority complex the Germans developed towards Britain there was an embittered controversy, and this gave them a point. It was a tragedy for Germany and Europe that old William I went on, in Bismarck's hands, until he was ninety and that his son, the Crown Prince Frederick, did not succeed until he was a dying man. For Frederick and his wife, Queen Victoria's daughter, had the liberal, constitutional ideas of the Coburgs like the Prince Consort, and were convinced that Bismarck had set Germany on a collision-course—as indeed he had. Bismarck regarded responsible Parliamentary government as 'the Revolution', and called the Crown Princess, who saw the danger ahead, maliciously, 'die Engländerin', though the English royal family were of as pure German blood as Bismarck himself.

I had a closer source of information in Spenser Wilkinson, who was brother-in-law of Sir Eyre Crowe, head of the Foreign Office. He was the author of the historic Crowe Memorandum, summing up the threat Bismarck's (like Hitler's) Germany constituted both to Britain and to Europe. Crowe had a German mother and a German wife: he knew what was brewing. Wilkinson was closely informed as to pretty little German ways and William II's odious treatment of his mother. One way and another my education was proceeding! In fact I cannot express how much I owed to these older Fellows at All Souls, from whom the youngster in their midst was learning, listening, watching, arguing all the way, and not only over politics and history. The dominant note of the college was public affairs; I rather regretted that it was not more literary—I could have spared Woodward for Aldous Huxley, or Dougie Malcolm for John Buchan, or H. W. C. Davis for even Belloc (Belloc, Buchan, Huxley had been defeated candidates, unfortunately: our loss). This dominant concern, politics and public affairs, had its influence in reinforcing my interest in politics—perhaps, without it, I should not have been so tensed up about politics. Ultimately, after a long deviation—not wholly a mistake, though it occasioned much heart-burning—it was not without use to the historian: the only *use* it ever had!

For one thing, we were much under the shadow of the tragedy of the 1914–18 war—one can see now that it heralded the end of European civilization, as we knew it, and the end of Britain's long and happy primacy in the world. There were reminders in the memorial in Chapel, and the photographs of the Fellows who had been killed. I made a secret cult of them, and would moon about the inner sanctum of the coffee-room looking at them: Raymond Asquith, the Prime Minister's son, a solid, masculine figure for all his coruscating wit; Foster-Cunliffe, Estates Bursar and baronet, hope of the young Conservatives; Patrick Shaw-Stewart, already one of the 'Souls' in London, of legendary brilliance and promise; a stolid Radcliffe, photographed outside my (later) staircase; and Anderson, a charming handsome boy, sunny and smiling in youthful officer's kit. I came upon a memorial to Radcliffe in Widecombe church in Devon the other day, his father squire of the parish. It was a hideous holocaust the Germans inflicted—and it was all to happen over again, needlessly: because humans will not learn. (I have learned, like Swift, that humans are idiots in all times and places; but there are degrees of idiocy.)

I was struggling hard to think out a position for myself, in arguments with others and with myself recorded in the Diary. There are attempts to work out a realist position not only in politics but in aesthetics. I was much influenced by what of Marxism I could get hold of, a rather esoteric body of thought at that time. I was obsessed by the prevalence of humbug in politics—no wonder in the age of Baldwin! There are Notes on 'The Myth of Public Opinion'—true enough: public opinion was manufactured and manipulated, the people had no opinion, rightly considered, as I knew from my own at home. All forms of idealism came under attack, even the social idealism of Tawney and Temple. 'The mental attitude that denies the existence of great 'bends' of interest, and indeed the necessity of self-interest in politics, seems to me hypocritical.' And it was: in all the teaching I had received from my tutors—acutely conscious of class as they were socially—this most important factor in history and politics was never once mentioned. I was as conscious of class in the one respect as in the other—some people commented on my acute class-consciousness; but what need to wonder? They were only half-aware. As for my own working people, the poor souls were unaware of their own interests—what a struggle it was trying to open their eyes to them, as a Labour candidate in the thirties! (Only too well aware of them today, to the neglect of everything else.)

The sage youth of twenty-three commented: 'On a purely realist basis, uncomplicated by idealism [I should now call it, rather, humbug], it should be possible to make accommodations by giving a point here and gaining one there.' This was not irrelevant to the situation, when the coal-strike had been going on for months. I thought that the objection from the point of view of English policy was that the appeal to idealistic motives was 'part of the game by which we have been successful. All very well when on the upgrade; but the danger is that when we are relatively declining, we may bamboozle ourselves by the same mentality by which we have bamboozled others.'

The youth had a point there. The humbug-mentality, played on by a virtuoso in the art, the most powerful man in British politics in all these years, Baldwin, kept the real issues befogged until the country woke up to mortal danger in 1939. A Fellow of All Souls, G. M. Young, given the task of writing Baldwin's biography, could hardly complete the task he was so sickened, and grew to detest the man. It was not the man who was detestable, but the politician.

The inner life yielded me my real satisfactions of mind, not politics, which provided nothing but worry and questioning— what Auden later labelled 'the Age of Anxiety' (he was nothing like so anxious as I was, and gratified himself much more). Such entries as these speak for themselves. 'Evening is coming on, and the spire of St Mary's and roofs around are veiled in violet mist. Looking towards Queen's, I see the trees drooping heavily to the lawn. Paris is in my heart: it must be a symbol of beauty in the contemplation of life. Health and joy in living seem to be coming back to me, at last, at last!'

The sheer beauty of the place constantly struck me, at any moment of the day or night. December twilight caught me coming back from the Library: 'Arrested at the corner of Chapel and Hall, I looked back at the twin towers above the roof-line, the half-lights of winter clothing the grotesque design with Gothick fantasy.' I remembered Newman taking the snapdragon growing beneath his windows at Trinity as a symbol of his perpetually being there (as he is, a bust on stone pedestal). At this point Woodward caught up with me: 'Thank God I'm here, and not in Birmingham!'—the commonplace reflection broke the spell.

Even the daily round, shopping in the town, had its charms, such was the zest of life returning. Going round to the best shoe-shop in the Turl, patronized by generations of those undergraduates who could afford it, I raised my eyebrows on paying my bill, but was consoled by the note that lay beside it: 'Dear Mr Ducker, Get on with my shoes. I want them before Xmas. Yours truly, ——.' There followed a well-known name. Coming back from Garsington on the top of the bus, I got a glimpse into the old family life of the High, when some shopkeepers still lived over their shops. I was on a level with the first floor where lights were being lit; in some rooms firelight flitted across wall and ceiling. One room in particular transfixed me, lit by gas above the fire-place. The family were at high Sunday tea in the next room; in this one the gas had been lit preparatory to their moving in. It was empty, waiting for life. 'But the bus moved on before anyone appeared; and so the room remains fixed in my mind, empty, familiar, expectant.'

It was like Henry James, for ever looking and watching. Naïf as I was, I was self-aware enough to jot down 'Narcissism: a Diary as one long love-letter to oneself'. Oscar Wilde gave it as his opinion that 'to be in love with oneself is the beginning of a life-long romance'; to this I added the gloss, without ever thinking of what he suffered at the hands of Lord Alfred—'and *much safer*!' A further reflection is more in the style of Palinurus (and what, contemporaneously, was Cyril up to?): 'Daily entries in a diary may be regarded as a kind of necessary excrement.'

My German lessons had been broken off by my illness; I now took them up again, though I never fully made up the leeway lost. Roger Makins had continued his, and was now off to the Continent to complete his preparation for the Foreign Office. Term over, I asked our poor old German teacher over to tea. Fräulein Pohl had taught at some Royal school for officers' daughters at Bath, and been 'turned away by a jingo staff at the beginning of the war'. She now earned her living by teaching all day and every day in her little attic rooms where she lived up a formidable number of stairs, up which one stumbled, in King Edward Street. Her lessons were unbelievably boring. 'She made an hour between lessons when she could come and drink tea with me here; and was pathetically pleased when I took her to see the Codrington Library, up to the Elizabethan Old Library, and into the Chapel faintly lit up for us by a few flickering candles. Poor soul, what a life! only one relation left, a sister stranded these difficult years in Danzig.'

It was the Fräulein who fixed up for me to go on with my German in the family of a Lutheran pastor at Hagen in Westphalia—a physical and spiritual environment more in keeping with her tastes than mine; at any rate the accent was said to be pure. The next phase in my education was about to begin.

2

My First Acquaintance with Germany

My immediately junior contemporaries—Auden, Isherwood, Spender, in particular—have made a great thing of their experience in Weimar Germany: Herr Issyvoo's *Mr Norris* and 'On Rügen Island', Wystan in peaked black cap sweeping snow in the streets of Berlin, the equivocal prose 'Letter to a Wound' which he had received, Stephen's Weimarish play, etc. I have made nothing of mine, though I was there before them and later was more involved through my anguished friendship with Adam von Trott. I kept it all to myself and my Diary, as certainly my first experience—I draw the title of this chapter from Hazlitt's famous essay—was lived to myself. I was bent on making up the time I had lost over my German through illness, by living in a German family—would that I had been able to live in a French family: a much better idea both for me and my contemporaries.

Oxford term over, I left Victoria for the Calais–Düsseldorf express on a glum 16th of December for a winter in Germany. Passing through Brussels at midnight, Cologne at breakfast-time, arrived at Düsseldorf I spent the day there mooching around. I noticed one rather fine post-war building, my first glimpse of the architecture for which the Weimar Republic is justly renowned. The Neue Presse was in half-tone brick, with vertical lines accentuated by sandstone ribs, the façade finished with small arches at the top, lattice-work in brick. Later, I could appreciate that this was a modern version of traditional Westphalian architecture, like the old Rathaus in Münster—and very good it was, better than what was going up in Britain.

Germany seemed to have plenty of money for public buildings, and there were nothing like the slums that existed at home, even in the industrial Rhineland. The Germans had no intention of paying the Reparations demanded of them for the war they had made and the destruction they had wrought in north-east France and Flanders; it is now known that they borrowed from Wall Street and the City about the same amount, one thousand million pounds, as they ever made over in Reparations. And unknown to us, they were already making the first beginnings in rearmament, upon which they were able to spend another thousand million when Hitler got them ready again to renew the war. As Amery said to me at All Souls, 'They so nearly brought it off the first time that it was to be expected they would have another try.' Their best historian today, Fritz Fischer, admits, what hardly any of them have been prepared to do, that both wars were but the crests of the long attempt of Germany in this century to achieve European domination and *Weltmacht*.[1]

All this was a closed book to me. Perhaps I deliberately closed my eyes as a young Leftist, indoctrinated with the disastrous nonsense put about by Bertrand Russell, H. N. Brailsford, E. D. Morel and the rest of them—that we were just as responsible for the 1914–18 war as the Germans were! There is not wanting an erratic historian today—a friend of mine in those youthful days— who preaches the same brand of irresponsible rubbish to the effect that Hitler was not much more to blame for the Second War than we were. A. E. Housman has a bitter comment on devotion to truth being the least of human passions. The fact that human beings do not care whether their statements are true or not is to me one of the most shocking things about them. An over-riding passion for truth has been one of the strongest impulses in my life—anyone can see that it has involved sacrifices from the point of view of expediency and 'getting on', a career, and all that. As to that, I do not care—I do not sufficiently respect humans, with their lack of standards. The truth, at all costs! Perish expediency, and secondary considerations. Here is one reason why I am an historian: *Ich kann nicht anders.*

Hagen, an industrial town on the edge of the Ruhr, was a gloomy enough place to have arrived at for the winter; but the sight of it was somewhat mitigated under snow—the first thing I noticed: 'the white limbs of the trees in the snow'. Nor was the typical bourgeois life of a Lutheran pastor's family the most

[1] See Fritz Fischer, *War of Illusions. German Policies from 1911 to 1914.*

stimulating to an ardent young intellectual who needed friendship more than anything, but—unlike those public-schoolboys, Wystan, Christopher, Stephen, or for that matter Graham, Evelyn Waugh, Cyril Connolly—did not know how to set about it.

When I arrived at the *Pfarrer*'s roomy, heavily furnished house there was an attractive Englishman—a Nairac from Mauritius, of French descent—who helped me to bridge the first days, translating for me. When he left, I was disconsolate. I was a defeatist about friendship, inured to caring more for the other person than he could possibly care for me: I 'allowed myself the brief indulgence knowing that it would soon end. But what would happen if I ever came across someone who was unwilling that it should drop? I persuade myself that I am willing to sacrifice everything to what I want to do with my life.' Now, an elderly man, I see that the overdeveloped will I had generated, in the course of the long struggle to get to Oxford, imposed too much of a strain on the young body. There were moods when I thought that the future might 'go hang, if there were any prospect of satisfaction in the present. But perhaps I am incapable of friendship?—I should demand too much from it. And so I live in a very real loneliness, all the more real because I don't notice it much when busy with my own ideas, reading and writing my Notes.'

I was for ever writing Notes for God knows how many projects, books on politics, history, literature, poetry; there is even a complete synopsis of a play on Swift. Swift obsessed my mind; during these early years I passionately wanted to write a biography of him. I went to Dublin to see all the places he knew; all the doors were opened to me, the Dean of St Patrick's showed me over the Deanery, from cellars to attics; I went to Laracor and Trim, and to Vanessa's Celbridge. But it was beyond me—and I had to get on with my college research in history; it is only some fifty years later, constant as ever to those early inspirations, that I have fulfilled it with *Jonathan Swift: Major Prophet*.

That lonely winter in Germany—where Wystan, Christopher and Stephen had such fun—I reflected, 'When I watch the attitude of other people towards each other, and then towards me, I don't think they put me on the same footing. It may be due to my holding myself aloof from their activities. But there remains a disquieting feeling that there is more in it than that: disquieting, even if it means that I shall be able by that quality to influence other people—for that destiny means no love or intimacy, no closeness of sympathy and no friends.' This was, in some part, prophetic; and today I have renounced even the desire to influence anyone.

I soon found somewhere to be alone in, as I had for years cultivated the intensity of solitude at Carn Grey—the wooded hills around Hagen. December 20th—'nach Mittag, N. geht nach Paris; am Abend, nach Bismarck's Türme'. On the hills outside the town were two memorial towers, one to Bismarck, fabricator of Germany's unity by the way of 'blood and iron'—the barbarian of genius; the other in memory of a Rhineland Liberal, Eugen Richter—for there was an alternative tradition in Germany, that of Liberal, responsible Parliamentary government. The tragedy for Germany, and for Europe, was that the former won out.

André Nairac was a happy extrovert, able to converse in German as well as French. That evening I walked up to Bismarck's Tower, 'partly to forget him, or at least not remember that he has ever been here [but who remembers him now?]. I think it is done now, but it means making a new start.' I was left alone, with the resources of the family and this raw industrial town.

Hagen reminded me of the Potteries, the only time I had been there—to lecture to the Workers' Educational Association, of which it was a foremost centre, thanks to Tawney. The ugly town sprawled in the valleys and up the lower slopes, but the upper were covered with pine woods. The forest extended all the way to I forget where: it made me think of the old romantic Germany of Jean Paul and Carlyle's tufted imagination. Earlier, it must have been a wilderness of a country, with sparse population strung out in tiny villages in the forest. I recalled a night at Garsington, when I had to find my way in pitch-black darkness down to the high road. I wondered whether the real Germany was not in the country villages and townships, the real England industrial, 'so that my political speculation may be out of focus through ignorance of it'. (Today, England is suburbia, my political opinions still more out of sympathy; but I do not care, for I do not wish to know it.)

As to the family, the middle-aged Pastor was a naïf sentimental soul. I paid 63 marks a week for my keep. On the proceeds he was able to make a trip to London, from which he came back with eyes wide open, and much impressed by the traffic—'Ach, der Riesenverkehr!' In his innocent way he was not without the typical German ambivalence towards Britain, admiration and envy so deep that it affected even him. 'Why should the English have got rid of our Kaiser?—he was a friend of England'. And so on.

I do not know whether the Kaiser's homo–erotic tendencies were operative or no; but Princess Bibesco, who was a close friend of the Crown Prince—'Little Willie' to the irreverent English—certainly knew, and seemed to think so. There was the awkward house-party at which an elderly General, tightly corseted and dancing as a ballerina, dropped dead and the Kaiser had to skedaddle from the incriminating scene. And he was a friend of the gifted Prince Eulenburg, who was highly cultivated and a civilized anti-militarist; so his enemies in the General Staff and Foreign Office framed him for his homosexuality in the usual way, ruined his career and ended his deplorable influence for peace.

Quite early in my stay, in the middle of the family evening meal, the Pastor suddenly came out with 'Why did the English send Oscar Wilde to prison?' I hadn't much sense, but just enough to realize that he was getting at the English, which Germans couldn't resist trying on. Here was a young innocent to try it on; nor had I much capacity to express myself in German, so I said heavily: 'Es war ein Eulenburg Kasus'. Consternation: the *Pfarrer* hadn't expected that a young Englishman would know about Eulenburg and the Kaiser. 'Sh,' he said; 'we don't talk about Eulenburg here.' 'Neither do we talk about Wilde,' I said smugly, having shut him up.

After that episode he went in for reading O. Wilde, and consumed *The Picture of Dorian Gray*, the silver hair starting from his head. The Germans knew that Wilde was one of the very greatest of English writers; we depreciated him simply out of English humbug. This was something to rub in, infantile as they were. Every informed person knows that there is a characteristic German combination of self-confident pronouncements with insensitive stupidity, a kind of wall across the mind. When I got to Munich, the musical Baltic baron in whose house I lived was able to condemn Milton, though he hadn't a word of English, as a mere Klopstock. He would not take my word for it that he was one of the first of poets. I had to tell him that the Italians had the perception to recognize that he was more of a Dante.

Similarly when the Pastor's eldest son turned up from university or *Hochschule*, an unpleasant pimpled youth of military bearing (he became a Nazi). I greatly admired Hofmannsthal's 'Ballade des Äusseren Lebens', and was fond of quoting:

> Wozu sind diese aufgebaut? und gleichen
> Einander nie? und sind unzählig viele?

The son of the house was able to inform me that the poem was written in a totally new and unique measure. I was able to inform him that *terza rima* was one of the best known of poetic measures, since Dante's *Divina Commedia* was written in it. The odious youth simply would not believe it. I said he could look it up and see that it was so. He ransacked his father's bookshelves, where he found a translation of Dante into German, and fortunately that was in *terza rima* too.

It was like the stupid-obstinate German woman my friend Rebecca West describes so well in *Black Lamb, Grey Falcon*—how recognizable these charmless characteristics were. That youth was afterwards killed in Paris, I learned. Well, what was he doing there? I remember the most sinister scene from my last visit to Paris, just before the Second German War, I was in the Rue de Rivoli, when suddenly there flowed down it a whole squad of German motor-cyclists, all similarly equipped, swerving into the Place de la Concorde. I shuddered at the omen: it was an exercise preparatory to the occupation of Paris in 1940.

The Frau Pastor was no beauty, dark, bony face, like one of those Madonnas one sees in German painting, Michael Pacher or Cranach. She was a kindly soul, with the usual middle-class female's propensity to talk about marrying and giving in marriage —never a welcome topic to this dedicated celibate. 'Sind Sie verliebt?' 'Sind Sie verlobt?' With not much command of the language, but well aware of what I was saying, I replied: 'Verlobt, aber nicht verliebt.' They thought that I was making a mistake: a great joke. The Frau had an insipid daughter to dispose of; would I like her to be my *Schwiegermutter*? (Nothing less). How old did I think the Frau Pastor? Considering she had a son of nineteen or twenty, I said firmly, forty-seven. The lady was greatly taken aback, another mistake: I must have meant *thirty*-seven. No, I held to it: *sieben und vierzig, forty*-seven. I had meant to put her in her place; the laugh turned against her: they all laughed at her vexation. Germans cannot resist *Schadenfreude*, even against one of their own, it is so deep in their make-up.

Only one denizen of the household had any appeal for me: the youngest, a charming child. But he was only five or six: not much intellectual companionship there, though he was rather fond of me and used to nestle up to me as I ploughed away at my German grammar. I am glad that he survived the war.

My 63 marks a week did not include German lessons; for those I went to an uninspiring ancient, Professor Haastert, who once surprised me. He had failed to take a post in England; I asked him when. He replied, 'Oh, that was in 1874.' Most of my few engagements, I notice, are in simple German: 'In die Stadt am Morgen die Bücher zu besorgen. Nach Mittag in die Wälder. Schrieb zwei Briefe am Abende'. And so on. On December 29th I went up into the woods in great excitement, 'after getting two long letters from Roger and Keith Hancock, raising the issues that have been struggling in my mind for the last two years. Is it to be the life of thought, or of action? Can I go back to where I stopped in poetry?—even now all the things that I most care for are bound up with that. Or is it better to go on with history and politics?—for here there is more work to be done in my generation.'

I argued the matter out with myself in the woods, where I sometimes stayed till nightfall. (It occurs to me now to wonder whether, in the advance of civilization, one could wander about in the woods up there alone today in safety—highly doubtful, now that the people are emancipated.) I did not like the thought that things work themselves out 'in accordance with circumstances, not all of them extrinsic'—and that was what happened in the end: my body finally revolted, and I was made to drop the idea of a life of action. Oxford was responsible for pressing me along that line: we studied Aristotle, who placed the values of an active contribution to the life of society higher than a passive life of contemplation. I was not made for the active practical life; I regarded myself as deficient here—all the more reason why I should rectify the balance, try myself out in politics. My will, aided by the pressure of the time, drove me into it, against my real nature—no young man of intelligence and public spirit could remain unaffected by the hopes of the time, the hopes of peace and disarmament, the League of Nations internationally, and internally those of social progress, a better deal for my own working class. Then, when things took a more sinister course in the thirties there was the urgent necessity to take a hand—one couldn't let up (though most fools did: many good lives were lost in consequence).

Here was the dilemma. Should I aim at a Parliamentary candidature? That would mean 'throwing over poetry and the life of the imagination, and probably that of historical and political thought as well. The chances are in favour of my deciding on the first group: it means lopping off less.' I am surprised today that the young man saw the choice so clearly. I staved off making the choice as long as possible, hoping for the best of both worlds— thought *and* action. Trying to keep going the two in harness, a double burden, in the event almost killed me. Thank God I never let go of writing, in the long *supplice* of a political candidature in the 'thirties, a hopeless struggle. One of the shrewdest, and to me most sympathetic of the Senior Fellows, Sir Edmund Craster— Bodley's Librarian—foresaw which way things would go, and that writing would win.

At this early stage 'one other person half-sees; but he is Dundas, who makes it a profession to look into other people's souls, especially in the lurid light of sex. He pronounced, "Much too complicated". I have precious little in common with him; he belongs to the pre-war generation, and is more interested in people than in movements and ideas. What he sees he won't appreciate; so he won't see more than I choose.' Anyway, I didn't want to know a lot of dons at Christ Church ('not knowing people is a great saving of time'). People at All Souls, and the public figures constantly passing through its portals, were immeasurably more interesting—however, they reinforced one's interest in public life and affairs.

'What I want is, of course, the impossible: some great romantic friendship that will be a source of strength and inspiration ... I believe that there is a power produced by the conjunction of two minds that goes beyond the potentiality of either taken by itself.' If the partnership of Rimbaud and Verlaine was sordid, look what it produced! And there were the still more creative friend-ships of Wordsworth and Coleridge, of Goethe and Schiller. But I was a defeatist; a note in the woods says, 'The romantic never happens; if it did, it would cease to be romantic.' One was left with one's loneliness, a main theme in the synopsis for a play about Swift.

Meanwhile, up in the *Wald*, there was

the contrast of rich tawny darkness under the pines with the blue mist in the valley: brown light of underwood, blue light above. In the town below a clock strikes five; lights begin to appear, workmen pour out of dark gateways and down the narrow wynds. A cluster of warm lights at the mouth of the hills like domesticated Pleiades brought to earth. And now, lights everywhere, filling the plain like a haven with a thousand ships, mast-lights through tangled spars of the pines. The railway line like a mailed serpent, rounding the curve of the foothills. Night coming on, the hollows of the wood darker and given up to the shades that haunt the night.

As I descended, footsteps crunching snow, lines came into my head:

No wind that blows
In that still country of the mind
Awakes the momentary beauty summer knows.

Nor in that wood
Now stir the thousand whispering sounds that run
Along the listening summer solitude.

The trees are still;
Only the soundless shift and drop of snow
Upon the ground the hollow spaces fill.

On the last night of the year, *Sylvesternacht* in Germany, we had fireworks and a brass band playing chorales in the square outside the Pauluskirche, the Pastor's church, which I did not attend. Abroad, I went only to Catholic churches, often to Mass, though no believer. On my way back I went out of my way into a tangle of streets near the Marienkirche, 'and was rewarded by coming upon a Lutheran church lighted up for service, the bells ringing. Down the dark street people were hurrying to be in time for church. I watched the ringers in the belfry, their dark shadows springing up and down against the lighted window.'

Then at the end of my engagements book—'a little poem on a book with the author's thoughts written in it, that will remain long after he has gone'. I think that was what confirmed me in the habit of writing Notes and keeping Note-Books: with these illnesses I could always hear 'time's wingèd chariot hurrying near' and was afraid that I should die with nothing accomplished. So, with the years, they piled up: scores of little pocket-books, in addition to the Diary, notes, phrases, observations, poems, fragments, historical memoranda, what places looked like, what people said—far more in number than Samuel Butler's, of which I am an admirer; and, if less amusing, many are naughtier, all authentic.

New Year 1927 began with a walk to Bismarck's Turm 'mit der Familie': hence no reflections, an impoverishment. With old Professor Haastert I was reading the stock poems of Goethe; in the Diary there are verse translations of the ballad, 'Der König in Thule' (not bad), and of 'Meine Ruh ist hin'—a sentimental poem at best. The family's level in reading was represented more by the low-lying Gustav Frenssen, who wrote provincial tales in Platt-Deutsch. They gave me a volume—long since disappeared. I really could not do with such fare. I was reading Emil Ludwig's life of Walter Rathenau, a figure who excited my interest: a great industrialist who was big-minded enough to be half a socialist; the creator of the Allgemeine Elektrizitäts Gesellschaft, who had saved Germany from collapse in the war by reorganizing her whole economy. A note says 'the organiser, if not of victory, at least of successful national resistance'. I was intrigued by him and bought his books, his biography and *Briefe*. For his services to

Germany he was murdered by the dastardly Freikorps, militant right-wingers who had the strongest elements of the nation behind them, who never accepted the verdict of 1918, let alone the Treaty of Versailles. These were not the only Germany, but they formed the Germany that really counted.

Other elements were to the fore under the Weimar Republic, and here we were on the edge of the Catholic Rhineland. A big new Franciscan church was being built up on the bare hillside; I watched the excavations being made, the plans taking shape, as at Oxford that autumn I had seen the foundations of Rhodes House being laid. The church was a skeleton so far—was it ever finished? —except for the façade with its archaic Teutonic sculpture, a barbaric Christ, hands outstretched to the unbelieving West. 'All up and down the hillside roads are being made and houses built.' I added innocently, 'It was surprising to see so much activity at a time when Germany is supposed to be impoverished and fettered.' How could they afford it all?

Even provincial Hagen was not without its cultural entertainments. There was an Exposition of local artists; I dutifully kept notes of what I saw—as I still do. There were individual paintings, a man ploughing with a white horse, a background of Rhineland chimneys belching smoke. Etchings, charcoal drawings and bronzes, all 'influenced by archaic Teutonism, the return to barbarism and the heroic age'. I took it for a return to the past, not a portent for the future, not so far away either: this was what was latent in the German soul—how much more civilized Paris, where we all should have gone, not Berlin!

Music, as always in Germany, was far better. The reader must imagine how much more difficult it was to hear good music in Britain in those days: wireless and gramophone were in their early stages, and I had neither. Intensely musical, I had only my piano, and in remote Cornwall only church music to go on. In the impoverished circumstances of defeated Germany, with the intolerable burden of Reparations, etc., a middle-sized industrial town like Hagen could yet support its own orchestra and conductor, Hans Feibusch. And this was so all over Germany: music was an industry. I soon became immersed in it to the neglect of the language, the scintillating Professor Haastert and the Pastor's family—still more so when I got to Munich and Vienna.

In the Stadthalle there was eighteenth-century music, Händel and Hasse and Jommelli; and I was electrified to hear the Romantic Symphony of Bruckner, of whom I had only just heard—not much performed in England till after the Second War. At another concert I heard Delius's 'Brigg Fair' for the first time—one had to come to Germany to hear it; but then, I reflected, he was a German. Even in Hagen one heard a pianist as good as Edwin Fischer, playing in a Beethoven piano concerto, or a whole evening of Schubert, Weber, Chopin, Liszt. At the Stadthalle concerts we had such a wide variety as Dvořák, Saint-Saëns, Dukas; Beethoven, Wagner, Berlioz's *Benvenuto Cellini*, Liszt's *Faust* music. At the Stadttheater we had *Lohengrin*, Humperdinck's *Königskinder*, and the *Puppenschuster*. Not bad going for a town of perhaps 80,000, under the heel of the conqueror—impossible to find anything like it in England or France!

For myself, I couldn't get on with the language on the old-fashioned diet I was being given, Goethe, Mörike and the *Deutsche Lyrik*. I was out of sympathy with it until I took up the modern poets for myself, Hofmannsthal, Stefan George, Franz Werfel, above all Rilke, greatest of them; or I was amused by a Surrealist, like Christian Morgenstern:

> Es war ein Knie geht langsam
> durch die Welt ...
> Es war ein Knie, sonst nichts

—the kind of thing that enraged the Nazis in the Weimar Republic. They had their own reply to it, and in those days, when they were a small minority, could afford to sing—what Adolf Hitler really thought—

> Ich hasse die Masse, die kleine, die gemeine,
> Den nacken gebeugt,
> Die isst und frisst und kinder zeugt.

As for the freedom permitted them and thugs like the Freikorps, murderers not only of men like Rathenau and a Catholic leader like Erzberger, but of many Liberals and Social Democrats, they showed what they would do with the freedom idiotically permitted them by the spineless liberalism of Weimar:

> Wir scheissen auf die Freiheit.

But of that side of the dear Germans, the most important side for the future, I was at that time unaware, like a good many other people.

In the bourgeois domesticity of the Pastor's comfortable parsonage I was translating Rilke's *Die Weise vom Leben und Tod des Cornetts Christoph Rilke*, his one popular work: it had sold a million copies during the war. It was not easy to translate, and almost impossible to render it into acceptable English, it was so deeply sentimental in the German Expressionist manner. So I did nothing with it: there it remains, heavily corrected, buried in the Note-Books along with the Swift synopsis and all the rest.

My nose has been kept close to the grindstone, what with three German tutorials a week, and my painful struggle every day with the newspapers. Then there are the concerts, a feast of music; my walks abroad in the country through the woods to ever new and unexplored land; a whole day seeing churches in Cologne—one might spend years there studying these and writing a book on their stained glass; and ever new books that I get hold of.

Since I had a crush on the young men killed in the war, I bought the Diaries of Otto Braun, a brilliant young scholar, a kind of Rupert Brooke, though not a poet. At that moment, 'an irruption from little Fritz, who comes in dressed up in his father's dressing-gown and little else, a round hat and bedroom slippers. He announces himself as the Herr Pastor. I tell him he's the Erzbischof, der Erzbischof von Hagen, and he goes out pacified.'

In mid-January, to my horror, there was 'a return of the old symptoms in my stomach. Dear God, I hope it doesn't mean that an ulcer is developing again. In some moods I feel myself to be a wreck, after all the pain that I have borne in the last few years, without giving in. And I mustn't give in now; there's too much to be done in the world, and what excitement and joy there is in looking forward to doing it. This evening I walked in the woods until the pain was only a dull ache in my stomach.' I noticed the white cups on the telephone poles caught, like birds, in the meshes of the trees. On the ground a little bird kept hopping along with me, piping a note to me now and then—lonely too.

I was frightened, and with reason. What I had not been told, was that the ulcer had never been dealt with. One of the disheartening things about being born into the working class was that there was never anyone to look to for help or advice—too ignorant: one was left to one's own. Nor can I acquit my doctor—a dear, highly sensitive Quaker—of blame: he should have told me, as he should have laid down a proper, if prolonged, course of treatment. As it was, I was left in ignorance. The ulcer remained, as I had had it ever since nineteen—all that overstrain and anxiety; at intervals it opened up and grew a little scar-tissue, again and again until in the end the whole normal passage through my stomach was blocked, and I was in a dying condition (as other people thought and told me afterwards) by 1938. There was then another major operation, in fact two, to short-circuit the infernal thing. I survived, only just: I found the arrangements of man were more satisfactory than those of providence. Enough! I hate to think of it.

> January 21st: I have been driven out of my comfortable seat in Herr Pastor's study, where I work at a little rickety table loaded with books, by a female member of his congregation who has come to check his church accounts or compile a list of the faithful. But from my new place at the dining-room window there is a pretty spectacle. Since early morning, from two to four when I was awake with pain again, it has been snowing. Now everything is white, and children are tobogganing down the street. As I settle myself to the afternoon's task of translating Rilke, I can hear their shouts, like a school-playground. The square before the Pauluskirche is dead-white, empty and beautiful, not a footstep to disturb the uniform snow.

Pressing on, I finished the translation and dreamed what a fine little book it would make with Gothic woodcuts. But there was no one to take these things up: I knew no one, and was too proud to ask. I didn't get started effectively until Eliot took me under his wing.

There follows a week's intermission—no Diary kept, 'explained by downright illness. Now that I am better again, it is like a bad dream to think of.

The strange and lovely lights gleam out of the dark
Suddenly as the tram goes on its regal way
Through shabby, squalid night-lit streets.'

February 2: the first day on which I have felt appreciably
better again; in fact, for the whole day I have been without
pain, though I am left weak and with all the convalescent's
eager desire to be out in the air again, drinking in with eyes
and ears everything that goes on. But I wonder what it was
that made me ill? A breaking-out of old poisons in my
blood, or a definite cause in something that I ate? I see that
I must be ever on the watch for my health's sake. During the
attack I was tempted to give up all the ideas I am struggling
for ... it seemed that all I could achieve was just to hold on to
life, for the sake of my mother and father. [His birthday,
January 31st, is the only note in that bad week.] The idea of a
great life must be thrown over, with all the strain upon my
energy—to lapse into a sort of Bradleyan valetudinarian
existence. [It came to that in the end.] It is curious that
Bradley did manage to achieve great work, but he didn't
achieve a great life!

Now hope begins to revive with health and spirits, and I
intend to go on with all the irons in the fire. I must read a
good deal of German literature while here, write poems—a
long autobiography to describe all the intense experiences
that form what I mean by my life, and books on Rimbaud
and Swift, essays on Jaurès, Rathenau and Marx.

In a Note-Book there is an ambitious note to ask Ramsay
MacDonald about Jaurès, and Lloyd George about Rathenau—
later I could have done, but didn't; as for Marx, I later met his
genial grandson, Jean Longuet. There follows a complete programme of practical work, teaching and lecturing, Oxford,
London, W.E.A. (fifty years later finds me occasionally lecturing
for the W.E.A.): 'I want to live and write for the young generation in thought and politics. What a programme for a sick man!
Perhaps it is only a sick imagination that would cheat itself with
such hopes.'

Feeling recovered, I went off for the day to Soest, in which I
revelled—seven medieval churches in green sandstone, think of

it! A little Hanseatic town left high and dry by the decline of the League, so that the town still stopped at the medieval walls, and beyond were orchards. I wonder if it was destroyed in the war?— ruined anyway, I'll bet.

Another day I spent in Cologne—a great contrast with my brother's initiation at the hands of a German Frau, as an ordinary Tommy in the Army of Occupation; I thought of him as I came over the Hohenzollern Bridge, a cold breeze blowing down the Rhine, but my initiation was to be in German Romanesque. Not so much the Cathedral—much of it nineteenth-century anyway— which the British were at such pains to spare in the Second German War, but the marvellous Romanesque churches, which were the real glory of Cologne, about which they were less well instructed. Many of those I saw that day must have been damaged. I spent the day in them, in the old town north-west of the cathedral. Even so I missed the oldest of them, Sankta Maria im Kapitol, which had served as model for the rest. There was the Roman idiom in the way the Gereonskirche looked straight down a broad street to the Dom at the other end. Afternoon sun fell on the eastern apse of the church, a pale streak of light out of the grey wintry day that lit up the arcade high up and warmed the stone with colour.

After the murky obscurity of St Germain des Prés, I was surprised by the splendour of the interiors, mosaics and painting, red, green, gold. St Gereon's, the Apostles' and St Martin's were busy with worshippers all through the afternoon, and as evening came on thronged with people for confessions, as the next day was some festival. Here one saw the heart of Catholic Germany. At St Andreas', near the Dom, there were litanies and intercessions going on all day. St Ursula's in a poorer quarter pleased me most, though inside the iron screen was locked so that one could only peer into the nave, but the mosaics stood out like burnished shields in the murk; beyond, an exquisite shrine of an early Gothic choir lifted the heart up, shining with the subdued white of a pearl out of the gloomy casket of the church.

What Cologne must have been like before the secularization following upon the French Revolution one could infer from all the open spaces where there had been a cloister—Andreaskloster, Gereonskloster—and there had been convents whence came so

66

many of the pictures I was later to see in Munich, medieval paintings of the Lower Rhine and Netherlands Schools. From Cologne came Roger van der Weyden's triptych of the Three Kings, and his St Luke Drawing the Virgin; perhaps, too, Joos van Cleve's triptych of the Death of the Virgin. So many of these treasures had been altar-pieces in the churches and convent chapels—one could hardly think the French Revolution and then Prussianization aesthetic boons.

As for the twentieth century, I never looked at the secular buildings; out of the corner of my eye I saw that modern Cologne was a city of banks, 'whole streets of them that I walked through, all quite new and garish and post-war'. There was Weimar for you! My last treasured impression was of the past—'a heavy, sweet-toned bell ringing from the Cathedral at the end of the day; as I settled in my compartment in the train, I could still hear it ringing high above the darkening town.'

My last day in the north I spent in historic Münster, which was heavily bombed in the Second War. In 1927 it was still unspoiled, and fascinating with the arcaded streets that went back to the Treaty days of 1648, which ended the Thirty Years War. There was the panelled Friedensaal in which the negotiations took place, the portraits of the negotiators dominated by the great Oxenstierna—of the saying that I have had reason to remember all my life: 'Do you not know, my son, with how little wisdom the world is governed?' (I used it as an epigraph later, after the Second War, for *All Souls and Appeasement.*)

In the Frauenkirche I was amused by a stern old lady under a formidable bonnet at her prayers; there were children playing down the aisle, every time they came her way she rose, scolded them, terrific grimaces and bonnet nodding, then immediately back to her prayers. Simple, unselfconscious old soul! I was most taken with the baroque façade of the Clementine Hospital, and the magnificent rococo palace of the Prince Bishops. After their day was over one wing fell to the Prussian military governor, the other to the civil governor; I fancied the two meeting at the head of the superb staircase. But how much more those eighteenth-century days appealed to me, the archaic rule of the Prince Bishop, the colour and swish of soutanes, clerical angels ascending and descending that staircase of a dream! Is it still there? If so, I expect it has all had to be rebuilt, after the cultural attentions of our age.

In German the word for ulcer, *Krebs*, is the same as that for cancer. When I explained to the Pastor and his wife what I was suffering from they wouldn't believe it; but when I held to it, I got the impression that they were the less unwilling to let me go. Before leaving I went to say goodbye to the old Professor, whom I had got to like, after a dozen lessons with him. (What I needed was someone of my own age, such as Wystan, Christopher and Stephen had no difficulty in finding.) After taking my leave I met him again in the Stadtgarten, which ran down a slope of the Goldberg. A curious contraption, which might be a war memorial or public lavatory (shades of *Clochemerle!*), caught my eye. The Professor said it had all been a horrible mistake: the Town Council had been so divided over designs that this had slipped in— it had been worse, with a mis-shapen figure like a monkey on top. We went over together. There were the names of the fallen, with Hindenburg's blessing in his own hand: 'True to their country, even to death. von Hindenburg'. For a moment 'I wondered if it weren't a satire on the dead men by those who had led them to death—like Orpen's ghastly satire on the Peace. The Professor had no such thought. He said simply, "My son is there among the names, my eldest son: he fell in Galicia against the Russians." A moment later, "and my son-in-law too, the husband of my daughter, whom I believe you have met."

3

Munich under the Weimar Republic

What a contrast Munich was to Hagen—a large historic capital city, full of splendid architecture, medieval as well as baroque and rococo, churches and palaces galore; theatres and two notable opera-houses, the big one for large operas, Wagner and such, the delightful little eighteenth-century Residenztheater, part of the complex of the royal palace, where they performed Mozart and where I first heard *Die Entführung aus dem Serail*. Munich suffered badly from bombing in the Second War, some of the losses—like the medieval and Renaissance glass in the Frauenkirche—being irretrievable; and I gather that a good deal of the *alte Stadt*, the historic centre with its narrow medieval streets, was destroyed and has been much rebuilt.

The author of these mischiefs, Adolf Hitler, had made his abortive *Putsch* with Ludendorff in just these streets that became familiar to me: the Residenzstrasse, the Odeonsplatz with its war memorial, the Feldherrnhalle, where—with his genius for propaganda—he later re-buried the 'heroes' who had fallen that day, only some three or four years before. There followed his trial for treason, also in Munich,which he turned into a triumph with his appeal to the inflamed nationalism that was far stronger with Germans than any Weimar liberalism. As a Czech said to me in a bus some years later, 'Ein Deutscher ist dreimal deutsch.' Hitler served only nine months of his sentence at Landsberg not far away, cosseted by all the comforts provided by Nationalist sympathizers, particularly women, and with the time at his disposal to write *Mein Kampf*.

It is astonishing to think that the whole historic drama of National Socialism, its rise and fall, the appalling career of Hitler with its evil consequences, the deaths of millions, the destruction in effect of a civilization, should have been wrought out between my innocent days in Munich, the Nazi capital, and now as I come to look back on it in 1975. In those days Hitler and his movement were only one of several groups that pullulated under Weimar, with the determination to overthrow the Republic and reverse the verdict of the war, which none of them accepted. They invented the lie of the stab-in-the-back, and Germans will believe anything —as indeed Hitler wrote at Landsberg: Tell people a big enough lie and they will believe it, e.g. that Germany was not responsible for the war, or was not defeated. He knew—for part of his genius was that he realized to his finger-tips that the stupidity of ordinary people is boundless—as he wrote also: 'Germans have no idea of the extent to which people have to be gulled in order to be led.' He knew too how to play on it—and led them with mounting success, supported by them to the very end. This conclusion of his he made the epigraph, or motto, of *Mein Kampf*: it was suppressed only in 1932 when he was on the threshold of achieving power by its means. He then put it into action.

In Munich in 1927 things had quietened down and we were not aware of him. When I asked my landlady, Frau Dr von Plunder, about Hitler she replied, 'Er ist ganz verrückt.' Ten years later, when she came to see me in Oxford she sang a different song: 'Aber er ist ein *magischer* Mensch'; she held forth on his appearance at the opera, his cultivated devotion to music—'ein *magischer* Mensch'. I reminded her that ten years before she had described him as 'verrückt'. She at once shut up. But where had she got the money to pay a visit to Oxford from?—they had none to spare when I knew them. Was hers a propaganda visit? Or had her journey been paid for to report on us at Oxford?—there was a great deal of that sort of thing in the later 'thirties as Hitler's—and Germany's—Second War was being prepared.

After Hagen I was much excited by the thought of Munich, 'half afraid of writing down my expectations and hopes, for nothing in actuality can be so fine as the picture one forms of it in the mind—perhaps the picture is even the best actuality.' However, I cautiously decided that things looked fair. Dr von Plunder was music critic of the leading Munich newspaper, his wife a professional singer; he of good Baltic stock, large and dark, long-nosed and hefty, she no beauty, her voice a bit overripe, with that sexy female vibrato I simply could not stand—why couldn't she keep the note clean and pure, and stay on it, like any choirboy, such as I had been myself? How I detested that fruity wobble, and still do. Anyhow, the life of this house centred on music, there was music at home, and people came to the house for musical evenings. Music was the leading industry in Munich; on top of opera, innumerable concerts and, since the Beethoven Centenary was in full swing, there was the chance to hear rare Beethoven works one would never hear again—like the early motet for the funeral of the Emperor Joseph, with its comic refrain, 'Josef ist tot, ist tot!'; or the funeral music for four trombones, played off stage.

I made the most of it all, immersed myself in music and sightseeing, nearly always alone—and so my German, instead of improving, went backward. Since I didn't like the language anyway, except for its poetry, I yielded to the temptation to read more French, which I respected and admired. (So had Rilke: he even published two volumes of verse in French.) The Plunders' house lay off the Ungererstrasse, which ran up to Schwabing, the highbrow suburb where musicians, painters, writers congregated. The house lay in the centre of what had been the estate of an old Herr Ungerer. The morning after my whole-day railway journey up the Rhine and across Bavaria, off I was down Ungererstrasse and Ludwigstrasse to the large brick Frauenkirche, with its grave of Emperor Ludwig the Bavarian, its fifteenth-century plaque of the Agony in the Garden, and its splendid green and gold glass that must all now have disappeared. Musical ladies to tea, and La Bohème radioed from the theatre. I was in luck.

The family belong to the best musical circles; they live in a large house surrounded by an enormous garden: two conditions I have long thought essential to the good life. Though my room is on the ground floor, is dark, has a hard bed with such a huge bolster that I shall have to learn how to sleep with it, and just outside my door is the heating-boiler that makes a continual gurgling—on the other side I have a whole bay opening out on the garden, covered with hard, frozen snow, sparkling now beneath the moon. Moonlight shines strangely through the trees: a landscape of a dream. The white coverlet is thrown back for me to get into bed, a big mirror put up to shave and dress by; in the corner my umbrella stands familiarly, on the table my gloves lie together, fingers pointed together oddly as if for prayer. I have been here for one day, yet the room is beginning to accept me.

It was indeed to be the scene of intense cerebration—and yet another ulcer.

Mid-February: 'I have been here exactly one week, and the times are rich indeed!' I spent the mornings in the Galleries, particularly the Alte Pinakothek with its wonderful collections, still not quite forgotten, its Roger van der Weydens, its Dürers— 'Maria in dem Rosenhag', his Italianate Peter and Paul—its Holbeins and Pachers and Patinirs—a new Germanic world to me. At a modern gallery I noticed Böcklins and Max Liebermann's portrait of the treacherous von Bülow, who double-crossed the Kaiser over the notorious *Daily Telegraph* interview. What a Byzantine lot those people at the top of Wilhelmian Germany were, with their mingled sycophancy and treachery, brutality and culture!

One morning wasted made me very cross. My mother had sent me a food-parcel. This had been held up in the German bureaucratic manner in the *Postzollamt*, to pay excise on it. I was summoned to claim it, and with difficulty ran the building down; when I got there, it was huge and I had to traipse all over the place to find Room 1103—there duly was my parcel, upon which I had to pay. When I opened it, there was a package of Cornish buns, baked three weeks ago, hard as bricks. I was so furious, I threw them out of the window, and sent home a rocket—they didn't make that mistake again. I know as well as the next man that they had done it 'with the best intentions', etc.; what maddened me was one more reminder of the ignorance of my working-class people, and people have no business to be so ignorant.

With the Ninth Symphony I had a marvellous chance; I had never heard it before. Now I was given the opportunity to hear it rehearsed all one morning and performed two or three nights later. In the mornings, galleries; in the afternoon, occasionally the Englischer Garten, where later the lunatic Unity Mitford, moon-struck on Hitler and with her family fixation on the Germans, shot herself—what inconceivable lunacies we have witnessed in our time! It all comes back when I look at her grave beside the lovely Windrush at Swinbrook: why be so daft? why? There is no need for it—still less for taking such people, or most people, seriously: they are simply without judgment or intelligence. A facile literary journalist—the light-weight son of a light-weight father—has been allotted a large sum to write the biography of this silly bitch. *Je ne vois pas la nécessité*.

Back in my room looking out on the garden, the nights were wonderful in the clear Munich air, the mountains only forty miles away: brilliant moonlight, a strange, unearthly glamour over the fields of snow: the very spirit of Winter. One afternoon I went down Leopoldstrasse to the University, and watched nostalgically the ebb and flow of student life; I should have made friends, but there was no time to join in the courses—I had to be back at Oxford next term to teach and get on with my research. So—across the street for more sight-seeing by myself, the magnificent Ludwigskirche, like a Venetian church with colonnades and campaniles. I was beginning to appreciate, what I learned to admire enormously, Italian baroque and rococo as mediated through South Germany: such a genius as Fischer von Erlach, his Hofburg at Vienna, and Melk on its bluff above the Danube. Later, Sacheverell Sitwell wrote a book about it; alas that I never saw the Bishop's Palace at Würzburg, with its Tiepolo ceilings, so badly damaged in the Second German War.

The Court and State Library closed, so that my desire for English papers and news went unsatisfied, I indulged myself by 'an expensive visit to the excellent bookshop between the Wittelsbachplatz and the Café Luitpold. What a pleasant neighbourhood, the *Platz* mainly enclosed by the family palaces of the Wittelsbachs, graceful eighteenth-century mansions. There is their Maximilian I on horseback, only a short carriage-drive to the Residenz and Hofgarten. They must have been very cosy here in Munich the past two centuries; "mais où sont les neiges d'antan?"'

Most of all I relished the medieval town, with the narrow streets and lanes between the ancient Court of the Wittelsbachs and the Rathaus: the Hofgraben, which must have been an open space surrounding the Hof in earlier days. I had a favourite little stationery shop there, kept by an old couple left behind by big business.

It reminded me of the chocolate-shop in the Rue Bonaparte in Paris, kept by two old sisters, which I patronized when I wanted a present for the lady who kept my pension in the Rue Honoré Chevalier, by Saint Sulpice. 'The poor old souls were very tired and nervous when such a large order for chocolate came so late at night from two foreigners, Jimmy B. and me. Their fingers fumbled as they tried to make haste over the parcels; one of them was quite harsh to the other, then broke down and said her sister was overtired and had been a long time in the shop that day. I loved the poor, pathetic old things; yet they didn't fail to overcharge us shockingly at the end of the performance.'

I explored pretty thoroughly the ancient part of the town, dominated by the twin towers of the Frauenkirche with their onion-shaped copper domes: into the Marienplatz and through the arcades of the Altes Rathaus, to the barber in a well of tall buildings between Petrikirche—how full of churches Catholic Munich was—and the Square. The barber bore an extraordinary facial resemblance to Jaurès—another of my heroes. 'Or was it merely his beard? For, come to think of it, the resemblance was quite as strong to Anatole France'—who then dominated the literary scene in Paris. The barber asked me if I were a Hungarian, judging from my dialect; I should have replied, No, merely from Ungererstrasse. Rather flattered at being taken for no downright foreigner, I said nothing; in fact, I had got along far enough in the language occasionally to dream in German.

Going out, I lingered to watch the scene from the platform at the end of Petrikirche overlooking the Viktualienmarkt. 'The worst of these coigns of advantage here as in France is that they smell abominably of stale piss. Looking across to the Jesuit church, the ice had collected in ridges underfoot, and it was bitterly cold. But how lovely are the baroque façades of the churches at night, when the firm lines stand out from the detail.' I watched the moon creeping up from the roof of the Church of the Holy Ghost towards the campanile at the east end; in passing through the Alter Hof, I saw the rime gleam blue in the moonlight upon its steep roofs and gables. After fifty years I still remember the sugar-cake extravaganza of the rococo church of St John Nepomuk, and the decorative magnificence of the Theatinerkirche, across from my favourite Café Hag with its rich variety of opulent, succulent

Kuchen displayed to tempt the greedy. (I rather think that this café was patronized by that other misanthropical teetotaller with a weakness for sweet cakes, the later *Führer* of the German *Volk*.)

As seen from the comfortable café the upper windows of the Residenz, where Wagner had besieged the unhappy Ludwig II for support (giving him nothing in return), caught not the sunset but the fresh blue light of the end of a rainy afternoon as if reflected in a pool. A threatening shower-cloud played a game with the light in the Domplatz, where Mozart spent the Christmas of 1774: the weather-vane lit up gold in high sunlight above our heads, while we were in darkness. In the deserted Alter Hof an old woman was dusting the windows in an upper storey, like some ghost of a retainer caught in her forgotten ritual, or a *revenant* in a Hawthorne story.

I cite these notes of the places where I walked half a century ago for the benefit of those for whom many of them no longer exist.

Back in Ungererstrasse I was much at home in my room—better than I had been at home in Cornwall in a miserable council-house overlooked by the neighbours, where one could hear *all* their noises and the demented shrieks of their children. One night I heard an unexpected exchange between two bus drivers and their wives on the ways of married life: said one lusty young bus driver to the others, 'I've 'ardly time to take me shirt off before she's got'n,' followed by sexy giggles. This was very unlike the domestic life of my room with the large garden in Munich.

I made a cult of my German garden—all part of the *culte de sensations* with which I excited myself and heightened my over-driven senses (I must have been stimulated by my interest in Rimbaud). We all know the sensation of being watched from outside through the window. I fancied that old Herr Ungerer came back to walk the garden at night and look in through mine.

When the wind is blowing in the pines outside, and there is a warm light behind the yellow curtains of the room down-stairs where a young man sleeps, then old Herr Ungerer taps a friendly signal on the glass door. One night the young man, half in fear, half in curiosity, gets up and watches the bent

figure down the pathway. At the bottom of the garden is a
fence; in former days the garden did not end there but went
right down to the church; the path still continues under the
fence into present allotments. For Herr Ungerer no fence
exists, he follows the path as in former days, his figure
vanishing from sight in passing through the high wooden
paling on the way to the church.

There follows a sketch for a story to account for this *revenant*'s
returning to the house—a story never worked up, too many ideas
crowded in on my mind, cheek by jowl with it in the Note-Book:
a comparison of Rilke with von Hofmannsthal, on Rilke's
Aufzeichnungen which I was reading, alongside of Gide's *Les
Faux-Monnayeurs* just out; a comparison between Rimbaud's
'Bateau Ivre' and 'The Ancient Mariner'; notes on Valéry's
Variété, on Aesthetics, the relative values of music and literature,
where music could express depth and simultaneities in time all at
once, which literature could not, not even the time-experiments
of Joyce and Virginia Woolf; yet literature could express 'tous ces
éléments intellectuels que la musique ne peut exprimer'. There are
notes on Beethoven's *Missa Solemnis*, which I heard for the first
time; another comparing Beethoven and Napoleon, citing
Goethe's disapproval of the later Beethoven as inhuman and
beyond nature, too stormy and tempestuous, and one comparing
his handling of masses of tone with Napoleon's handling of
masses of men. Both exacted the utmost from their material,
Beethoven driving the voices in the Ninth Symphony and the
Mass almost beyond endurance, as Napoleon did his men in his
later campaigns. There were curious points of contact too, not
only over the *Eroica*, but in Beethoven's republicanism and
Napoleon's latent Jacobinism.

These are only a few points from the Note-Books; a great deal
of cerebration went on behind the yellow curtains at night, after
the day's expeditions into the town and all the music.

No company for a young man in the place, I was consigned to
this basement room on its own, away from the life of the house.
Always a prey to night-terrors, I was not afraid by myself down
there; but one night of storm 'it seemed the wind was in the
house, and the rooms above filled with the sound of innumerable

feet hurrying here and there: all the dead things seemed to be awake and listening in the dark, stirring and rustling, sleepless. When day at last comes, a high wind is in the garden bending the tops of the pines; a break in the clouds and the winged sea-horse in the plaster fountain gleams among the trees, his turfed mound flaked with fallen scales.'

There was always the garden to take refuge in in its different moods, pacing up and down the gravel while phrases or verses came into my head. One little poem I did publish subsequently; it began:

> I ran into the garden: for there
> The air was cool, and morning crystal-clear;
> The winter sun a brave show made
> Of throwing summer patterns in the glade.
>
> And from their haunts among the trees
> The nymphs and tritons and the Naiades,
> Fantastic figures in the shade,
> Unto the fountain silent music played ...

Or there was the garden at night, after rain, the paths rain-wet, reflecting a grey light, the moon hidden. 'The lights of the town glint through leafless branches. A wind wakes like the inwash of a tide along some southern shore. In the wind I hear the voice of a woman singing in the night. Or is it the dream of a woman singing, some woman dead, whose voice was heard once in the garden?'

The prosaic thought that it might be merely the voice of the *gnädige Frau* did not occur to me.

For once there was going to be company, and I was graciously bidden upstairs to a musical evening. Professor Quidde was arriving with his wife: a well-known name in Germany in those days, for he had been prosecuted for *lèse-majesté* against the Kaiser before the war. A respected classical scholar—as it might be Gilbert Murray—he had published a biography of some Roman Emperor, perhaps Nero or Caligula, where there were deleterious comparisons with the ridiculous *Allerhöchste*. I think he was imprisoned, which made him a bit of a hero in Weimar days. His wife appeared to me to have stepped out of a Gainsborough portrait of a lady in blue.

She was indeed a distinguished old girl. After playing the cello all the evening for a Beethoven trio, a difficult late Brahms trio and a sequence of *Marienlieder* lately composed by Dr Plunder for his wife's fruity voice, Frau Quidde sat down to try the piano, took off her rings, and played a delightful piece. She then turned round and asked whose it was. Dr Plunder said Schubert—and indeed it was very like one of his 'Moments Musicaux'; she told us it was from a piano sonata of Rossini that had remained in manuscript with the King of Italy.

An American lady provided comic relief. Her husband had a great idea, to write a book on God and the English Language. Apparently the Bible was not written in Hebrew and Greek, but in English, only in Hebrew and Greek characters. This could be proved from the Pyramid:

> the Pyramid is his one devotion, he lives for the Pyramid. He has undertaken to make her appreciate the Bible; this was what she had never previously been able to do. Of all her family she was the only one that was unorthodox; she had always been able to see things without preconceived notions, she was broad. [She was—absolutely enormous.] When she was only three years of age she had been beaten for asking 'Why?' Herself had always asked 'Why?' As for ordinary people who went about without thinking, swallowing what they were told, she often wished she were like them. 'Why am I different from them? Why can't I take things for granted?'

It was a favour to know so much of her husband's plans: she oughtn't to have told me so much. She didn't think he would find a publisher in England, with his unorthodox ideas. I suggested he might try America. No, he wouldn't do that: the orthodox would be down on him for his ideas. But he was brave and never troubled by what they said, and neither did she.

After the *Marienlieder*—if only she could express what she felt! But she had always been like that: she must be silent after hearing such music. She had sung all the leading parts in opera; but if anybody spoke to her before half an hour after singing, she felt she should strike them in the face. Now why was she like that? I said it was an interesting psychological problem. Oh, psychology; she had studied psychology deeply, for years she had been a teacher of psychology. But why was it that when she wanted to say how much she loved what she had heard, she couldn't? Not a word had she spoken to Dr von Plunder; and as for Frau von Plunder, she thought she had a heavenly voice, and yet she couldn't tell her so for the life of her. At the end of the evening I passed her holding forth to Frau von Plunder with the rest. 'With that wonderful voice, what a crime it is you are away from the stage. A thousand thanks you *allowed* me to come,' etc.

Once or twice I met my hostess in the town and entertained her to tea; another time, when she felt tired, would I take her home in a taxi? When I came to leave for home with all my luggage, two heavy suitcases and a smaller one, she thought a taxi unnecessary and expected me to travel to the railway station by tram. I reminded her. One more little indication of German insensitivity to others. One day I took her (I always paid, of course) for the day up into the mountains to Garmisch-Waxenstein. It was the first glimpse I had ever had of mountains, from the train going out of Munich; what an excitement to see them there on the horizon, some forty miles away, looking like the blue fringe one sees in the background of a Mantegna. Getting up into them among the snow was still more exciting; we went up the Zugspitze by mountain-railway, the altitude going to our heads and making us quite hilarious. I have still not forgotten our delicious lunch of mountain-trout. On our way down we got stuck in the suspended cage, like a rat-trap, in which we were descending: a horrid half-hour with an abyss of 500 or so feet yawning all round us. Young, I took it better than I could today: indeed, today I wouldn't go up it at all.

In return I was once taken to a fashionable, 'artistic' lunch given by a rich German-American woman, who kept an opulent flat in Munich. Again, a first experience—I can have been invited only on the score of being an intending writer. No evidence of taste, plenty of wealth; a long lunch-table presided over by one of those ugly Thurber women with straight fish-mouths one saw in the *New Yorker*. What put me off was the sycophancy of the Plunders to money—talk of 'the pornography of power', it was nothing to the German sucking-up to American money.

A night or two later I caught sight of her surrounded by her court at a lecture on the Frauenkirche given in a fine room in the Residenz. I couldn't attend very well for just *looking*: dark panelled room, gilded baroque figures and busts, over the fireplace 'Maximilianus et Elisabetha'; audience sitting at long tables with their beer glasses, faces caught up out of the gloom by the white light of the film-screen. I thought it looked like a Rembrandt night-scene; and 'there was my American German lady who, in spite of her kindness, I don't much like, with underjawed hollow face and fat neck turned to the screen, plump beringed hand fondling her glass of dark wine. Beside her sat a pretty fair woman, who blushed self-consciously when she thought people were looking at her, a conspicuous gown of black shining with silver ornaments.' It never occurred to my uninformed mind that they were probably a lesbian couple.

One way and another, in spite of all the outcry about Reparations and the Treaty of Versailles—against which the Germans mounted a campaign which took in the Anglo-Saxons, aided by such irresponsibles as Keynes and Russell—Munich under the Weimar Republic didn't give the impression of being impoverished. Musical life was at a far higher level than anything in England, except only for London: constant operas, big and small, concerts, theatres, galleries, literary events—and, even so, I was hardly aware of all the painting activity going on; though the high-point of the Munich Expressionists had been before the war, with Kandinsky, Franz Marc, Kokoschka. One evening there was a crowded theatre-event presided over by Stefan Zweig in memory of Rilke, who had died that winter. When I arrived at the box-office, the person in front of me got the last ticket—and I worshipped Rilke! Saddened and maddened, I offered extra money for a ticket—to be told gruffly, 'Das geht nicht bei uns.' I have not forgotten—and would offer double to have got in.

Music every night, and at home reading French, my German was falling back—I had made no attempt to follow old Spenser Wilkinson's advice and take a dictionary to bed with me. (One of my Cornish friends, a handsome fellow, who in Rome had an Italian mistress, found one night that she, when he thought of leaving, had taken a dagger to bed with her.) In the Herkules-Saal of the Residenz the complete cycle of Brahms's chamber works was being performed; since this also was a first experience I didn't have time or knowledge to differentiate between early and later Brahms (which I now find much finer than earlier). I was much taken with the dark looks of the young cellist, unmoved, self-contained, withdrawn—he reminded me of Roy Harrod at home. In the Prinz Regenten Theater there were Schiller's *Wallensteins Lager* and *Die Piccolomini*; I even saw *Caesar and Cleopatra*, for Shaw was practically a German author at this period, his plays were everywhere, lucky bounder. When I asked a Frenchman why they didn't perform Shaw, he replied, 'Parce qu'il a insulté les Français'; I replied, but he has made a fortune insulting the English!

In the large National Theatre one saw the big operas, Wagner's *Walküre, Fidelio,* Strauss's *Rosenkavalier* and *Ariadne auf Naxos*; in the enchanting little Residenztheater we had Mozart, my first *Figaro* and *Die Entführung*. In the former I saw a rare performance of Pfitzner's portentous *Palestrina*, conducted by the composer, doyen of Munich music as Strauss was at Vienna. I still remember that opera, in spite of its longueurs, though I've never heard any of it since: there was a splendid moment when, after long hesitation and inability to write, the polyphony of the 'Missa Papae Marcelli' burst forth. I remember too the fluttering bird-like hands of the composer—and that, like Furtwängler in Berlin, when Hitler took over, he went in with the Nazis.

In addition to all the German music, concerts by the Cathedral choir, we had a visit from the Don Cossacks Choir—I went to both their concerts—in those days before Hitler and Stalin together plunged Europe in terror again and Russia was cut off from the West. At their second concert, one of church music in the bleak Lukaskirche—'what a genius for ugliness these Lutherans have'—I had an opportunity of observing the stalwart well-drilled Russians more closely. One episode rather disturbed me: the clear relationship between a tall dark bass and his friend, a young fair alto. The tall fellow came up to his friend, and quite naturally placed his hands on the other's hips, letting them rest for a moment before the latter disengaged. Sex-starved and alone, I at once thought of a story *à la* Gide, whom I was reading. I did not know of Nijinsky and Diaghilev's 'Il m'est absolument nécessaire de faire l'amour trois fois par jour.'

At the end of the month I was unwell again; I thought it was from late nights and enjoying myself too much. In fact it was my old enemy; it took its regular course and, unbeknown to me, deposited one more growth of scar-tissue, then I recovered. The process, I now diagnose, took about a week, pain at night, at the *end* of the process of digestion where the beastly duodenum was; when I could, next day, I would take a gentle walk by the Isar or in the Englischer Garten (a duodenal ulcer would have given Unity Mitford something serious to think about). March 5th: 'ill all night and most of day with pain'. Then, indomitably, to a Beethoven Concert, Fifth and Seventh Symphonies, Knappertsbusch conducting, with whom Dr Plunder conducted a running feud in the *Münchener Neueste Nachrichten*: he used to call him 'Meister Dreieckige'—he certainly had an unimaginative triangular way of conducting. After a week, 'at work all day revising *Die Weise*, ideas for two poems. Bad, restless night; 12 noon, got up, the morning after the night before.' A note on recovering says,

'After days of pain it seems as if I look upon the world with new eyes and see, as if for the first time, how beautiful it is to live. Even the greyness of this late February evening is a wonder. There is a silver dust of dew on the pines; the birds are coming back and fill the air with the beating of their wings. An elder blackbird walks sedately on the marble brink of the fountain; the coloured papers we hung upon the trees to greet the spring still flutter, faded and tattered. The noises of the outside world, the traffic that came singly into the sickroom, all is now only an ordered murmur like the familiar inrush of the sea. A low bough of a tree lays a light touch on my shoulder: I turn to see what ghost follows my footsteps in the night.

Vexed and disappointed at my setback and wasting time, as I considered being ill, I took refuge in the Diary. 'I wonder if I am cheating myself, a kind of self-abuse, in playing with all these ideas and planning all these works, without setting myself to making works of art of them?' Actually, I was too young, they wouldn't have been good, any more than the early plays, novels, etc., of Wystan, Stephen and Christopher: *The Dog Beneath the Skin, Trial of a Judge, All the Conspirators* have no permanence in them, unlike 'The Waste Land' or *Sons and Lovers*. One's work is better at the end, after a lifetime of experience—like Brahms's Clarinet Quintet, the Alto Rhapsody, the *Vier Ernste Gesänge*, the Intermezzi, as against the early trio and sextet; Strauss's *Metamorphosen* and wonderful last songs for soprano, against the appalling vulgarity of the *Sinfonia Domestica* or *Ein Heldenleben*. As Rilke had written to the young poet who asked his advice about writing, to become a poet one must have gone through a great deal, 'viele Erfahrungen haben'. I had little or no experience of life.[1]

Now, at twenty-three, 'I haven't time to sit still and devote myself to the work that is nearest my heart: there is so much to learn, so much to think and do.' Moreover, had I 'the courage to make the choice, and decide on writing as the main business of my life? There are so many people writing nowadays, and so many cleverer than I, that I should merely add one more to the number of scribblers.' This was much too modest; but in recent years Maurice Bowra used to reflect how wonderful the 1920s were, when we began. There were still alive and writing Hardy, Kipling, Conrad, Shaw, Yeats, Robert Bridges (absurdly depreciated at present, as Kipling was twenty years ago); among novelists, Wells and Bennett in full spate, besides Belloc and Chesterton. There was all Bloomsbury, Virginia Woolf, Strachey, E. M. Forster, their outliers and friends, Katherine Mansfield, Middleton Murry (a far better critic than people realize), Eliot; among the still young and promising, D. H. Lawrence and Aldous Huxley ... What is there to compare with that today?

Then there was the temptation of the life of action, partly to test myself; but was it possible to combine that with the life of the imagination? 'The Diary is a witness of the long hold it has had upon my mind. How many times, in the night, when I have been in pain or illness, have I thought, if I should die there is my Diary left as a remembrance of my thoughts and all my enthusiasm for the lovely things I have seen.' It was all I had to show for my

[1] Or again, 'Verse sind nicht, wie die heute meinen, Gefühle (die hat man früh genug)—es sind Erfahrungen.' (*Malte Laurids Brigge.*) ('Verses are not, as people think today, feelings (one has those early enough)—they are experiences.')

intense and incessant activity of mind. 'When my mother came to see me when I was desperately ill in Oxford, I told her never to forget what I wished done, that my Diary should be put in safe hands. If I should die, that would be the only way of providing for my mother and father; it worries me that I haven't insured my life and have no money to leave them. I was afraid that they wouldn't remember about the Diary, or think it all a dream.'

Poor souls, what could they have done about it? They knew no one, understood nothing of the passionate concerns of my mind. It is pathetically comic to think of 'safe hands'—what safe hands were there? I must have instructed them to keep my letters; for from this time they begin, with a long diet laid down for my father. He, too, was complaining of stomach-pains; and this worried me. Poor young fellow, I refrain from quoting the solemn detailed instructions—I am sure they were not adhered to. My father, like old-fashioned working people, had more faith in nostrums and was always plaguing the doctor for pills. When I sent home money, I found by a side wind that the credulous fools occasionally spent what I sent on football pools—I made an almighty row about that when I found out. I don't know how seriously they took it, or whether it stopped them—but there you have ordinary people. The conscientious youth of all those years ago, worrying about their health and providing for them, when it was he who needed the advice and care; but that was beyond them.

So much for working people!—it may be imagined how I valued the privilege of being one of them.

'Still he wished for company'—and then an opportunity opened up that was not really in my line. A young woman in Munich had been studying the violin for three years; she reminded me of an early girl-friend of mine at home at Tregonissey, who had been learning the piano for years, similarly without much promise. Dorothee Schnellhorn was very much like W. W. to look at: placid, kind blue eyes, fair wavy hair with a little snail-whorl at the temples, a friendly smile, a cold wet nose with a tendency to dewdrop. But wasn't this an opportunity thrown by Providence in my way to broaden my experience? Equally, 'might it not be a trap for my complete freedom, a sacrifice of the future?' I liked her mother much more:

> an affectionate motherly type who does her best to get her daughter into the best musical circles and forward her appearance on the concert platform. All that side of the business is new to me, the exigencies of the artistic life of Munich. The daughter talks to me of the beauty of the life devoted to art, how she hates having to curry favour with influential people, and is happier all alone up in her rooms in Elisabethstrasse, with her violin and her music. For all that, the young lady has been terribly anxious to get me to take her to the *Fasching* balls and dances; once I was nearly caught, but there weren't any tickets left. A narrow escape from wasting a precious evening, which might be so beautiful elsewhere! At these concerts I find myself always let in for taking the young lady and bringing her back. The only occasion when her mother and I went alone, we had to tramp a long way afterwards through wet windy streets to drink tea with the daughter at the top of five flights of stairs!

Once arrived there, my attention was held by the magnificent view over the city at night: a deserted square beneath, campanile on one side, dark against the streaming light and traffic of the Leopoldstrasse, the main thoroughfare. I found Dorothee 'very attractive, for a German girl', but inert and passive, rather defeatist about her musical prospects, as well she might be. When the *gnädige* Frau von Plunder brought my breakfast down to my basement room next day I learned a little more. Dorothee was no chicken; she had been married at seventeen, divorced and was now twenty-six, though she looked twenty. Her husband had been forty-two when they married, an officer in the Navy; at the time of the Revolution he became a musician, and thus they met.

It was good of the lady of the house—who had herself been a prima donna, if not very prima—to let me, if a trifle maliciously, into the secret. Though I hardly needed warning: 'I don't like being pressed and beguiled at the same time: the game is too obvious, and my eyes are too wide open to take much pleasure in the game of life—perhaps, after all, it is the reflection of life that interests me.'

My attack of illness followed, and I did not see her again for a week or ten days. I hoped that I had caught this attack in its early stage; 'but the fight has left me weak and pale, as I see when I pass in front of the big mirror in my room.' When I went to see Dorothee, she was in bed with flu. I had brought

a big bunch of white hyacinths that I carried in vain through the streets two days ago, quite worn out with looking for Elisabethstrasse and disheartened by oncoming pain again. She was looking at her most attractive, with two long tresses reaching to her waist—and nobody the whole afternoon and evening to look after her. [More inert than ever, one could hardly have got into bed with her in that condition.] So I made tea for us both, hunting around in the tidy kitchen for everything. After tea and a purposeless talk—at least it came to no point—I sat down to the piano and played to her. Then for her supper I boiled her a couple of eggs, which she ate with satisfaction enough, though I received no praise; she said that I was good to her, I said it was boring to be virtuous. That seemed to strike a chord with painful mem-ories—or so I thought, and went off to make a nice concoc-tion of orange and lemon and sugar. I wondered what was passing through her mind, and decided that disinterested friendship on her part would be even more boring than the path of virtue on mine.

So that was that. A year or so later her brother turned up for me to entertain at Oxford—which I duly did: a good-looking German type, upstanding and fair, blue eyes like Dorothee, with more to say for himself, not at all listless and inert, but no more responsive either.

Recovered from my setback, I resumed my explorations of the town: visits to my favourite bookshop, buying Stefan George's poems, offset by Valéry and Paul Claudel. 'I put myself in good humour by giving my small change to a poor old woman who sat shivering with a few papers and a forlorn bunch of flowers at the corner of Odeonsplatz, blue with cold and bruised rings around her eyes. I wondered why more people didn't notice her or take some pity on her.' Thence off in better spirits through the

Post Office, occupying a fine baroque palace, to my favourite medieval quarter. A placard noted where the church of St Michael had stood, built by Louis the Strong, destroyed in 1815.

> March 4th: I was worn out by the experiences of the evening [seeing *Fidelio* for the first time], and by so much cerebration that accompanies my long walks alone in the open air. So I had to leave off writing early, and off to bed with Paul Morand's *Ouvert la Nuit* [a popular, well-thought-of writer at the time.] My wanderings had led me along the banks of the Isar, then wooded with pines and birches, the stream clear and swift-flowing. There was a fountain, beside which I watched, until lights began to come out around it and the grotto behind, a bridge below. Across it was Munich, magnificently spaced out on either side of the Leopold-strasse, running straight to the other side of the city, to end with a church spire. And so back towards Schwabing through the English Garden.

Munich had no more ardent admirer than this young Englishman.

Heavenly spring weather was coming on. One afternoon I went out to Nymphenburg, which enchanted me, sitting light and airy amid its vistas of waters, the long canal along its axis. Sun and air were intoxicating. I thought 'what a fairyland these old Electors made for the games of a princely life, this palace of windows and mirrors, silver and delft, the park with its statues and cascades, and bosquets amid the many waters'—in one of them the exquisite Amalienburg, which I have still not forgotten. 'There I met a woman, who, though not old in years, had had many troubles and bore a great sorrow.' Alas, I have no memory of her, or of her story, true or not, of which she must have disburdened herself to this improbable confidant. What is significant is that solitary experiences were far more intense—I think it is Henry James who remarks on that—and remained more in the memory.

A day at Schleissheim by myself, for example, I still recall, the very look of the mirrors in the palace; whereas I have no memory of a day with the family out at Grünwald, father and young son racing down the side of the valley, Frau von Plunder and I walking more sedately up the village to look at the mountains. 'Two men were driving a little plough, drawn by two large motley steers.' But at Schleissheim I was in my element: 'Three palaces set in parks and woods and fields. I went alone, armed with pencil and note-book, so there was a better harvest of pleasure than at Grünwald or at Nymphenburg. There's always so much to see and reflect upon, take delight in, when one goes alone.' I quoted Rilke's description of his own solitariness, 'when one has nobody and nothing, and one goes about the world with a trunk and a box of books, and even without curiosity.' My curiosity, however, was insatiable—at least, curiosity of the eye—and the harvest was a longish poem describing how everything *looked*.

The Altes Schloss seemed to be used as a kind of Hampton Court, inhabited by whole families, a stalwart young fellow in green uniform on guard. A stream ran through the middle courtyard: I watched a woman washing linen in the sunlit water. The former dining-hall of the palace had become the chapel, where I rested in the cool stillness; on one side the altar, 'Königin des Friedens, Bitte für uns', on the other, 'Heiland der Welt, Erbarme dich unser.' Then the tell-tale date, '1916'. Here was what, for ordinary simple folk, the ambitions of their governing classes had led them to. I felt sad for them: 'Nothing in the rest of the day was so intimate as that moment.'

From the simplicity of the Old Schloss I went over to formal terraces and marble galleries of the New. 'If I have seen all that baroque grandeur before, knowledge and experience are accumulating: I can now make comparisons, the beginning of criticism.' Nymphenburg was gayer and more Italianate. Here on the walls were scores of vanished Max Emmanuels and Karl Albrechts, with their Amalie Maries and Maria Antonias—one could imagine the salons and staircases filled with them, the corridors rustling with the swish of their silks and satins.

Among the pictures I was taken with a realistic Jan Massys of 'The Tax-Collector', gloating eyes, devouring mouth, and spectacles half-way down his nose, the money well within reach, a deep red the dominant colour. In a small wainscotted room a Clouet of a daughter of Henri II, a pathetic face painted in dead whites; and a small portrait of the Emperor Maximilian I, unforgettable from his nose—the like of which I had noticed only with Federigo Montefeltro of Urbino. Upstairs was a Kneller of Henrietta Maria—evidently a copy of an earlier portrait.

To end with was a charming little garden-palace, Lustheim, to close the vista of the long canal: inside, all green, pink and purple marbles, picked out with gold and silver, painted ceilings. More intimate and *familial*, but empty now, one missed the more the Electresses and their entourage flouncing in and out. Outside there was considerable activity: workmen cleaning out the fountains, cutting the quickset hedges; women, in orange and purple woollens, red and white kerchiefs round their heads, sweeping the brown leaves into heaps. 'No picture—Pre-Raphaelite or Impressionist—can describe the rhythm of their bodies as they bent after the long white rakes in broken line; nor evoke the pungent smell of the dead leaves.' (All the same, Millet haunts me.)

All is recorded, however, in the poem, which took me two days writing in the garden; then off in the evenings to Beethoven concerts—the Ninth Symphony again in the Tonhalle, and Pembaur playing a programme of piano sonatas at the Odeon. There were three more Beethoven concerts before I left Munich—what a feast, and what luck to have been there during the Centenary celebrations! Yet another concert at home, at which we had a Nardini violin sonata, a Bach cantata, sung by Frau P., and the *Marienlieder*, again, of the Herr Doktor. I was reading Franz Werfel's novelized biography of Verdi and went to hear *La Forza del Destino*, otherwise *Die Macht des Schicksals*, and, for my last extravagance, Strauss's *Der Rosenkavalier*.

My last few days in Ungererstrasse were days of domestic disorganization and largely wasted, I noted. For myself I was writing long letters to my brother in the midst of his wife-troubles, trying to plan his future as well as my own, wondering whether we couldn't set up something together at home, dreaming of taking the Plunders' house for the summer and bringing my mother and father out. How innocent and sanguine!—they had hardly ever crossed the Tamar; I was too loyal to the family, then, shouldering their troubles as my own.

In Ungererstrasse the faithful Rosa—the maid of all work, upon whom everything was put—had revolted and decamped. Grimly ugly and with a thick delivery, well on the way to being an old maid, as I feared, she had one only outlet—an addiction to having her fortune told by the stars; even cards would do. So one day I told her her fortune from the cards, in the hope of saving her some money from fortune-tellers. She still thought that the stars were better—it all depended on the planet you were born under. Her growing antagonism to the *gnädige Frau*, who made a slave of her, was brought to a head by her interfering with a fortune-telling letter from Paris.

The house was forlorn without her. I wondered whether there would be any breakfast, and went to forage for myself in the kitchen quarters, where all was desolate from last night's meal. I explored farther into poor Rosa's little room: all tidy, bed unslept in, nothing but a table, chair, large cupboard and a small glass. She had never before been away from her post; she had left quite suddenly, taking us all by surprise: that, at any rate, had not appeared in the cards. Her place was taken by the pretty nurse-maid, blooming round apple-cheeks, merry dark eyes I have not forgotten—at whom I wickedly made a pass: in vain.

It was just as well that I was off to Vienna. Before leaving I went nostalgically, in a way that early became habitual with me—as later, going round the garden at the Huntington Library on my last day to say goodbye to it—for a last tea-time in my favourite Café Hag. There was a funeral party of women enjoying themselves in the opposite corner. I had noticed how much German bourgeois enjoyed the pomp of funerals, and remembered Swift's observation that the merriest faces were to be seen in mourning coaches. Mourning seemed as strict for the men as the women, ridiculous tall silk hats, long frock-coats, black kid gloves. The women talked away with subdued pleasure. I suppose the event gave them all a sense of self-importance. Rain poured dismally in the streets, people running along under umbrellas. I sheltered on the doorstep to look my last at the familiar front of the Residenz. No wonderful colours this evening, no pale blue water-lights reflected from the sky, turning the windows to pools. Only the big red marble portal to confront it, bronze figures reclining awkwardly upon the pediment: Temperantia holding an antiquated carriage-lamp, clearly out of fashion; Fortitudo with so hefty a phallic weapon that one would hardly need fortitude so equipped.

Was the cult of nostalgia a part of the *culte de sensations*, straining my nerves along with my sensibilities? I went for a last time into the garden late that night, tempting whatever ghosts might be abroad.

The wind was cool, a tang of awakening earth; little night creatures went scurrying along the paths. At the corner by the big elm, a bough of the two-branched fruit tree had been hacked away. 'Who has done that?' I said, and was frightened to hear the words spoken aloud in the dark. On my way back to the comfortable green lamp showing in the window, a strange man was standing in the path. A strong light from a street lamp outside dazzled my eyes, and when I looked again there was nobody there.

4

Vienna: the Spring of 1927

Looking back on it now after half a century I see clearly that Munich had not been fundamentally affected by the First War — the Wittelsbachs had retired into the country: that was all, for the rest society went on much as before. But the life of Vienna had received a dire blow. Before the war it had been the cosmopolitan capital of the variegated Austro-Hungarian Empire, with a glittering society of princes, Czech, Hungarian, Polish with their immense estates, as well as Austrian; at the apex, the Habsburgs with old Franz Joseph himself an historic monument going right back to the revolutions of 1848 — and the reaction. People recalled nostalgically the brilliant sky-blue uniforms of the Imperial Guard, the dashing cavalry. The city was impoverished and had known recent destitution; poverty was visible, prostitutes and disease perambulated the streets. I had read C. A. Macartney's book, *The Social Revolution in Austria*, which made him known to Richard Pares and me: together we got him made a Research Fellow of All Souls later on. On the outskirts of the old city the big *Siedlungen*, the working-class tenement houses looking like fortresses (but were not, as Dollfuss subsequently found), were beginning to rise: Red Vienna.

Living my inner life, I was aware of the tragic background, but no more: I was not out to explore it, but to educate myself. Watching and observing all the time from outside, a lonely outsider, I was absorbing what really appealed to me: music, poetry, pictures, not politics — my political interests were as yet theoretical, not practical. For ever looking, bent on *seeing* — though too innocent to know what a *voyeur* was, and not yet having read Henry James — I was taken with the lines of James Stephens, which spoke for me:

Everything that I can spy
Through the circle of my eye;

Everything that I can see
Has been woven out of me ...

Closing it, I yet shall find,
All that is, is in the mind.

There was the train standing at the platform, on April 6th, 1927, with the exciting placard: München–Kufstein–Innsbruck–Brennero–Bologna. Italy!—would that I could go on, like Goethe, to Italy, with all that the Mediterranean meant for the barbarous North. But I could not afford it—I was sending money fairly regularly home to help my parents. In Hagen I had received an encouraging letter from dear Warden Pember: 'The opportunities for travel when one is young should always be seized: I myself let too many of them slip by.' G. M. Trevelyan told me much the same. I suppose they got caught in the toils of family life; I got caught in the toils of politics and a political candidature, which tethered me and was nothing but a grief to the spirit. When I did get to Italy ten years later it was all too brief a visit and I was in a moribund condition.

The compartment was largely taken up by monks in black, Benedictines or Dominicans, whom I observed with fascination. Their leader was striking, with close shorn hair and full black beard in contrast. Black eyebrows and eyes so dark and scrutinizing (but he was being scrutinized too) as to give the face a sinister expression, especially through a sly underbrow manner of switching the eyes from one object to another. He was conscious of his good looks, stroking his glossy beard and giving the moustaches an upward turn with a quite secular slickness. The small part of his cheek that was visible revealed a dead white skin of the finest texture. His characteristic gesture was to run his hand down his regular nose, pressing the clean-cut nostrils together, and so to the beard on his chest. I was fascinated: what a pity so handsome a type was dedicated to celibacy, but, on the other hand, what a splendid cardinal he would make! He dominated the conversation, plunging his hand into his leather case, hunting for papers in the pocket of his long cloak; when he got up for his bag on the luggage rack, I saw he was wearing a long over-gown, but underneath a scarlet belt round the waist of his cassock. Evidently a monastic dandy. (I wonder now what his sex-life was?)

Besides myself—half a monk, and wholly celibate—there were two secular occupants: in my corner an obstreperous cripple, who had the exhibitionism that went with his condition, was over-dressed in what he fancied were the tweeds of an English sports-man. He had been on a tour of the New World, and couldn't wait to tell his café-friends what he had seen. He was well provided with luggage—evidently well off—and with cameras and photo-graphs; also with a brandy bottle from which he would take swigs. Consumed with curiosity and anxious to make an impres-sion, he could not resist asking the striking young lady, clothed in a leopard or possibly two, 'Was sind sie, Fräulein?' Treating him with obvious disdain, she said, 'Ich habe eine Menge Kinder', and turned away to me.

In those days after the First German War the English had great prestige, and English books and plays were much to the fore on the Continent. She was reading Margaret Kennedy's *The Constant Nymph*, which had a vast success at the time. This was a sore point with Geoffrey Faber, our Estates Bursar at All Souls. He had given up a lucrative partnership in a family brewery to venture out into publishing, with small cash resources. It happened to him to turn down *The Constant Nymph*, which would have made the fortune of his struggling firm—as Kingsley's *Westward Ho!* helped to make that of the Macmillans in their early days. Years later Faber's made a similar mistake when Eliot turned down George Orwell's *Animal Farm*, on obscure grounds of doctrine. I recall these failures of judgment to show that publishers can make bad mistakes—not Faber's alone, though they did lose yet another successful author.

The young lady had not much discrimination; she talked with equal enthusiasm for Galsworthy, Shaw, Elinor Glyn and Robert Hichens. Had I read *The God Within Him*?; I should. (Not bloody likely.) And why hadn't Elinor Glyn published anything lately?—she was so good. I hazarded that perhaps she was worn out, and turned the conversation to contemporary Germans who interested me more. She liked Stefan Zweig, though she considered the second story in his latest, *Die Verwirrung der Gefühle*, 'schrecklich'.

Franz Werfel she hadn't heard of, and was at sea about Rainer Maria Rilke: she thought he was living in Munich, she knew someone who knew him, and how interesting he was to talk to. (Rilke talked to no one, and anyway was now dead.) I wrote her down as a woman of fashion, good-looking too, 'to whom much must be forgiven'.

With so much of interest in the compartment I do not recall much of the journey—mountains, skirting a lake (was it Chiemsee or Starnbergersee?); but I do remember my thrill at first seeing the historic Danube, not blue but murky with the wash of melting snows. As we approached Vienna a marvellous mass of a palace-monastery rose up above the opposite bank: Fischer von Erlach's Melk. (No Socialist *Siedlung* could rival that.) Arrived, I took up my abode at the Pension Számvald, kept by Jenny Wagner, at Hörlgasse 4, just around the corner from the big Gothic Votiv-kirche of the later nineteenth century.

Next morning I began my exploration with the Ring surrounding the city—not badly damaged in the Second German War—penetrating to the cathedral, as usual: Stefansdom with its lofty spire. In the Kohlmarkt a poor old woman, with lined face and blue apron, was dragging herself helplessly along on the pavement by the shop-windows. She wasn't a cripple, but so weak that she could move only by clutching window frames and door-posts. Plenty of well-dressed women passed without taking notice. I was just in time to see an improbable office-clerk, with supercilious pince-nez and pencil case sticking out of his waistcoat, go up and hand the old soul some *Groschen*. I was too late to give her anything, but from a distance watched her painful progress—and then reproached myself all the way to Stefansdom: the middle-aged clerk had at least an act of charity to his credit. But then—'not a hair of their head should be hurt' ... I reflected.

Opposite the Cathedral a man with an appalling diseased eye was selling toy contraptions. The underlid of the eye had dropped, and the inside, raw and horrible, was turned outwards to the world. I couldn't approach him, but shuddered and turned away. I suppose now a case of syphilis, rampant in post-war Vienna, with its cult of the feminine. I remembered the tricks such types as Jack Loam had been up to, to avoid serving in the war: swallowing concoctions to simulate asthma just before examination, eating soap to produce palpitation of the heart, etc.[1] Across from the Augustinerkirche, a one-armed man held a basket of unwanted wares, with two small parrots drowsing on a perch.

'The sights of a great city! My long-planned sonnet-sequence on them! The smells of these narrow Viennese *Gassen*, particularly the peculiar odour by the congregated fruit stalls in Freyung.'

The afternoon I spent in the Volksgarten and the Hofburg. Here, at the old heart of the Holy Roman Empire, the embryo historian came into play. The ancient courtyard was dominated by Francis II's statue to the Emperor Ferdinand, Charles V's brother: a Victorian conception with respectable allegorical personages sedately representing the virtues. From my Schools reading at Oxford I recalled the other side to Francis II's virtue—his uxoriousness, his wife remarking during her last pregnancy, 'The pitcher that is always taken to the well ends by being broken at last'; and it was so. Put up in 1846, Metternich's smug taste was discernible in the thing—only two years before the catastrophe of 1848. I thought I recognized his sententiousness in the inscription on the gate into the Burg Garten: *Justitia Regnorum Fundamentum*. (How much justice did Venice and Lombardy get after 1815?) At that time I was more sympathetic to Napoleon than I am today—today I agree with Pitt; I didn't like the self-complacency of Metternich which breathed through the boring state papers I had had to read, particularly his 'Survey of the Moral and Material Progress of the Empire' during his ministry.

Naughtily I thought of Metternich and Guizot shaking their heads together over the dangerous liberal course Britain had entered upon with the Reform Bill of 1832—they were sure it would lead to revolution. When the revolutions of 1848 knocked both of them off their perches, they met in perfect safety on a London platform. The English governing class had been right to make concessions and institute reforms in time. 'Still, I would give a great deal to know in every detail how Vienna looked and was during the great Congress—a better show than Versailles after all.' Thus the budding historian *then*.

The oldest part of the courtyard bore the date 1536 above the gateways.

[1] Cf. *A Cornish Childhood.*

What contrasts the Hofburg has seen! The Spanish influence, with its solemn ceremonial, dominant in the later sixteenth and seventeenth centuries; the French inflexion in the eighteenth century—more light! One has only to glance at Joseph II's great courtyard that faces on the Augustinerstrasse to see how strong was the hold of Versailles on the courts of Europe and royal minds. Then 1848-9, with mobs swirling through the buildings. And the long sunset of Franz Joseph's reign, the illusion of security which led him to 'perfect' the work of Maria Theresa and continued by Joseph II: so the inscription over the declamatory nineteenth-century gate with vulgar cupola and statuary.

This referred to the erection of the Dual Monarchy at the behest of the Hungarian aristocracy, assuring their dominance over the Southern Slavs, and the German-Austrian ascendancy over Czechs and Slovaks—the whole thing reversed after the Second War, the secular struggle of Germans against Slavs finally settled in favour of the latter. The Germans, historically speaking, have cooked their goose.

It need not have been so, if only they had known how to behave with decency and moderation—or just moderation would have done. For here we come to an overriding lesson of history: moderation pays best; hubris is almost always followed by nemesis—witness Louis XIV and Napoleon, the Kaiser and Hitler. And a less obvious, sickening lesson: how impossible it is to get peoples to follow a reasonable course, to work towards rational solutions in politics, giving each his due. The break-up of the Austro-Hungarian Empire left a number of fragmented states, a power-vacuum for Germany to break into the moment she was able to resume the march of aggression. The right solution for Austria-Hungary was to allow the Southern Slavs to become an independent state; then to reorganize the Monarchy as a federal state, the Czechs as equal partners with Austrians and Hungarians. This was what the Archduke Franz Ferdinand favoured, whose murder at Sarajevo in 1914 precipitated the First War. This would have been a better base for a central European state, with more hope of permanence. The Hungarian aristocracy vetoed it—and in the end paid a bitter price for doing so: their extinction. Concession is better than extinction.

When the Czechs got their chance in 1919, they were not much better: they bit off more then they could chew, and included three million Sudeten Germans in the new Czechoslovakia—thus giving Hitler his chance to overthrow their state. It might have been possible to get along with one million Germans within the gates, but not three. I made this point to Dr Beneš when he turned up at All Souls, a ruined man, after Chamberlain's sell-out at Munich. Wouldn't it have been better to have bitten off less? He agreed that it had been a mistake. Then why not have been more moderate beforehand? The Czechs paid a bitter price in turn for *their* foolery.

Such is human idiocy in politics; such are the lessons of history. For, of course, history—which is the record of human conduct in gross—has its lessons: it is one of the most important points in studying it. Where should we be if we didn't learn from our mistakes?—human survival depends upon it. This consideration shows up the quality of a contemporary historian, A. J. P. Taylor, in his comment on a German admiral's admission that 'Hitler's entire war was a crime, and remained so—even if it had ended better for Germany!' Upon this Taylor comments, with cheap cynicism: 'The time has surely long passed when we have to make moral apologies for one side or the other in the Second World War.' This is to reduce human history to the meaningless—quite apart from its inhuman reduction to nullity of the innumerable lives sacrificed to crush an evil thing that perpetrated the worst crime in history, in its extermination of the Jews. The fact that such a statement can appear in the *English Historical Review*—and that people do not see through it—is another indication of the decline of standards in our time.

However, back to the spring of 1927, when we thought that we had learned our lesson from the First War, and there was altogether more hope about in the world—though it proved a false dawn. The evidences of impoverishment were there for all to see in the historic complex of the Hofburg, expressing the whole history of Austria for the educated to read. 'Now everything looks neglected and peeling, the nineteenth century no less than the sixteenth: it's all one. The oldest part of the complex, with a clock-tower and little spire, is now a branch of the inadequate Post and Telegraph service. Through the gateways of Ferdinand, Maria Theresa and Franz Joseph there rushes a neurotic stream of noisy cars, covered with advertisements of chocolate and margarine.' But I still remember the perfection of Fischer von Erlach's Riding School, after years, and the monumentally heavy nineteenth-century palace of Gottfried Semper, heavier even than Buckingham Palace with its 'Grossmutter Denkmal', and dwarfing the charming Hofgarten. Franz Joseph, with his simple tastes, didn't live in it: he preferred to be out at Schönbrunn. I still remember my surprise at his Spartan iron camp-bed.

That night I went to hear *Salome* at the Opera, with Strauss himself conducting—the outstanding link with better days—and came back through the Hofgarten, all the lamps shining on the rainy paths.

After such a day I stayed at home next morning, reading Baudelaire and writing up my notes. A long Note appears on the theory of Class War, which I was wrestling with—trying to think out what I thought for myself about Marxism, instead of swallowing it whole, like my friends of that time, Jimmy Crowther, Maurice Dobb, Ralph Fox, or a later friend like Christopher Hill. I was intellectually obsessed by Marxism, long before it became fashionable with English intellectuals: but I did not want to 'give myself' to it, as those did, any more than I wanted to give myself to anything or anybody. I wished to think out what was true, and would not commit myself a millimetre beyond. I am grateful now for this working-class horse-sense; it is significant that those friends of mine were middle-class, with their feet less on the ground, less realist. The criticism of *A Cornish Childhood* which I most value today is a tribute (from the *Manchester Guardian*) to its *realism* of outlook. I had here the advantage—as elsewhere all the disadvantages—of my working-class roots and background. I wasn't going to subscribe to anything that took me out of my depth, so there ensued a prolonged struggle to bring the theories of Marx, another scion of the middle class, into keeping with my working-class experience, without illusions.

The struggle was a prolonged one. In all these Notes that I was writing—when I might have been enjoying myself like my contemporaries, Evelyn Waugh, Graham Greene and Cyril Connolly, or my immediate juniors, Auden, Isherwood, Spender —I was working my way, unbeknownst at the time, to a book: *Politics and the Younger Generation*. When it came out, it was disconsidered by my seniors, like R. C. K. Ensor, who contrasted it unfavourably with G. D. H. Cole's *The World of Labour*. But it wasn't intended to be the same kind of book: Cole's was a factual and descriptive study of actual conditions, mine was an attempt to construct a general position from which to view politics, history and literature. It had an influence at the time upon the younger generation it was intended for. But it came out at the time of the catastrophe of 1931, from which we may date the ruin of Britain. So what matter now what I thought about politics then?

On the other hand, useless as my speculations and efforts turned out to be in the realm of politics—we shall see about that later— the intellectual effort I put into thinking out a position for myself has served me well throughout life: *I knew what I thought and what I did not think*. What of Marxism I agreed with—with its illuminating emphasis on the importance of Class in society (about which one heard nothing from lectures or tutorials at Oxford)—has had a stimulating effect and permanent importance in my work as a historian of society. I can still claim, in some salutary sense, to be a Marxist historian; when I look at my first little book, *On History*, which turned out to be a programme for my future work, I find that I can still agree with it. That would not have been the case if I had committed myself to the dubious elements in later Marxism, Dialectical Materialism, for example: the gospel laid down by Lenin's intellectual arrogance, as Russian as any Orthodox Patriarch, in his *Dialectical Materialism and Empirio-Criticism*. Have you read it, dear reader?—it is unreadable—or any of the present generation who think themselves so 'committed'? I wrestled with all this Marxist stuff forty years ago, before they were born—I still possess quite a good nucleus of a Marxist library, Pokrovsky, Bukharin, Krupskaya, Radek, Trotsky, a number of the comrades who were shot or murdered with an ice-pick.

The opinions of the young about politics are of little value— political like historical understanding requires experience and mature judgment—and I was no exception to the rule. So I will not trouble the reader with my speculations in the 'twenties in this field, merely enough to illustrate the overriding theme of this Autobiography, one's self-education, a Cornish Henry Adams. Even so, these speculations were in the field of theory, not practice —that came later. But fancy devoting a wet morning alone in Vienna worrying about the gospel of Class War according to Marx!

I thought that the lack of explicitness in bourgeois political thinking was perhaps deliberate, keeping the working class in ignorance, another way of exploiting their dependence; and that the explicit recognition of class-conflict might 'militate against class-war in practice'. So evidently, like the much-abused Kautsky, I was a Revisionist. 'The Communist argument that Communism is pushing the class-war to its conclusion in the classless state is extreme idealism, and dubious even in theory.' I might have added that it was just as much humbug as the bourgeois muffling up of the fact of class-conflict; and as for 'the withering away of the state' in classical Marxist theory, what a cruel delusion! Was there ever a heavier imposition of the state with reinforced apparatus— enormous armed forces, police and security forces, forced labour camps, internal and external spying, torture, brain-washing, drugging, etc.—than in Soviet Russia? The state 'withering away'—with a K.G.B. 750,000 strong! What bitter disillusion-ments of earlier hopes we have gone through in our time!

I reflected, if innocently, that 'calculated bourgeois obscurantism led to accentuating class-divisions. If the end of political activity is not the disintegration of society but an organic whole, it is only by realizing the pressures of class interest and the weight exerted by economic conflict upon political action that we can limit their scope and counteract their effects.' Here was Revisionism again— the case for Social Democracy, not Communism. 'This means, in practice, a system of graduated taxation of incomes above a certain level, and a levelling up at the other end.' I am still in favour of that, provided that it does not cripple the operation of incentive throughout the economy: which means that such a pol-icy needs careful consideration and delicate handling.

There follow pages of political theorizing—for which I have not much respect today (except in the work of a scrupulous mind like John Plamenatz)—about different conceptions of the state: the hierarchical and organic, as with Aristotle or Catholic theorists, and the cellular, whether Utilitarian or Communist. In the 1920s the Communists appeared to me to be like the early Puritans, 'a chosen people whose function is to bring certain ideas into the world, their ideas being a good deal more important than themselves. From their theories the modern world has much to learn.' Not many people saw that in England in the 1920s; no wonder I was out on a limb on my own, little understood by anybody (Henry James: 'Nobody ever understands *anything*': a sentiment with which I have had much reason to agree all through life.) There follows the conclusion, again a Revisionist one: 'The best preservative from Communism may be to adopt what is valuable in its ideas and absorb them into the modern body politic.'

From this chaff, without colour or savour, smell or touch, I turned to what was more congenial to my mind, literature and the arts, music most of all, and secondarily painting. I was reading Baudelaire's prose-poems, which struck a sympathetic chord in my own new experiences of life alone in a great city—Paris, Munich, Vienna. (It was only later that I came to add London and, much later, New York—but always alone, like Santayana.) Baudelaire was describing New Year in Paris: 'délire officiel d'une grande ville fait pour troubler le cerveau du solitaire le plus fort.' Much of Baudelaire's poetry, unlike other poets—especially English, springing from the countryside—was inspired by city-life: 'C'est surtout de la fréquentation des villes énormes, c'est du croisement de leurs innombrables rapports que naît cet idéal obsédant.' Many years later Princess Bibesco, Proust's friend, pointed out to me, beneath her windows in the Île St Louis, the exact spot where Baudelaire wrote, by the parapet over the Seine, one of his most famous poems. At so many points Baudelaire spoke for me. I had meant to write a sonnet on the poor women who came out of their hovels in the slums of St Aldate's to see the great go by, in Commem. week in those days. Very well: 'C'est toujours chose intéressante que ce reflet de la joie du riche au fond de l'œuil du pauvre.'

It struck me as a curious coincidence how often it happened that

the things I have been thinking about on my own one day have occurred again in my reading the very next day.

Yesterday I thought for a long time about the life of great cities, today some of the original thoughts appear with renewed force in Baudelaire. The prose-poems are no other than the things that strike me in going about the streets and looking at the poor people, all the hideous and lovely things of the teeming world, singled out, infused with the breath of indignation, and given the colour of the life of the mind. I hadn't thought to find in Baudelaire a great proletarian poet!

A Note next compared music with other arts, suggested by hearing Liszt and programme-music like *L'Apprenti Sorcier* for the first time while abroad.

Such music is in essence an attempt to extend the province of music into other spheres: the subjects and inspiration— the *Faust* Symphony, *Totentanz*, etc.—are taken from outside music; even the formal development is conditioned not by musical considerations but by literary exigencies. It looks as if this nineteenth-century attempt has spent itself; in spite of Stravinsky [i.e. of the earlier period] and others, the traditional lines are still unbroken, and these moderns are still 'experimental' in their work. Is the attempt in its nature impossible, the sphere of music being so pure, so much *sui generis*?

This answers the question implicit in Valéry's *Avant-Propos*. The future is still with literature; for literature has such illimitable possibilities that it can extend itself into the spheres of other arts, making some of their ground its own, without changing its character or sacrificing its identity. Compare the influence of impressionistic painting in modern literature, Pre-Raphaelite in England or through Stefan George in Germany; and the musical extensions of Rimbaud and Verlaine.

One hardly knows what to say about this now, in the crack-up of all the arts along with contemporary society. 'Modern' painting is now hardly recognizable as painting—so devoted a lover of painting as Kenneth Clark thinks of it as at an end; 'modern' music is hardly recognizable as music, when one listens with combined tedium and exasperation to the music of a Pierre

Boulez or much 'contemporary' stuff, the clotted groups of notes of a late Tippett piano sonata, for example. One is the less surprised, however much disheartened, because such work reflects the dissolution of contemporary society. The classic arts depended all through history, not upon the people, always and everywhere beneath them, but upon a leisured class, educated and intelligent; when this has collapsed into the abyss of the masses, with mass-civilization (no word for it) and the mass-mind (A. E. Housman knew the word for that), there is likely to be little creative future for the arts.

This is, paradoxically, corroborated by (a) the fact that Soviet Russia and Communist countries in general prefer and patronize, in the most conservative fashion, the art of the past and its imitators; while (b) contemporary society elsewhere, feverishly trying to find something new, produces only dissolution, in the arts as in society itself, along with everything else, morality, ethics, philosophy. The cult of Wittgenstein is the cult of an end to philosophizing.

More fruitful than general speculations were the particular reflexions that occurred to me as I walked the streets of Vienna. (Another lonely street-walker in Vienna before 1914 had cogitations which effectively contributed to the end of our civilization.) Still nourishing the hope of writing a biography of Swift—while looking for material among my *Nachlass* for this volume of autobiography I found an entire Note-Book besides the synopsis for a play on the subject—I coupled him in my mind with Baudelaire. There was a comparable savagery in their irony about life, an undertone of reproach against God for what he has created in man. I might have added the cult of filth, from some obscure psychological reaction. I noted Baudelaire's destructive nihilism, and that he too was an inverted moralist—a destroyer of bourgeois morality.

Cornwall, too, was in my mind. At home, at St Austell, there had been in the Victorian age a queer old Dr Biddick of Biddick's Court, who went his rounds by night. His disappointment in love had made him into a misogynist—a variation on Miss Havisham in *Great Expectations*. There should be a story in him. Biddick's Court is still there today, but I'll bet no one in St Austell knows how it came by the name—and I had forgotten it myself until I looked up these early Note-Books. In the old burying-ground I had noted the slate headstone (now vanished) to the four young fellows, one a Nancarrow, drowned on a Sunday afternoon a century ago, in crossing the bay from Mevagissey to the Gribbin.

I fulfilled that intention to commemorate them in my best poem, 'The Old Cemetery at St Austell'—to be discouraged by Cyril Connolly, my precise contemporary at Oxford. He wrote nothing creative himself: *Enemies of Promise*, to say why he couldn't write a book, and *The Rock Pool* to prove it; *The Unquiet Grave*, mainly written by Propertius or Lactantius, Flaubert or Baudelaire—for the rest, literary journalism, which Wystan Auden summed up with regret that Cyril should simply have become the best reviewer in England. For myself as a writer, there was a strange paradox. Too sensitive and proud, I was all too easily discouraged from outside, often by people with no confidence, some with no ground of confidence, in themselves; while, within my own inner fortress, I was totally undiscourageable, for I lived for myself alone my own inner life. The real writer needs, especially in the discouraging circumstances of today, a combination of the sensitiveness by which his spirit lives, with an outer toughness towards all that would discourage him. I fear I did allow myself to be discouraged, at any rate from publication; and I have not forgiven those who discouraged, for that is the cardinal sin. The first-rate are all encouragers—such people as Eliot and G. M. Trevelyan, Neale and the Sitwells, who all eventually encouraged me. But I had a considerable barrier to surmount, in the London literary clique, nearly all public-school and middle-class, who knew well how to promote each other's interests, wrote each other up in the literary weeklies, and—so far as they could—ignored me. I was never one of the clique, so that now when they look, either in person or posthumously, for support, scrounging in death as in life, nothing is forthcoming.

On the more superficial plane of success with the public—which is much more a matter of concern with them than with me—there is yet another paradox: that an unpopular writer (with them) should be popular with the public. I never suck up to their trends or their fashions, or curry favour with them or fall in with their trendy humbug, or fear to say exactly what I think: I write my books for myself alone—and the public responds, into many hundreds of thousands. That paradox should give literary journalists something to think about; they might find it a rewarding inquiry.

Resuming my perambulations I completed my round of the Ring, up along the Danube Canal to Schotten Ring, which I fancied as another Boulevard St Michel, the so familiar 'Boul' Mich''. (And what a spectacle it presented in the break-up at the Sorbonne in recent years! What a contrast with the blithe and hopeful, the civilized, 1920s!) I perambulated in the rain as far as the baroque Karlskirche with its remarkable design (I suppose also by Fischer von Erlach) of two wings projecting from the façade to enclose two columns. This too was another *Votivkirche*, put up by the Emperor Charles VI—of the War of the Spanish Succession—in 1713, with the inscription, *Vota mea reddam in tempore timentium gentium*. This was the war that occupied most of Queen Anne's reign, famous for the triumphant partnership of Marlborough and Godolphin, and abroad of Marlborough with Prince Eugene, of whom there were other memorials in Vienna. Though my money was getting rather short, I bought myself a good engraving of this fine monument, which I still possess. In the Karlsplatz there was a traffic jam; among all the cars and lorries 'there was an old-fashioned wagon loaded with the stiff bodies of young calves, and little tongues, hanging helplessly over the side.' Odious, carnivorous man!—enough to make one a vegetarian.

In a café I observed 'the usual group of gossiping women, with a few odd men about. The woman at the bar, with sleeves turned up and serious expression under pince-nez, impressed me by the determination with which she spread butter over the bread. A cripple's face was of an ideal, almost unbearable beauty: unbearable to me, for the expression was one of uncomplaining endurance of the suffering life had wantonly thrust upon her.' What a contrast with the vanity of the crippled young traveller in the train! An illustration of the theme of Baudelaire's *saeva indignatio* at the end of 'Mademoiselle Bistouri'. My mind went back to the poor seamstress I used to see sewing away morning, noon and night, at her window opposite the Luxembourg, I suppose in the Rue Vaugirard: 'her head always bent over her work, the eternal throbbing of her sewing-machine in the tiny squalid room.

Outside, in the Luxembourg gardens, where the trees were blossoming into a mist of delicate green foliage, children with their nurses were bright and laughing, cool breezes under the alleys in the hot sun. Only once did I see the seamstress look up from her work: an accursèd accident of birth had turned one side of her face into a shapeless mass of purple flesh, like a folded flower in flame.'

Next day, on with my explorations in the historic part of the town; I spent the afternoon in Freyung church. For its Cornishry I was reading Hugh Walpole's *Jeremy and Hamlet*, which I found 'a falling-off from *Jeremy* and more carelessly written'. I suspect that this youthful judgment was true enough; Hugh Walpole became, with popular success, a slipshod writer, his later books unreadable—at any rate by me. I was intrigued by his Cornish connexion. His father had been a Canon of Truro Cathedral in its early days; the youthful Hughie went for a time to the small boarding-school which used to stand, angular, gabled and Victorian beside the village street at Probus, presided over by Mr Handsomebody. I much miss this idiosyncratic building as I pass there today, its place taken by a petrol-filling station.

Hugh's earliest and best book, *Mr Perrin and Mr Traill*, reflects something of this vanished school. In the early days of success, he had a seaside villa at Polperro, before that quintessential Cornish fishing harbour was ruined—he left it when he found American admirers penetrating into his bedroom. Perhaps his best Cornish connexion was his policeman, Harold, who looked after him most of his life and gave him the emotional assurance which that neurotically trepidatious temperament needed. My predecessor here at Trenarren, Canon Shirley, was a close friend of dear Hughie. The only time I set eyes on the writer—a name to conjure with, with the great-hearted public in those days—was down on the beach at Hallane, where I was preparing to bathe alone. Finding myself watched by these two elderly satyrs, I was cheated of my dip—and cheated them of the spectacle. Nor did I meet the beloved Hughie, a generous, kindly soul, well inclined to young men. Think what I have missed all through life by this standoffishness!

However, next day I had more than enough of human company. In a corner of my gloomy room in the pension there was a doorway, blocked by a large cupboard; this made for a certain intimacy between the inhabitants on either side. The woman who lived next door was quite a personality, of considerable bulk and inexhaustible conversation. What made something of a bond was that she had spent most of her youth, until the middle of the war, at Falmouth and had relations of the remarkable old Cornish name of Uglow (pronounced 'Youglow'), familiar to me from the music-shops and piano-tuners of my youth. Her father had been a Yorkshire manufacturer, who made a fortune and retired to Falmouth. The two daughters inherited his money; one settled down, but this one was determined to see the world.

> With her bulk and pluck, and an equal store of vulgarity, she is capable of fending for herself anywhere. Talking to her, at the end of an hour—for conversation with her was to be measured by the hour—I feel as if bathed in ink. But I haven't been in contact with anybody to whom I could express everything easily for months, and I haven't been in the company of such an ordinary type for years. Living to myself is, after all, rather highbrow society. With this large-hearted, large-breasted soul, I heard the tale of all her friendships, courtships, disappointments in love, failures to marry; all her prejudices, her views about Society (with a capital S), the working classes and strikes—and diminished dividends; all her acquaintances and relatives, their various histories and circumstances: until the complete story of her life was open to me like a Thomas Mann or, rather, Sheila Kaye-Smith novel.
>
> Though I detest the sentiments and the commonness of this Yorkshire commercial type, I confess to a solid respect for the woman. I can't transcribe an account of her life: it would take the rest of the volume. My fear is that, by the time when I can transcribe it, I shall have forgotten the people who move in and out of the scene; but the chief character I am not likely to forget.

This was what happened—a whole novel, from her loud mouth, lost. Conversations with her were interminable, and rather held up my dedicated sight-seeing. Something similar happened to David Cecil, when he was caught in an hotel in Munich by another compulsive conversationist, Elizabeth Bibesco (formerly Asquith), who kept him up into the small hours talking. He felt he couldn't stand it, and early next morning, taking his shoes in his hand, he stole silently down the corridor past her door, and took the train out of the city to Berlin.

I was made of sterner stuff. Miss V. was making the carpet for her new flat, and when she left I missed the snip-snip-snip of her scissors, the firm footsteps on her parquet floor, the hoarse voice talking fluent but shocking German to her young 'cousin'. She much wanted to engage me with him. When he turned up in my room I was surprised by his youth: it crossed my mind to wonder if he were precisely her cousin, he was just my age, rather nice-looking, Viennese-dark. But he smelt of garlic, which I couldn't stand; so the acquaintance was not permitted to ripen.

Nor was another, of a more questionable character. This was a middle-aged American, engaged in gun-running into the Balkans—half a forefinger was missing—who was more than anxious to make the acquaintance of the young Englishman. Protected by my armour of (not complete) innocence—I had not had the advantages of a public-school education—I managed to keep him at arm's length when he showed signs of becoming sentimental. Shortly his mistress turned up, so his sexual needs were provided for.

What a contrast this was with the domestic life of the Lutheran pastor's family at Hagen, or even the musical household in Munich! Another evening I was pertinaciously pursued by a prostitute—I remember her fluffy white fur—along the pavement practically into the pension. What with prostitutes, mistresses, women on the loose, their boy-friends, gun-running in the Balkans, it was more like the scenario of a Graham Greene novel, as it might be *Stamboul Train*.

Conversations with Miss V. took place at night, one going on until 2.45 a.m.—as bad as Elizabeth Asquith! This rather cramped my style for concerts, until she left. However, I did get to a Richard Strauss concert, at one of which I heard the *Festliches Präludium* and the horrible *Sinfonia Domestica*. A crisp note described him as 'the completest expression of the twentieth-century bourgeois in music'. This is not to decry his operas, or the finest works of all, his last: the *Vier Letzte Gesänge* and the *Metamorphosen* in which he summed up the grief and disaster to the Germany of which he was so conspicuous an ornament. One afternoon I went, in pursuit of a grander spirit, out to Heiligenstadt, walking up the slopes past the house where Beethoven was supposed to have lived at some time. I remember the external stairs, a rambling low house; and beyond, up the slopes into the *Wald* where he took his walks. Viennese folklore said with the young Schubert, and that the deaf great man would stop to make a musical notation with his stick. Alas, it does not appear that the irresistible young genius knew the older, of transcendent genius.

I went a good deal to Stefansdom, three days in succession in Easter week to Tenebrae, with its ceremonial putting out of candles. Old Cardinal Piffl—a living link with Franz Joseph and the Empire—came across in procession from his palace across the street, the ground floor of which was occupied by shops. A tubby little old man, complexion the colour of his purple, he was accompanied by his suffragans, canons and seminarists: a relic of better days, he was at least better than his successor, Innitzer, virtually a collaborator with the Nazis. A feeble creature, after the coronation of Pius XII Innitzer was to be seen on the balcony of St Peter's handing round sweets to the assembled prelates.

One evening I went to see *Parsifal* at the Volksoper and was not much taken with it, particularly its imitation of the ritual of the Church, the communion service. In the last act my attention wandered: 'The pure drama of the last scenes of Rimbaud's life came over me suddenly and possessed me.' Nor was I much pleased by the Czech woman in the box who took me under her wing and expatiated on the beauties of Czech opera, and how I must see Smetana's *Bartered Bride* at Prague. My experiences on the Continent had sickened me of ordinary humans' national exclusiveness—but how much worse was to come!

Another evening there was open-air cinema propaganda for the Social Democrats, who were in control of the city government. Under their aegis a quarter of vast *Siedlungen*, working-class housing settlements, was taking shape. I remember what an inspiration they were to the remarkable Socialist clergyman at Leeds, who inspired a similar development there in those days—

and what a criminal mistake Dollfuss made later in firing into these arenas to crush Viennese Social Democracy. *Everything* played into Hitler's hands, and what use he made of it!

That evening a thundercloud hung over the mountains, with wonderful effects of light—a fat Jew from Cologne remarked to me, 'entzückende Beleuchtung!' Down in the city one could hardly breathe in the narrow sultry *Gassen*, the sweaty atmosphere of the fag-end of the day, the smell of the drains and rotting vegetables. Posters admonished: 'Sichert den Mieterschütz— Wählt Rot!' ('Protect Rent Control—Vote Red'). People bustled about, hot and bothered. Suddenly a woman's voice burst forth from an upper window above the square, like birdsong when I opened my garden-door in Munich in the early Spring mornings, like rain falling upon the thirsty square. Men stood still for a while, and then moved on about their business with brisker step, light in their faces.

With my passion for the past, and my ambivalence about religion, on Good Friday I made pilgrimage with the rest to the Sepulchres in the churches: at Stefansdom, St Elisabeth im Deutschen Haus, Petruskirche, Franziskaner Kirche. In the ancient courtyard of the Deutsches Haus a door, with evergreen bush on either side, led down to the Sepulchre. In the walls were fragments of memorials to former guildsmen, under the wooden gallery a tablet to say that Mozart lived there from March to May 1781. Next evening there was an *Auferstehung* procession at the Votivkirche—all these aids to the religious life of the people: what was I doing among them, who didn't need them, though I hungered for something, I knew not what? Watching and waiting, as usual.

The grey façade rose behind the mounded trees of the garden in front, spires gleaming with the whiteness of naked bodies as night came on. Through the spring leaves the church appeared as behind a veil of a thousand emeralds; high above, between the spires, a star shone, and as I moved up the street the star moved until caught in the crown of the topmost angel, keeping watch with folded wings from the gable over the plains of the city. Jostled by the crowd of sweating mortals on the pavement, I fear that at the corner there will be waiting that woman who follows me with the dark despairing eyes.

On Easter Day I summed up: 'I've got to know my way about Vienna; I've been down almost every one of the little streets in the old part of the town, and often into the inner courtyards of the charming eighteenth-century palaces crowded in the *Gassen*. I've been all through the Hofburg, paid two lengthy visits to the chief gallery, been thrice to the Opera and into a score of churches. Reading: Baudelaire, and a biography of him.' Late in getting up, I taxied down to the Cathedral, in time not to miss a note of the Kyrie of Beethoven's Mass in C, written for Stefansdom. Somehow, in those days, Easter after Easter I managed to hear pontifical High Mass at a Roman cathedral: one year it was at Notre Dame, another at Bordeaux, at Chartres, then Dublin, now Vienna. It was a splendid ceremony here, what with the music, the hundred lights and vestments, the Cardinal in white and gold celebrating, putting on and taking off his mitre, two bishops as deacon and subdeacon. The sombre black oak stalls in the choir were covered with embroidered red silk, over the Archbishop's throne a white canopy. But the enclosed pew up in the gallery of the choir, that had been the Habsburg pew, was empty, looking dusty and neglected amid the splendour of the sanctuary.

Well—could Communism or Socialism show anything that was half so appealing?—all the mystery and magic of the Mass, Beethoven's music, the tenderness and passion, the falling cadences the utter silence in the vast church at the Elevation, everyone kneeling. (Thomas Hardy: 'Hoping it might be so.')

The crowd that filled the church was interesting to be in. On entering I made the mistake of moving along by myself, filling a place whenever anybody turned and went. But few people turned or moved at all. Just as I was in despair of getting any further than the crossing where the crowd was thickest, an idea possessed four people in line of whom I was last: like sheep we moved, along and up into the choir-aisle, an instinctive herd movement, led by a stocky determined middle-aged man; I brought up the rear. It was curious to watch the undecided movements of humans, going up the chancel or coming down, moving alone or in pairs, in contrary streams, in confusion.

Always, and everywhere, sheep.

Easter Day was crowned for me by my first hearing of the *Meistersinger* under Weingartner at the Opera. It appealed to me far more than *Parsifal*, especially the Nuremberg night scene, which 'caught something of the flavour of Shakespeare and the sixteenth century'.

Next day I resumed my inadequate education in the arts— starved of such things all my regrettably proletarian life—

spending another morning in the Kunsthistorisches Museum, splendid gallery. The Venetian room was brilliant with Easter sun lighting up one side: I watched the light passing across the pictures, calling them to life, now glowing, then fading. Of all the pictures that spoke to me Palma Vecchio's 'Holy Family with St John' was the glory of the room: a fig tree in full leaf as background for the Virgin, with the foothills of mountains typical of the earlier Venetians; rose-coloured lights on white bodies, a rich colouring that made the picture glow. To the vigorous impressionism of the Titians I preferred Palma's clarity and quiet perfection. A Moretto da Brescia's 'Saint Justina' was something new for me: the figure sloping to the left countered by the curve of the great reed over her right arm, evidently her symbol. Colouring sombre, the patron all in black; the saint's outer garment a dull gold, her white unicorn of chastity heavily shadowed with greys and black, with the bough of a tree overhanging figures. I made notes too of the Fra Bartolommeo 'Madonna and Child'.

The budding historian was more at home with the historical portraits, names he recognized, features he wished to learn. Here were the Archduke Albert and Philip II's favourite daughter, the Infanta Isabella Clara Eugenia, to whom he bequeathed the government of the southern Netherlands—what remained to Spain after all those fatal decades of war and struggle. A wonderful pair of Rubens portraits, rich in black and gold, brilliant red background. Albert had a typical Habsburg slope of the head, a shrewd calculating look; the Infanta, a reserved and monumental stateliness, painted however in secular finery, unlike her later portraits in the habit of a religious: the two sides of the Spanish royal house. As against the rich voluptuousness of Rubens' paint, gold lace and jewelled ornaments, the Clouet of Charles IX was of an anaemic pallor—but an interesting character-study: the decadent Valois youth, with faint growth of hair on petulant lips; a shifty look in the wide dark eyes, refined and lovely feminine hands.

Who, I wondered, was Rubens' Elizabeth of Bourbon, with a face like Henri IV? And here was Van Dyck's Prinz Rupprecht von der Pfalz—our own Prince Rupert of the Rhine: a handsome boy, brown hair, dark eyes, in black satin with gold chain, buckled belt attaching hilt of sword, which he was to wield with such effect in the Civil War. In the corner a white hound looks up at the young master—always fond of dogs: a black hound of his haunts the terrace at Windsor. A companion portrait of his elder brother, the Elector Charles Louis, showed a slightly older lad with reddish hair and rather Habsburg-sloping face. An early Van Ostade (1621–49) showed the derivation of the English landscape school clearly enough: a splendid piece, sand-dune country with two magnificent trees in the centre, upper boughs blighted and bare. At an inn with hanging signboard, a traveller on a white horse halts for a drink brought by the innkeeper; an old man and child struggle up the rain-wet road, a dog following, chicken scraping at front. It never occurred to me, in my aesthetic innocence, to question the adequacy of subject-description in painting, to consider mere form devoid of content; it occurs to me now, fifty years later, to comment on the silliness of concentrating on the latter, mere form-criticism, to the exclusion of the first. This is totally unhistorical; for one thing, quite untrue to the aims and intentions of the painters themselves, to whom the subjects appealed, upon the rendering of which they then lavished their gifts. So do not let us be discouraged by the silliness of art critics any more than by that of literary critics.

The diarist commented modestly, and reasonably: 'I sat there a long time before the Palma Vecchio, and made a few notes.' (An elderly man now, I still continue my lifelong habit of making notes on pictures in art galleries, very much so in the United States, where the galleries are the best things to see—often for fear

I may not see the pictures again, though I have managed to revisit a good many.)

In 1927 I felt that

the total result of making notes on pictures is to realise the hopelessness of translating from one art into another [a subject that much worried me then]. The humiliating feeling of one's life being too short, and one's capacity too limited, oppresses one; it becomes a nervous obsession, such as I have with books, obsessed with the insane desire to know everything. ['When I have fears that I may cease to be' ...] It's impossible, as I well know; but I proceed on the assumption that it isn't. Never once have I allowed that there is a limit to my faculty of learning. Yet such a limitation is essential in these days when there is such a multiplication in every sphere of knowledge. Moreover, the ideal of universality is the greatest danger for the instinct of creation.

Today, I wonder whether there wasn't something in that: whether sheer intellectual ambition was not cramping to the creative? Still, one can but follow one's own nature; such a tension in itself is a stimulus to creation—provided the body could stand the burden the will placed upon it. A scientific schoolfriend had confessed that he had

had to recognise that there was a limit to his faculties: one of his most acute disappointments was to have to admit that he had no kind of creative originality. In his research in physics he had been successful with the spade-work, and up to a point where a leap of the mind was necessary. I reflected that just where his mind stopped short, for the leap with him never came, was the point where with me certainty only began. For I have always felt that at the last moment I could depend upon rising to the occasion; often when adequate preparation has been lacking, something in my nervous system leaps to the call. I have relied upon that in any number of examinations, and in the two critical examinations when it was a question of life or death: in both my operations my mental attitude was just that before an examination, only with every faculty trained on the end of surviving. There may seem to be a difference between this intuitive nervous concentration and the original leap of the mind; but I feel that they have the same source in a certain physical constitution, though I don't know enough Freudian psychology, or physiology, to trace the working out of dispositions I am instinctively sure of.

There I was again—wanting to know still more in another field: comic, if it weren't so serious. For, of unbelievable obstinacy, I was determined to go on as before, putting strains on myself which nearly killed me in the 'thirties—a second peritonitis, a third and a fourth operation! Still I would not give in—though I was made to give up practical politics, an unrelieved blessing.

A comparable contrast existed with my treacherous Oxford friend, Otis, who had made me a similar confession of his limitations. He was a public-school boy, brought up to the exposure of his fellows, therefore gregarious and dependent upon society. He was at his best in company, where he shone, and appeared to have every confidence: it excited him to be the centre of interest and admiration. But this was only outward.

'Out of society, and alone, he is nervous and without confidence. He hates being by himself, and can't bear the loneliness of his own room; it is just because of his nervousness that he has to go out into society and, in losing himself, finds himself. [I understood, but couldn't appreciate, that state of mind.] My trouble is in complete contrast to his. Where he has this outer confidence, if only in appearance, I have an inner: my happiest times are when I am alone, I do all my best thinking independently and by myself, without help or stimulus except that of reading. My way is planned; where most people are at sea in the uncertainty of the times, I am decided as to the way to go and only long for the time when I can lead others along the way.

Cheated of this latter intent by the catastrophic break-up in our time, the dissolution of society, there remains the inner confidence, a fortress to fall back upon. In the evils of a world in chaos and confusion, through all the tragic experiences and falsification of hopes we have gone through since 1931, the practical solipsism I have arrived at is perhaps the most satisfactory rule of life for such an evil age: live as best as you can to and for yourself, achieve what you can within you, making yourself as independent as you can of circumstances and even of people, for as often as not they fail you, or cannot come up to expectations, or cannot achieve what they have it in them to do. Expect nothing of others, or of outer circumstances; live within yourself, a free and independent spirit. Never set your sights by the approbation or disapprobation of others: they are not worthy of it, and what they think doesn't matter to your inner being, if you possess your own soul.

This is, if not a good, then the least unsatisfactory gospel I can offer in bad times. I find it succeeds very well. Now you know, dear reader, what I really think. Few people in truth understand me—and I am not anxious that they should. But it's odd that one or two of my more intimate friends have never grasped it: I suppose it's beyond their comprehension.

By twenty-three, it strikes me, I had the situation fairly weighed up.

> With all this inner certainty, there is yet the outer confidence lacking. I am never sure of my effect on people; I cannot depend on them as I can on myself. I see clearly the part that has been played by my struggle against circumstances, and the consequent sense of social inferiority. This uncertainty, I tell myself, will disappear with the justification of achieved work. [That was longer in coming because of the double strain I imposed upon myself—all the richer and the more varied in the end, having succeeded in surviving: the real triumph!] My dreams show that the outer uncertainty needs to be fought down: in them, nothing ever goes right with me.

In fact, understandably enough, my dream-life reflected an acute anxiety complex: I am always subjected to some test in which I fail. I have to arrive at a dinner-party, but can never get there in time, or arrive at all; I have a lecture-engagement, but cannot get to the hall; or, worst of all, a part in a play and have been far too busy to learn the words; a speech to make—it used to be a sermon to preach—and words utterly fail me: a situation that never arises in real life, I am relieved to think. It used to awaken me; but now the discipline is complete: even in half-sleep I know that it is only a dream and, when I wake, I shall be in complete control.

I couldn't make out then why my anxious dreams were always of failure. 'Some of the elements, including that of sex, I spot; but why it should come about in that way I can't think. Perhaps the dissatisfaction that permeates the half-light of my dreams may be not only due to my hesitation before the secrets of life, but also to the long waiting and preparation for the days of achievement, where only, I know, I shall find my full development.'

Initiation into the secrets of life—for what that was worth—was available to me in 'the long manœuvres of the prostitutes at the corner of Hörlgasse', which I watched along with everything else, always from the outside. Along with 'the slow black cars down below, creeping like big obscene beetles with their antennae feeling forward into the night. Or the man who stopped to talk with his shadow at the other corner; while the stale and fetid breath arose from the mean streets with approaching summer.'

That afternoon, a Note says, 'Schönbrunn with the democracy': that and no more, except for 'a woman whose teeth were a mass of decay and gold'. Perhaps I was tired; but the charm of Schönbrunn was unforgettable—for sheer delight one puts it above Versailles or the English palaces. My stay in Munich and Vienna brought home to me the pull of Italy upon South Germany, and how much lighter and gayer the baroque of Southern Europe is than Northern. One memory has survived—that of Maria Theresa's Chinese room, with its collection of Oriental porcelain fancifully displayed, not as in a museum in boring glass cases, but upon brackets, in corner cupboards and cabinets. Outside on the terrace was the spot where a sentinel had been posted during the past century and a half, no one knew why—until it was discovered that the Empress had placed him there to guard the first crocus of the spring, and the order had never been rescinded. A pointer to the static rigidity of the Austrian Empire, it was also a tribute to its civility—can anyone imagine such an endearing aberration in Soviet Russia, though it might have happened under the Czars?

Next afternoon I spent in the gardens of another palace, the Obere Belvedere, built for Prince Eugene, Marlborough's companion at Blenheim and with a comparable record of victories (killed in the end).

.   .   .   .   .

In the open space before the palace children are playing, and old people walk up and down with sedate irregular steps under the sycamores. Spring has thrown a green shawl around the shoulders of the pollarded trees in the alleys. Two foolish happy lovers sit on a bench, with no eyes for the sun and the wonder of spring. Little winds rouse a swirl of sand, a momentary ghost by the water's edge. The Easter sun shines coldly over the sheet of water before the house, lighting up the columns, the achievements of arms, the eagles of the great dead. A cold wind sweeps the surface of the water; behind the walls the sun is sinking, the shadows lengthen over the grass, and the bell of a church nearby comes to me over the water like the bells of Mylor over the Penryn river. How often have I stood again by the water's edge, listening to the bells of that Sunday evening, while the freshening wind blows cool across the creek.

An old woman in blue apron and white cloth over her head, age in her limbs, fear in her blue eyes: I cannot and will not see her. Yet, when I turn away, my eyes follow the retreating figure down the avenue between the elms, until the imploring hands held out to heedless passers are only a gesture in the pattern of distance. Leaving the garden, with its narrow terraces down the steep hillside, I note the little house where Bruckner lived and died, in 1896—the face of a priest speaks from his medallion. The palace itself, with all its memories and glories, now passive and dead behind its shuttered windows: silence and stillness after the fever and dust of its day.

It made a strong impression on my mind, in particular the contrast between the southern gaiety and many-windowed sunniness of its conception, and the grand, stately gloom of Blenheim, which I was to come to know well from the inside.[1] Nor could I have dreamed that I should one day make the acquaintance of one of the children that used to play in those gardens of the Belvedere: Queen Mary's favourite niece, the Duchess of Beaufort. I rather think that the Schwarzenberg Palace, in the same quarter, was not open to the public; but indeed

---

[1] Cf. *The Early Churchills.*

Vienna was full of the closed palaces of the old Austro-Hungarian nobility who had withdrawn to the country. Charles Henderson, to become chief of my Cornish friends, made the acquaintance of some of them, glad to take in English paying guests, who (then) had the money—and a wonderful time he had in their Alpine retreats, romantic castles on their precipices, villas beside their lakes, days in the woods.

Bent on educating myself, next morning I was back in the Museum, 'where I spent most of my time with the van Dycks, Rembrandts and Velasquez.' The last I have never forgotten: there was a smallish room wholly devoted to Velasquez' portraits of the Spanish Habsburgs, Philip IV and his children, the little Infantas in their elaborate great drums of farthingales, the blue eyes and flaxen hair of the family, the features emphasized by their inbreeding until it all ended in the poor invalid Charles II and the War of the Spanish Succession. I noted too some pictures of English interest: the Holbein of Jane Seymour; the Hogarth of his wife, with nut-brown hair and black ribbon round her neck; hair drawn back from full forehead by jewelled clasps, a prim self-assertive mouth. I noted a typical Reynolds beauty, a young lady in pale lemon, leaning forward cheek on hand: a pale oval face, her golden hair piled up in a coiffure at the back. A Raeburn, and a Gainsborough Suffolk landscape besides. It was consoling to see that these held up well beside the grandees: a Virgin of Antonello da Messina, a little heap of cherries in her lap, while hands from an unseen person offer a glass of water; Joos van Cleve's miniature of the Emperor Maximilian holding a red carnation; or Hieronymus Bosch, so much appreciated by Philip II, illustrating a 'Going to Calvary' with a macabre Dickensian humour.

The afternoon I devoted to the *Nouvelle Revue Française*, as often all through those years, when it was the leading literary journal in the world, in which the best French writers appeared— then numerous: Gide, Paul Valéry, Paul Claudel, Cocteau; Mauriac, Montherlant, Paul Morand, not, I fancy, my friend André Maurois; Jules Supervielle, whom I especially appreciated, Jules Romains whom I did not (any more than I do today's mixed-up, popular sentimentalist, Sartre); Giraudoux: *La Guerre de Troie n'aura pas lieu*—but it did take place; and Drieu la Rochelle,

who came to a sticky end in it as a collaborator. A regular
subscriber, I built up a fine file of the *N.R.F.*, in request for
replacement for war-time losses at Oxford: now in an American
university library.

There had arrived a long letter from Otis, 'as I might have
known it would, the day after my writing and thinking about
him.' I do not seem to have kept it; did he keep my letters, I
wonder? After his malicious attack on *Politics and the Younger
Generation* I ceased to know him: 'not knowing people is a
great saving of time', most being not worth knowing; he
qualified.

> In the evening a charming walk through the oldest part of the
> town between Stefansdom and the *Postamt*, where I sent off
> *Jeremy and Hamlet* to L. [one of my young relations whose
> education I was encouraging—to not much point ultimately,
> ordinary folk not being very educable]. After posting my
> parcel, back into the sombre court before the old university,
> its baroque front built by Francis I and Maria Theresa, on one
> side, the painted façade of the Jesuit church on another. I
> went into the church for a while, the usual little crowd of
> believers kneeling in the pews and before the side altars. A
> bell began to ring out over the Square; I went out to see the
> agile figure of a young fellow pulling at the bell-rope before
> a window of the tower. Tea and papers in a café in the
> Graben. Last, an organ recital in Stefansdom: I haven't heard
> such playing since I last heard Henry Ley at Christ Church or
> Marcel Dupré at Nôtre Dame. A longish Passacaglia by the
> not very inspired Max Reger [I am still of the same opinion
> about him]; a Mozart adagio arranged from a string quartet;
> a Bach cantata, 'Ich will den Kreuzstab gerne tragen', and the
> Toccata in F, which fills me with exultation whenever I
> hear it.

I find a note on 'the splendid anger of Bach toccatas, rushing
forward to their conclusion, like a war-horse proudly tossing its
mane in the freedom of the field'.

The second of the Strauss concerts confirmed my impression of
the first.

I was irritated last time by the *Festliches Präludium* and the *Sinfonia Domestica*, and this evening I was put off by *Also Sprach Zarathustra*. These works attempt to impose themselves and force one's judgment by their technical ingenuity and the resources of an enormous orchestra. But they are irredeemably vulgar. Everything to seduce one is woven in, even to scraps of Gregorian plainchant; if anything could win me over, that would, for critical detachment dissolves when I hear the plainsong of the Church. But these things fail to redeem the patchwork on to which they are sewn—a genius for pastiche. The offensive bourgeois that Strauss is! I can't think of anybody who sums up the display, the opulent sensationalism of the Europe of 1890–1914, better than Strauss. The good side seems to be that of his operas, and the best of them, the *Rosenkavalier*, is so because it is nearest to Mozart. I felt disgusted by the capers executed around perfectly good themes; *Zarathustra* seemed to me to have no unity and no development. One can see to what extent Wagner is responsible for these latter-day lapses. The motive-system may serve a purpose in opera, but even there how one longs for some relaxation from it in any given work!

What these reflections imply for the considerations on the arts that have occupied my mind in Munich and here I am not sure. They seem to point to a conclusion that the attempt to push music into the sphere of other arts, in which Wagner was a prime mover, is unsatisfactory. It has produced interesting works by the way: almost the whole of Liszt, most of Strauss outside the operas, a good deal of Berlioz and such composers as Dukas. So far from discouraging my hopes of exploiting the bordergrounds of the arts, it goes to back up hopes for the future of literature. The attempt of music fails because of its essential purity of nature; literature wins by its very 'impurity': everything goes into it. This is clean contrary to Paul Valéry's view of the future of music and literature

—derived from Mallarmé's bias in favour of reducing everything, including sense, to music. Optimistically I concluded that my position was intended to sweep up the theorists of pure aesthetics—whispering the last enchantments of a leisure class—into 'a wider and firmer intellectual structure for an uncertain age'. It was meant to be less refined, more common and comprehensive.

'I am tired now; but the night-walk homewards through the gardens of the Hofburg was refreshing. The young sycamores in the avenue are getting fuller in the leaf; the day has been sultry, but a breeze brought out the aromatic smell of the opening buds. The Votivkirche was at its best: the lower part of the façade carved with a thousand shadows in the half-light, the spires and pinnacles like calcined bones.'

April 23rd: as I write the date, I remember that it's a red-letter day in England now: St George's Day, Shakespeare's birthday. Rather appropriate for an incident that happened to me in the Hofburg this morning. I went to see the Habsburg Treasuries. In one were the coronation jewels, except for a crown and a few things carried off to Madeira by Karl and Zita [the last Emperor and Empress]. I noticed an elderly woman who had something English about her, showing another about the place. In passing we exchanged glances; her eyes were weak and red, as if she had been crying. On I went, much taken with a cross of the Order of St Stephen, which Maria Theresa wore every day. The coronation cope of the Holy Roman Emperors was of exquisite Saracen work, made at Palermo in the twelfth century. I was fascinated by the Oriental patterns wrought in gold on plum-coloured silk: the central line a stem of the Tree of Life, branches spreading out to form the orphrey; on either side a lion, a comical brute as his tail and head have to meet for the sake of the design. He is killing a dragon, the features of both beasts picked out in scarlet. The edges and borders were trimmed with seed-pearls, not burdened with over-large jewels as in contemporary European work. To think that this was what the Norman kingdom of Sicily could achieve!

My mind went back to the one and only piece of Sicilian-Saracenic work in Cornwall—the fine rare ivory casket in which the bones of St Petroc were kept, chief treasure of Bodmin Priory: delicate metal work, exquisite painted roundels. After the Reformation it was kept safe away from the public for centuries among the borough's possessions: now on show in the parish church.

The treasures were scintillating, the achievements of man's best quality: his artistic inspiration, and the craft of his clever, ape-like hands; the chased leather carrier for the imperial crown, Charlemagne's patterned sword-hilt and scabbard, plaques from the crown and crucifix surrounded by large globular Carolingian jewellery, painted miniatures from the Gospels, ivory scenes from the bindings of medieval manuscripts. And last, something quite out of the tradition, but no less touching: the cradle, gilt and eagled, of Napoleon's clever, impassioned son, the young 'King of Rome', known to the Austrians as Duke of Reichstadt.

Passing from one Treasury to the other, I ran straight into the little old woman, who probably planned it; for she asked apologetically, 'Sie sind kein Amerikaner?' She was overjoyed to meet somebody from England. She was English, but hadn't been home for half a century; she spoke without a trace of foreign accent, sometimes relapsing into German when she couldn't find a phrase. With touching self-deprecation she was afraid that I wouldn't recognize her for English. She had married an Austrian army officer, now dead, and was living on a pension and her small savings. It had been difficult living in Austria all through the war: many of her closest friends had been nasty to her; it was hard to bear, 'it was so uncalled-for.' I consoled her with the thought that Germans living in England had had as bad a time. (By no means all, however: an old nurse to the family at Hatfield lived on in the House, cheering every German victory; and Belgium? 'But the Belgians were so unkind to the Germans.' Very characteristic: unredeemable egoism).

The old lady said that the Austrians had turned like that in imitation of the Germans, for it did not really lie in their character (but what about Hitler?). The Germans, she said, were responsible for a great part of the trouble, and the war. There was William II, 'no better than a clown', always making so much of the Army. And all the nationalist boasting! 'This was just what my New Englander thought, at my pension in Paris; and it is what Miss V.

thinks here.' This was educative, too; for, remember, I had been brought up in the pernicious Leftist rubbish of Bertrand Russell, H. N. Brailsford, E. D. Morel and Co.—Cambridge and Garsington—to the effect that England was as much to blame as Germany for the war. I now was learning better for myself in Germany—and all that happened in the subsequent decade, the 'thirties, corroborated it.

Did she ever go back to England? No; she was an Austrian pensioner and couldn't leave; besides she had no one in England now, all her friends were dead. She had a son here, a doctor. I said I owed my life to the doctors. This pleased her: 'Not many had a good word to say for them.' She was quite touched when I told her that her English was perfect; she said what a joy it had been to meet someone from England again. 'I promised her on parting that we would try to meet whenever I came back to Vienna. A poor little friendliness that, for I may never come back.' And, in the event, I never did.

'At the gate of the Hofburg we parted and went our different ways: I along the pavement before the Michaelskirche. For a moment I watched the couple going along the opposite side of the square: her companion and my poor old friend in her field-grey costume, walking along with short uneven steps. They turned the corner; and went, I suppose, for ever out of my life, as I from theirs.'

The evening before there had been another *Verbindung* with England, of a sort: an excellent production of Shaw's *Caesar and Cleopatra* at the Burgtheater. As I had noticed, Shaw was practically a German author at that time, performed everywhere, looked up to, venerated. Lucky dog! English writers in those days enjoyed the prestige of their country to carry them upwards, both in Europe and in America. Nothing of that for us: we have had to work our passage, everything against us—except for the language itself.

That same afternoon of my encounter, I was 'drinking milk in the Prater with the democracy.' It may be seen that, for all my Marxist thinking, my attitude towards the people has been consistent throughout my life. Nothing odd about that: the Communist opinion of the masses could not be more realist, more devoid of illusions about them; nor their whole system be based more clearly on their conviction of the unintelligence of the masses. Not that a grand working-class type like Ernest Bevin had any illusions either (his last words were 'The buggers won't work'; true enough). It is only middle-class intellectuals who suffer from these delusions—and have helped to undermine and unstring our society by them.

Actually the democracy wasn't drinking milk with me, but beer, watched with disgust by me. 'A repulsive dropsical old man sits at the opposite table: a *nouveau riche*, with bulging purple bags under his eyes. He surely votes *Einheitsliste!*' An election was on; this was the combined list of all the parties opposed to Social Democracy; the silly working class, of course, having no sense of unity, allowed themselves to be divided between Socialists and Communists—as in Berlin right up to the take-over by Hitler, which they so richly deserved by their ineptitude, and which they had done so much to bring about. Or, as in Spain, where they were divided three ways, among Socialists, Communists and Anarchists(!)—so that they lost the Civil War, poor idiots, and got the Franco they asked for.[1]

The real sympathies, if not of my mind, then of my spirit are betrayed next day—my last Sunday in Vienna—by a note: 'Blast the Election! It prevented me from hearing a Bruckner Mass in Stefansdom today.' I heard a Ferdinand Schubert Mass instead in the Augustinerkirche; when I had had as much as I could stand I went off to the Nationale Bibliothek to see the illuminated manuscripts. Here was another fine Fischer von Erlach building, an architect of the same class as Mansard or Wren, each of them with a capital city to improve, Vienna, Paris, London—though far more of Wren's work in London has been destroyed.

Here, behind the courtyard dominated by the equestrian statue of the unfortunate Joseph II, was a collection of manuscripts of outstanding quality, some of them of English interest. For example, the Gospels of St Cuthbert, from the Irish–Anglo-Saxon school, as early as the ninth century: where can they have come from? Perhaps from the monastery of St Gall in Switzerland, of Irish foundation from those early days when Ireland gave light

---

[1] Connolly admits his similar disillusionment: 'Nor am I so certain that the Spain which would have arisen out of a Republican victory would have been what we had hoped for or that a European war would have been averted.' *The Evening Colonnade.*

to Europe, instead of murderous bombs; or perhaps from the manuscripts so eagerly sought by Boniface, greatest of Englishmen, to civilize the Germans. More within my ken was a fifteenth-century psalter, written and illuminated for Humphry, Duke of Gloucester, that early book patron and benefactor of Oxford, whose books were scattered at the (culturally) deplorable Reformation. There was a Sacramentarium in Carolingian script, but with Anglo-Irish decorations—evidence of those early cultural exchanges.

A last dash into the Museum enabled me to carry away in mind some of the Renaissance riches—a glass beaker set with pearls and gold for Philip the Good; Augsburg watches, Nuremberg plate, Viennese porcelain, Italian majolica; armours of Maximilian I and the Emperor Sigismund, or Ferdinand of Tyrol—such as I see regularly now in the Metropolitan in New York. Grandest treasure of all was the Fugger Sarcophagus, with Greek sculpture at its freest and most natural. And, endearing in its gaiety, the complete altar set—candles, crucifix, figures and all—in Dresden porcelain, white and gold, a gift from Saxony to Maria Theresa, who occupied such a living position still in the tradition of Vienna, to any cultivated mind. O what riches, for a sensitive youth to feed on in his heart with thanksgiving and carry away to nourish his mind in the years to come!

That evening I went off to the Opera to hear *Lohengrin*, the only time I have heard it—but with Jeritza singing and Strauss himself conducting. I had hoped to come back to England via Prague; but I had now left myself not enough cash—what with spending so much on books (my form of drink), on concerts and opera. Most of the books I bought in Vienna were French—I had rather gone off German, associated in mind with Fräulein Pohl, Professor Haastert, and the Pastor's family in Hagen. My accent was pure, North German: I said *Bischen* and *Mädchen*, not *Bissel* and *Mädel* like South Germans, but I never had the feeling for the language, or the respect for it, I had for French. 'Geb' uns unser tägliches Brot' sounded comically like rustic English; and I agree with Matthew Arnold—against Wystan Auden—that English needs the precision and clarity of the French influence, not more of the Teutonic. Look at what appalling results it had in Carlyle and Carlylese!

Next day I spent in bothering about passport and tickets, yet once more—how I have always hated this chore! Before 1914 people could travel almost anywhere—except Russia, of course— without a passport. Think of it! Traipsing about the streets I watched a woman dragging a recalcitrant calf, with noose around its nose, down to the railway line; and, in a café, a Japanese coping gingerly with chocolate cake, while some meticulous women disputed about which end to open their eggs. Swift's Big-endians and Little-endians were evidently still much to the point with ordinary humans.

My first acquaintance with large cities induced in this country-reared youth two distinct moods. When all was yet new and strange the crowded spectacle excited and attracted me; it was a wonder to see spring in the foliage of squares and gardens, or sunset behind palaces like the Belvedere or Nymphenburg, still more moonlight fantasticating towers and spires like the terraces of Babylon, such as I had been awed by as a child in John Martin's engravings in the only book we possessed in the house, the vast *Home Preacher*. (I now own a late John Martin landscape, painted in the Isle of Man, a great rarity.) My second mood was odder. When tired with tramping and perpetually watching, worn out with sights and sounds, taking in everything, I got a curious *fixe* against the irregularity of great buildings, plastered with decoration and all the bright lights, signs and advertisements. I longed for simplicity and uniformity, for the buildings to go in long regular lines, quite straight and white, without break or decoration. 'So that one's eyes', I wrote, 'might find rest in the simplicity of the lines, refreshment and renewal.' I wondered if this was the secret of Greek architecture, and if one would ever grow tired of the lines of the Parthenon, of any Greek temple. (Alas, I was never to see one). Even the wonders of modern building, St Peter's or the Karlskirche, *tired* the mind: much more the restlessness of the nineteenth century, the confusion and chaos of the twentieth. 'Perhaps only the Greek and early medieval are free, for the mind to feed upon their infinite simplicity, without ever exhausting itself. They have this quality of absolute sufficiency and satis-factoriness characteristic of the greatest art.'

Inadequate as this early wonderment may be, it represented some inner inflexion of mind; for, uninstructed as I was, I instinctively responded to the simplicity of archaic sculpture and, as against freedom of expression, always preferred the restraint and control of Romanesque or early Greek sculpture to later. This fixation on simplicity and disciplined restraint had a curious parallel later in my political thinking: as against heterogeneity, let alone pullulating anarchy, I wanted uniformity and homogeneity. I even had a hankering after reducing everything and everybody to oneness—I could not bear the proliferation of differences, the way things naturally were in the world, left to themselves without order and control.

Perhaps this was a reflexion of neurosis, brought on by overstrain and exhaustion in the 1930s, as my earlier feeling about great cities reflected tiredness and saturation.

Anyway, I was homeward bound, to digest it all, calling in on the Plunders at Munich, to collect books and things I had left with them. When I arrived, they were sitting down to supper upon what they really liked, this (musically) cultivated German couple: a mess of raw meat, with a raw egg sitting on the top of it. They apologetically invited me to share their supper—I hadn't met that while staying with them, though I had met raw fish at the Pastor's in Hagen. I could away with one no more than the other—one more notch in my count of latent barbarism under the musical culture. Next day I mounted the train for Ostend, where I slept, by the sound of the sea once more; the day after I crossed to Dover and was back at Oxford by nightfall.

I used to regret that I hadn't gone to a university abroad and stayed longer; but for one thing, I hadn't the money, there were not the facilities that proliferate now, and perhaps I was mistaken in thinking so. These months abroad, I can see clearly now, provided me with what the Grand Tour provided young English aristocrats with in the eighteenth century—and more. Going to yet another university was not what mattered—after all, I was not going in for German, either history or literature, thank goodness. How Miss E. M. Butler, the best authority in the field in our time —and what excellent books she wrote, little enough appreciated, by far the best on Rilke, for example—disliked both, though her subject, and Germans too! (She much preferred French, rightly.) It is a curious thing how unpleasant even Germans of genius are—Wagner or Nietzsche, Frederick the Great or Bismarck or Luther; she saw how unlikeable Rilke was, for all his genius.

No—my equivalent to the Grand Tour answered far better. Culturally starved as I had been for years in a working-class home, I had now been given my opportunity by All Souls—and I think made the most of it: one way and another I had taken in quite as much as I could absorb, laid in a stock for years to come, perhaps the foundation for a lifetime.

5

All Souls from Within

And what meanwhile—since this is intended as a portrait of a generation, a picture of a society in transition by a social historian —were my contemporaries and friends doing?

Graham Greene, having given up hope of becoming an oil magnate with the Asiatic Petroleum Company, was at Nottingham serving an apprenticeship in journalism with the *Nottingham Journal*, with Cecil Roberts as Editor, who became much later a friend of mind. Both Graham and Evelyn Waugh were very rude to Cecil, and I am bound to say that the poor boy, who had gallantly supported his mother after the early death of his father, showed himself the greater gentleman. Graham found Nottingham dismal and Dickensian—for all his education at Oxford, no idea of the fascinating historic character of that Midlands capital, before it was largely destroyed after the Second War.[1]

'When I read Dickens on Victorian London,' says Graham, 'I think of Nottingham in the 'twenties. There was an elderly "boots" still employed at the Black Dog Inn, there were girls suffering from unemployment in the lace trade, who would, so it was said, sleep with you in return for a high tea with muffins, and a haggard blue-haired prostitute, ruined by amateur competition, haunted the corner by W. H. Smith's bookshop.' Graham found cheap lodgings for himself and his dog Paddy 'in a grim grey row with a grim grey name, Ivy House, All Saints Terrace. My high tea before work consisted almost invariably of tinned salmon which I shared with Paddy, so that most days he was sick on the floor.' We see the stage set early for the cult of squalor that runs all through his subsequent work. 'I was earning nothing and learning very little on the *Journal*, and I had begun again to draw

[1] Cf. *Times, Persons, Places.*

an allowance from my father who could ill afford it.'[1] So Graham left to try the literary life in London.

Evelyn Waugh—with a crisp comment on his Third in the Schools from his tutor, Cruttwell—had betaken himself to the art school, Heatherley's, celebrated by Samuel Butler's picture, half realist, half caricature. But Evelyn's heart was still at Oxford where he had had such an uproarious and drunken time. He has a characteristic description of a party in Beaumont Street given for him by rich and comic John Sutro, talented mimic. 'John's party consisted of Harold Acton, Mark Ogilvie-Grant [the handsome 'House' man who killed himself], Hugh Lygon [the original of Hamish Lennox in *A Little Learning*, and Sebastian in *Brideshead Revisited*], Robert Byron, [heroic opponent of Appeasement, who perished in the Mediterranean], and Richard Pares. After luncheon which was hot lobster, partridges and plum pudding, sherry, mulled claret, and a strange rum-like liqueur,' they went their various ways drinking all day and all night. 'Next morning I drank beer with Hugh and port with Preters [i.e. Hugh Molson] and gin with Gyles Isham, lunched with Hugh and Desmond Harmsworth. Harold and Billy [the Acton brothers] saw me off at the station.'[2] Back to London, to be supported by Father, to whom Evelyn had always behaved intolerably—though Chapman and Hall, their publishers, were doing badly in the slump—until he got the prep. school job in North Wales which inspired *Decline and Fall*.

Richard Pares had been what Evelyn calls 'the friend of his heart', and was to become my dearest friend at All Souls. But Richard did not enjoy drinking, and so he and Evelyn drifted apart. 'I loved him dearly,' Evelyn says, 'but an excess of wine nauseated him and this made an insurmountable barrier between us.' Richard had the sweetest nature and was the most amusing and cleverest of companions. Evelyn has an account of a decadent dream of Richard's, and I remember a vivid one which ended with 'Here the Great Explorer Woodward met his end.' At the bottom of Richard's character there were determination and stoicism, which led him to a life of dedicated scholarship; when struck down by multiple sclerosis in middle life, at the height of

[1] Graham Greene, *A Sort of Life*, 156, 168.
[2] Evelyn Waugh, *A Little Learning*, 212–13.

his powers—the finest eighteenth-century scholar in Britain—
never have I witnessed such heroism, nor did a word of complaint
escape his lips. It fell to me to pay tribute to him at his memorial
service in Chapel at All Souls—we had received a message of
apology from Evelyn for his non-attendance: I could not but think
of the irony of their story, their glad youth and promise, all that
past known to hardly anyone there, stored up and laid away in my
memory.

At this time Richard himself intended journalism—we all had
had our taste of it as undergraduates, contributing to *Isis* or
Cherwell, the *Oxford Outlook* or *Oxford Magazine*. Richard had
had an invitation from the powerful Editor of *The Times*,
Geoffrey Dawson, under whom that paper was sometimes regarded as the All Souls parish magazine. He kept an eye open for
possible recruits, and twice made a bid in my direction, which I
didn't for a moment consider. Richard was to serve his apprenticeship on the *Liverpool Post*, but could no more bear it than Graham
could Nottingham—if Richard had received a call straight to *The
Times*, he would have been caught. As it was, he settled for
academic life and, the son of Professor Sir Bernard Pares, a job
was found for him at London University; indeed all university
doors deservedly were open to him, never a rejection.

Cyril Connolly was another very close friend of Richard. With
his Third in the Schools—a Brackenbury Scholar of Balliol!—he
had gone down to live the literary life in London. Richard told
me that Cyril meant to write the biography of his fellow Anglo-
Irishman, Swift, and what a brilliant book he would make of it.
He never got round to doing it, but wrote little pieces in the *New
Statesman*, and lived as companion with naughty old Logan
Pearsall Smith—'living off Logan', I called it—in St Leonard's
Terrace, in Chelsea. This was in fact no sinecure, for Logan was
an acute manic-depressive, who played cat-and-mouse with a
succession of young men who hoped to succeed to his bachelor
inheritance—Robert Gathorne-Hardy has told the remarkable
story in a book worthy of it. Cyril began his *Enemies of Promise*
characteristically, in the afternoon: It is after lunch (omelette,
vichy, peaches).'[1] The subject is the Predicament of the writer,
which they are always holding forth about nowadays, instead of

[1] Cyril Connolly, *Enemies of Promise*, 3.

getting on with it. It starts, again characteristically, from the platform: 'The predicament is economical. How to get enough to eat?' I could have told him, quite simply: '*Work*. Cut down your eating and drinking to what you can afford. Cut your garment according to your cloth.' When Cyril came to see me at Oxford he rushed greedily to see the comments I had written in the margins of his book, and was relieved to find that—apart from a few passages marked 'Two silly pages on the politics of literature' or 'Writers don't *understand* politics'—most of the comments were appreciative, even laudatory.

Harold Acton had gone down, with 'a liberal allowance' from his parents, to live the literary life in Paris, starting off with Desmond Harmsworth, a charming acquaintance of mine; who deserted however to be married. Harold was 'irritated by the symptoms of incipient slavery which he already betrayed.'[1] So Harold settled for an apartment in the Île St Louis, which I was to come to know not until forty years later, as a friend of Marthe Bibesco. There Harold was perfectly *à son aise*, hobnobbing with the fashionables, Gertrude Stein and the Sitwells, Picasso and Tchelitcheff. So he was now on his way, and has written it up beautifully in *Memoirs of an Aesthete*, his best book.

Peter Quennell, the only one of the group I did not know and did not make the acquaintance of until much later, had gone down rather earlier than the others—propelled by the authorities—to live the literary life in London. He too was taken up and given a start by the Sitwells; he had a literary family—at least they wrote books—behind him, but he is singularly reticent about his life in his book, *The Sign of the Fish*. What is the point of being reticent if you choose to write an autobiography?

David Cecil, after a spell of teaching at Wadham, also went to live the literary life in London—I missed him sadly, when that time came, from Oxford. However, with the seriousness of mind of the Cecils, which I greatly respected, he got forward with his books, in spite of marriage and the joys of family life—he married into the literary circle of the MacCarthys and Bloomsbury, which was a help. And later came back to a full-time career as a professor at Oxford.

Justice of mind compels me to say that they all, in their various

[1] Harold Acton, *Memoirs of an Aesthete*, 169.

ways, were set to fulfil themselves in their work. I was the most belated of them, for reasons which will become clear.

And what of my immediate juniors, between whom and me were but two or three years, so little, with my backward start, as to make them practically my contemporaries—except that, with their prep.-school and public-school background, they were far more sophisticated, and naughtier. Auden was already up at Christ Church, and during the next year or two I was to see something of him. Isherwood, who had known him from their prep. school, describes him as he was at this time: 'His small pale yellow eyes were still screwed painfully together in the same short-sighted scowl, and his stumpy immature fingers were still nail-bitten and stained—nicotine was now mixed with the ink.' Wystan had rooms in Peck—Peckwater quadrangle—which are recognizably described, as also the idiosyncratic, ill-fitting, smelly clothes he shambled about in. 'There was a workman's cap, with a shiny black peak, which he bought while he was living in Berlin, and which had, in the end, to be burnt, because he was sick into it one evening in a cinema.' How ill-regulated, how awful they were!

Frightfully unappetizing as this apparition was, he apparently suffered no frustration in his sex-life. His friend tells us: 'His own attitude to sex, in its simplicity and utter lack of inhibition, fairly took my breath away. He was no Don Juan: he didn't run round hunting for his pleasures. But he took what came to him with a matter-of-factness and an appetite as hearty as that which he showed when sitting down to dinner. His manner of describing these adventures bore all the marks of truth. I found his shameless prosaic anecdotes only too hard to forget.'[1]

Actually one of those named above corroborated this: Wystan could always, on the brief train journey to London, make a contact. All this side to Wystan, since he became a world-renowned figure, has been carefully relegated to the background. On his last encounter with Cyril, Wystan said, 'I'm afraid I have become dreadfully square, you know.' But why hush it up? We all of us *knew*.

At the House he was much disapproved of by Dundas, for

[1] Christopher Isherwood, *Lions and Shadows*, 183, 189, 195.

whom I had no great love; but Ernest Jacob took up this startling recruit to the Eng. Lit. School, who duly collected his Third, like the rest of these young geniuses. As to Wystan's genius I had no doubt, from the first or second reading to me of his poems. He would come over to All Souls and read them aloud after lunch, sitting in the big quadrangle of a summer afternoon. Their originality and force struck me at once; Wystan had the providential good fortune to achieve early a personal style of his own and, such was the strength of his personality, to impose it on others, the head of a school. If genius means energy of mind—certainly it is a characteristic of genius—no one had it more markedly than Wystan, channelled into poetry. All the same, since poetry demands other qualities too, is it likely that it will last as securely as Eliot's? Eliot's *moves* me much more.

There came a hot summer afternoon when Wystan suggested that we adjourn from the quadrangle at All Souls to his rooms at Christ Church. Along we went and up the corner wooden staircase. On entering, I was somewhat surprised at his sporting the oak, i.e. shutting to the outer door, locking us in. He next proceeded to draw the blinds and close the shutters; turn on the green-shaded light, like an office-lamp, and read to me letters from a friend in the Mexican Eagle Oil Company, describing his adventures with the boys. I had never had this educational privilege before and—registering primly (to myself) 'a Fellow of All Souls doesn't do this sort of thing'—I was determined not to appear priggish, but huddled farther into my chair. I must have been in a fine mixed-up state of mind, for I have no memory whatever of the stimulating adventures regaled to me. Never embarrassed—a middle-class attribute—I began to wonder a little ... and great was my relief when I heard the deep notes of Tom resound outside. 'There, it's four o'clock,' I said, 'I always have tea in the Common Room at All Souls at four o'clock.' With that, I rose and went.

Somehow, after that, Wystan was never so much at ease with me. I continued to see him from time to time, even in later years in New York, but we never became 'close', as they say in America. In fact, I was more close to him in the last years of his life, when he spent some months with us at All Souls. Obscurely, I was determined to make it up to him—his life had in fact become bleak—

and he gave me the last book of poems he brought out before his death inscribed: 'With Love, from Wystan'; to which I see I added, 'how nice after all the years.' Besides his genius, Wystan was—unlike some of the acquaintance above—a gentleman.

This is not the place to go into his poetry. How much of it will last?—much of his later verse is sheer prose, cut up into lines. His way of life in America was antipathetic to poetry; and indeed Robert Lowell commented to me that there was something uncongenial to English poets in the American environment. How much Wystan lost by uprooting himself! it is the most dangerous thing for a poet to tear up his roots, and become rootless. One sees what he lost, from the inspiration of those earlier poems:

O love, the interest itself in thoughtless Heaven,
Make simpler daily the beating of man's heart; within,
There in the ring where name and image meet,

Inspire them with such a longing as will make his thought
Alive like patterns a murmuration of starlings
Rising in joy over wolds unwittingly weave

And make us as Newton was, who in his garden watching
The apple falling towards England, became aware
Between himself and her of an eternal tie.

Compare that with the poem that emerged from a 'Fifth Avenue dive'! I once asked Wystan in New York, over his favourite 'Bloody Mary', if ever he went back to the limestone country in the Pennines that had inspired him. 'No. I could never go back,' he said sadly. 'That was Paradise.'

One wonders whether, in the end, Louis MacNeice may not emerge as the finest of those poets. Him I never knew, but I used to see him about Tom Quad after Mary Ezra, then just a girl, who was the daughter of Marie Beazley, my undesired Egeria. Louis stood out rather singular, among the poets, as an enthusiastic hetero. I looked upon the young couple with no friendly, but an envious, eye. Louis married her. It all ended sadly when she went off to America with a handsome pugilistic-looking Ukrainian, who wrought devastation among hearts at Oxford—and whom I met, years later in Los Angeles, dusty and deflated, defeated by life. While Louis wrote heart-achingly:

The whole of my year should be hers who has rendered already
So many of its days intolerable or perplexed
   But so many more so happy;
Who has left a scent on my life and left my walls
   Dancing over and over with her shadow ...
So I am glad
   That life contains her with her moods and moments
More shifting and more transient than I had
   Yet thought of as being integral to beauty ...

How lucky *we* were not to be bothered by such an encumbrance!

And Stephen Spender? Isherwood has a somewhat romantic description of him as he was at this time: 'blushing, sniggering loudly, contriving to trip over the edge of the carpet—an immensely tall, shambling boy of nineteen, with a great scarlet poppy-face, wild frizzy hair, and eyes the violent colour of bluebells ... His nose-bleeding (now long since cured) was famous at this period. Without the least warning, at all times of the day, the blood would suddenly squirt from his nostrils.'[1] I see him like that now, on an early visit to my dark oak-panelled rooms in the front quad, handkerchief held to that organ, dabbing furiously at his blood-stained face.

Such was the poetic Oxford to which I was returning.

I was returning, however, not to the literary life, but to the life of a don. While I was away, Woodward and Cruttwell had fixed up a term's teaching for me with St Edmund Hall—last of the medieval Halls. It was to all intent an independent college, run by its admirable Vice-Principal, A. B. Emden. The only relic of its dependent status was that Queen's College had the appointment of the Principal, and they proceeded to appoint their superannuated Chaplain, one Cronshaw, to the job. Emden took this like the good Christian he was, held on his way and did all the work, and eventually succeeded. He was the only creator of the Hall's success—charming in the intimacy of its small quadrangle, its dining hall and Caroline chapel, with pretty seventeenth-century library above used for the dons' dessert after dinner. The

[1] Ibid., 281, 283.

charm of the place was its smallness of scale—today ruined by the giantism that afflicts our time, a hall the size of Christ Church, overpowering buildings that ruin the roofscape of the High.

I was very glad of this addition to my resources from teaching for the History School. The stipends, then, of Prize Fellows of All Souls were but £300 a year—plus rooms, service and dinner. No one in those gentlemanly days would have dreamed of getting up in a College Meeting and proposing a rise in his salary—it was considered a sufficient honour to be a Fellow of All Souls, as it was. For the rest, we went ahead for ourselves—took on teaching from other colleges, examining of every kind, for Oxford as well as other universities, School Certificates, Oxford and Cambridge Joint Board; lecturing for the W.E.A. or extra-mural bodies; reviewing, writing articles, eventually books. All these activities I went in for, and more; determined to be as independent as possible, I did not scrounge for college jobs, let alone for every conceivable allowance—family allowances, housing allowances, travel and research allowances, allowances to purchase books for oneself(!). The decline of our society has produced a world of scrounging.

I enjoyed my teaching; but, of course, took it too seriously, like everything else, and worked at it too hard. The reader may wish to know how the famed 'tutorial system' worked at Oxford. Undergraduates came to me in couples each week of term. One set each undergraduate a subject for an essay, within the required field of the Syllabus for the Honour School, and suggested the reading for it with the lectures to attend. Next week one heard the essays read and criticized them. Besides this, one took a share in the college entrance examination, examining for Scholarships. As Fellows of All Souls we were not supposed to take more than twelve hours' teaching a week, for our research took priority. Actually I sometimes undertook fifteen hours' teaching—too much; today, I gather, full-time college tutors feel themselves overburdened if they have ten—and we were merely half-timers.

Tutors are at their best when young, before staleness and boredom set in; I was keen and had to do a certain amount of reading in the subjects I was teaching—one day when I was wholly free a note records twelve hours' reading. No Trade Unionist would approve of that. In reading for my own Schools I had emphasized the nineteenth century and thought of making that my field of research. Woodward advised me against that—it was his own period. I was teaching the sixteenth century; perhaps these two factors settled the matter for me. I had been drawn to the Tudors from my boyhood, and I am still at them.

By the tutorial system, in my time, the dons were sacrificed to the undergraduates—naturally in a modern mass-university with thousands of students, many of whom ought not to be there, they cannot hope for the constant contact we had at Oxford, often prolonged into the vacation by reading parties. 'Sligger' Urquhart at Balliol used his Swiss chalet for this purpose: Richard, Roger Mynors, Cyril Connolly, were of the elect regularly invited there. Ernest Jacob used to have them, often in his favourite fishing places, on the Ribble or in Scotland; Otis figured in these, I never had—couldn't afford it.

I cannot say that my pupils gave much back; on the whole they were a conscientious, stodgy lot—but they were not slackers. One bulky pair of twins I recall from their consistent mispronuncia-tions: they always said 'Straakey', for Strachey. One or two of them became good scholars: notably John Armstrong, now a leading authority on the fifteenth century, who discovered and edited a tell-tale chronicle of the Usurpation of Richard III; another was Hanson, who became an eminent bibliographer at the Bodleian—I met him again, a fortnight before he died, at the Huntington Library in California. A third became a professor; another professor graduated from among my Merton pupils. Neville Williams, I am proud to say, has made a name for himself as an historian and is now Secretary of the British Academy.

Evidently I was thought a stimulating tutor, for shortly I was in request from Lady Margaret Hall. Among these girls two stood out: Veronica Wedgwood and a very pretty companion, some-thing of an heiress, Welsh with a winning smile, sexy voice and engaging stutter. I found her rather distracting, and she did her best to distract her tutor, not much older than they were. Once, on the excuse of going out to a party, she came arrayed in an evening frock, rustling silk and all the colours of the rainbow—I was fair game. Veronica, clever girl, played herself down, never made a mistake and—like so many of the Wedgwoods—rather gone to the good, allowed her companion to make the running and glamourize me. I made no move, however: I wasn't going to be caught: I wasn't going to marry anybody, not even of my own sex—which would have been easier, and offered fewer problems. One evening at a Shakespeare play in Wadham Gardens—O those summer nights in the Oxford of fifty years ago!—she announced to me, rather tauntingly, that she was marrying: a rather long-nosed fellow, who became a doctor, but did not live long. The announcement gave me rather a pang—as it was intended to.

Such was the background; in this way a good deal of my days, my time and energy, was spent. I was doing too much teaching, especially for one who did not intend to become a full-time tutor, or a professor, but meant to be a writer and, if possible, to combine that with politics. Nor do I wish to bore the reader with the details of the tutorial work on which I spent myself: it was not my real life, successful as I was at it—that remained, as it had always been, my inner life. It shows how much teaching took out of me, that during my first term as a tutor I kept no Diary. Only Notes remain.

One of these remarks on the Generations, as portrayed in the dining car on my way back: 'Repulsive old men, sensualists with grinding voices. The war generation represented by younger men around me: the steady sort, but not to be burdened with too great responsibility, bent on enjoying life.' I was reading Lawrence's *Seven Pillars of Wisdom*, which he had written as *his* piece of work as a Research Fellow. His closest friend in college was Lionel Curtis, a remarkable man in himself, to whom Lawrence opened his heart: his most intimate, despairing letters are all written to him—a tribute to Lionel's own quality, if any were needed.

Curtis was a combination of prophet, evangelist, constitution-maker and contacts-man. One of Milner's Young Men, the Kindergarten, along with Geoffrey Dawson, Bob Brand, Dougie Malcolm among the Fellows, Curtis had had a considerable influence in forming the Union of South Africa, in putting across Dyarchy, dual control, in India, leading eventually to self-government—for which Kipling never forgave him; and in the Irish peace-treaty, with the Irish Free State, and partition in Ulster. He could have said, with Napoleon, if he had known

French, 'J'avais le goût de la fondation, et non de la propriété', for he was a prolific creator of institutions, of the Royal Institute of International Affairs, Chatham House, for one. For these public purposes he had a magic touch with millionaires: he could do anything with them, generous men, though nothing with academics. He was, however, the chief inspirer of the Oxford Society.

Many are the stories I could tell of him, but I am not writing his biography: Geoffrey Dawson told me that only he could—and in the event it has never been written, a loss to the history of our time. (I have a sketch of him in my *Private Lives*.) He believed himself, intolerably, to be a prophet; what made him tolerable was that he was warm-hearted and lovable. He had disciples of his *Civitas Dei* all round the world; I was not one of them, but I was fond of him, and he was fond of me.

He had created a charming place for himself at Kidlington, in the old part of the village—a large thatched cottage beside the upper Cherwell. I had been reading *Revolt in the Desert*, the shortened version of Lawrence's famous book; Lionel invited me out to read one of the ninety rare copies printed—we had another locked away in the coffee-room—and I spent a happy afternoon on his lawn reading in it. 'The green turf came up to the door, hollyhocks, gillyflowers, roses by the wall; beyond the privet fence, prim strawberry beds. A Cherwell summer: the drowsy buzzing of flies, the soft motion of birds' wings.'

After tea we walked to the kitchen garden; giant cauliflowers, blackcurrant bushes veiled in nets. A cage-contraption caught my eye, a dusky-coloured creature rustling and stirring inside. A rat? No, a starling. On seeing us the poor creature opened its wings and beat frantically against the wires. On the underside the feathers were a lovely fawn; but near the breast the wing had been torn by its efforts to get free. What was to be done? An accident, I innocently thought, and told the Just Man that he had accidentally caught a bird in his trap. No reply: his anger that the starlings came and ate his fruit left him speechless. He turned away to talk to my friend. Could I steal back, when they had gone on, and set the bird free? There was the wild creature, palpitating with life, still struggling vainly against the wires, would go on getting weaker from hunger and thirst. Miserable, I was too weak to interfere. Another effort, now feebler: couldn't he put an end to the struggle at once? No: the bird was for Jezebel, the cat.

I had seen that lovely creature playing all alone in the garden: coat of slate-blue and terrible eyes of jade: stealthy movements of grace and a sudden leap into the air. For a time I couldn't tear myself from the little tragedy of the cage in the cabbage-patch; and then, with a 'Not a hair of their head should be hurt', I meekly followed the Just Man up to the mill, to approve the good work he had achieved in clearing the channel of sedge and banking it with gravel.

That night I wrote my note on 'The Just Man and the Starling'. At twenty-three my outraged sensibilities were all with the poor wild creature; today, a gardener myself—here at Trenarren we haven't a cherry or a berry for ourselves for the birds—my sympathies are with Lionel. Time has passed; I am now more than his age then.

Lionel, perhaps not really a marrying sort, was married. He had proposed himself for the hand of the elder daughter of the Cecils, Mima, who became Lady Harlech, on condition that this did not interfere with his mission in life. This was not thought good enough for a Cecil, and he settled for his secretary, a handsome piece devoid of any sense of humour, but much approved by Nancy Astor with her feminist sympathies. She had been baptized Gladys at the font, but this being considered rather lower-class, she had been renamed, more grandly, Patricia. The daughter of a clergyman, out of a small Devon vicarage, she described me as a 'peasant'. So I was amused when I saw her once put firmly in her place by Bishop Headlam. Lionel had walked us from Oxford across the fields and along the Cher—in those days when all was open—and we were a large party for lunch. Patricia called on the Bishop to say grace. Though I had no social experience, I would never have made that mistake. The Bishop said grace resentfully, and then said loudly, 'You did wrong to call upon me to say the grace. In the first place, I am not your chaplain; and in the second, it is your husband's duty to say grace in his own house.' There was a dead silence. I did not laugh, but the peasant saw well enough that the poor lady had revealed her lower-middle-class origins.

Lionel recruited, as an Associate Member, Sir Robert Borden, war-time Prime Minister of Canada; with Lionel's connexions around the world he recruited the most interesting of these Associates, besides others who were his guests. André Siegfried came for a couple of terms from Paris;[1] Abraham Flexner from New York. This last had his useful influence in America. Flexner —another creative founder—had been promised a large sum of money to start yet another university; after his experience of All Souls he preferred to create something of the same sort, and laid down the blueprint for the Institute of Advanced Studies at Princeton, though it subsequently became under Oppenheimer more scientific than he intended. Ernest Jacob recruited Le Bras, a fat little medieval canonist, a Breton, who became Rector of the University of Paris. From Dublin I managed to get Myles Dillon, who used the opportunity to study the Celtic and Sanskrit manuscripts in the Bodleian: he ended up as President of the Irish Academy. Lionel's guests were legion: Smuts came several times from South Africa, so too Jan Hofmeyr, Herzog and Justice Feetham; John Dove and Lionel Hitchens from old Milner days. (When Lionel first set eyes on the Cornish Lionel in Chapel at New College, evening sun filtering through the stained glass, 'it was love at first sight'—a sentiment that would at once be mis-interpreted today. It made me smile—but there *was* that emotional element binding the Kindergarten together. Lionel Hitchens, of that Falmouth family, was obliterated by a German bomb in London in the Second War. He had not been an Appeaser.)

These elect and distinguished Associates of the inter-war years have been characteristically followed today by a mob of Visiting Fellows, academics, mostly of less interest and distinction. Such a large scheme—correct enough in principle, but undertaken on too generous a scale—was virtually forced upon All Souls by the Franks Commission, whose main charge against the college was that *'it was not spending up to its resources.'* Here is the Keynesian *cliché* that has bankrupted the country: Spend—Spend—Spend,

[1] He always carried a copy of La Rochefoucauld in his suitcase, as William Faulkner always carried a Shakespeare.

never save anything for a rainy day. Is it any wonder that the country has exhausted its resources, has an astronomical indebtedness abroad when before 1914 it had vast investments in the outside world? That was how we had no balance of payments problem: today a debtor country, at the mercy of Arabs, able to buy up historic houses like Mereworth—or the whole country, if they chose. A contemptible society—the country which I myself can remember as the first in the world.

All Souls was quite right to opt for Visiting Fellows: a service to Oxford to bring distinguished men from abroad, and for them to come. But not to bring Tom, Dick and Harry for a jaunt at this country's expense, from rich countries like U.S.A., Japan and post-war Germany (having lost the war!). Half-a-dozen elect persons a year would have been enough. In English universities today anyone has only to get up and propose *spending* money— and every third-rate academic will vote for it. So All Souls committed itself to fifteen of these persons a year!—And, to support them, pledged itself up to the hilt, bought large properties both at Iffley and in North Oxford and built complexes of flats to house them, besides maintaining and feeding them. For this purpose the college committed its revenues up to the limit—no surplus as in my day (with £300 a year as a full-time Fellow); of this I much disapprove—one should not live right up to one's income, let alone go beyond it.

But prudent economy is old-fashioned. One of these recent Visiting Fellows, not ashamed to run up a considerable debt to the college, had the face to tell me that my attitude to money was out of date. It is true that I much object to having my hard-earned savings confiscated for the benefit of spendthrifts, or engulfed in tax to compensate constant strikers, inveterate slackers, silly students who ought not to be at a university. No reactionary, I am all in favour of those who qualify to be there and make the most of their opportunities—though when I think of the struggle I had to make, with *one* university scholarship for all Cornwall, which I simply had to get or fall by the wayside, it makes me angry to think what young fools today will throw away, or destroy, or vandalize—when everything is done for them. Another such Visiting Fellow from Scotland—whom I watched guzzling glass after glass of the college wine (I have lived all my life at All Souls as a teetotaller; people who cannot afford to drink expensive imported wine should go without)—made the mistake of letting me know that he was using the opportunity to correct O-level papers. He could perfectly well do that at home—that was not what the expensive Visiting Fellows scheme was for.

What a contrast between now and 1927!

This is the place to make an important point about the group of Empire and Commonwealth men at All Souls. They were a recent growth, an excrescence on the real college tradition, which was never Tory but Whig; with the venerated Warden Anson, who virtually recreated the college and was the real maker of its distinction in the past century, Liberal Unionist, still not Tory. Warden Pember, whose sole idea was to keep things going exactly on Anson's lines, was a Little Englander Liberal, who could not bear the Empire-Commonwealth-Round Table group (they had been put across him by powerful Geoffrey Dawson, Estates Bursar before Geoffrey Faber). Though I was a Labour man, I was much more sympathetic to them and their idea of the Empire. They thought of it essentially in terms of 'trusteeship', trusteeship of and for native races in the backward areas of the world, certainly *not* exploitation. They were devoted to what they considered their duty and—indubitably Christian gentlemen (I was neither, but wished to be fair-minded and saw them as they really were)—moved by the motive of service; self-important, yes, but not motivated by their interests.

And I still think they were right. Lionel Curtis, for example, was a liberal about South Africa, not in agreement with his friend Smuts, let alone Boer reactionaries like Herzog. He was a friend of Lugard—whom he brought to All Souls—of the marvellous achievement in Nigeria: his heart would have been broken if he had seen the appalling events, the massacres of hundreds of thousands, after the British left. Or similarly in the Sudan. Or in East Africa. Or, for that matter, in India, between India and Pakistan. It has all been a ghastly tragedy, which we owe to the Germans for making a Second War. Of course, the British Empire as such would have been phased out, in the natural course of events, but it would have taken place more gradually; there would have been two or three decades in which to train up services, administrative, educational, medical, technical. It would have been in the best interests of the blacks themselves.

So it is not surprising that I, as a young Labour man, was much more in sympathy with this group—as indeed was Keith Hancock, an Australian, who belonged to it and wrote Smuts's official biography—than the academic Fellows. Woodward, for example, was given to supercilious pooh-poohing of them and their activities, though he had no objection to receiving Rhodes money for a tour around the world. No love was lost between him and Reggie Coupland—another creation of Lionel's—who built up a fine monument of historical work on Empire and Commonwealth history: basic works on East Africa, Nigeria, the Nationalities problem in the Commonwealth, on Wilberforce and Livingstone, besides serving on Indian and Palestinian Commissions. (Woodward was ploughing the sands of diplomatic history.) Over this difference of inflexion Richard Pares, in spite of his research into the Old Empire and the West Indies, was with Woodward against Coupland and the Empire group. This was because he was an academic *pur sang*, and he shared Woodward's middle-class inferiority complex about the public figures. An outsider to both, I had no such complex; if the truth be told, I found the men of the world more interesting, more varied, more generous, and one could learn so much more from them than from small-minded academics. I proceeded to learn from them. G. N. Clark noticed very early on that, as between Richard and me, inseparable as we were, Richard was the uncompromising doctrinaire; I was at bottom a compromiser, and a moderate.

What with teaching, keeping up with my old friends and making new, reading avidly as always, no writing, term passed quickly. Booth, my Anglo-Catholic friend who had taken me under his wing as a choirboy (no more), brought *his* friend to lunch; Jimmy Crowther came for the week-end; I kept up with my Christ Church cronies, dear Tom Lawrenson and Robin Burn. Maurice Bowra came to dine; then Driberg: he made no impression, for I have no memory of it—but he was supposed to have one of those Victorian china plates with 'Thou God Seest Me' erected over his bed. (I never penetrated his bedroom.) Chamber music I heard at the Holywell Music Room, said to be the oldest

in the country: Jelly d'Aranyi, a friend of the Pares family—
wonderful as it seemed to me: a concert of Ravel, new to me,
César Franck, Beethoven.

Too busy to keep up my Diary, I yet wrote Notes. Here was
another visit to Lionel's garden at Kidlington.

Blue sky, but pallid like pearl; summer wind, the silver birch
shaking its boughs like feathers, gleaming white in strong sun.
The straight paths, edged with carnation and forget-me-not,
go down to the river; the lawn starred with daisies, beyond
orchard tawny ranks of tulips, like poppies, in long grass.
Banks of sedge shudder in the breeze, between them I know
the river is there, swirling on beneath the trees to the city
miles below. The water meadows are golden with butter-
cups, the heavy sheep prostrate around the trunk of a willow,
lambs crying in the quiet of late noon. Bedstraw and stone-
crop upon the dry wall that encloses this paradise amid the
fields.

But my old enemy was at me again; for I still remember this
'Summer Dawn: May 25th, 1927'.

Before me, at my attic window, a picture of life secret to
myself alone, everything taken by surprise, it is yet so early.
The garden, the trees, the grey walls are drenched in the
waters of sleep. All my senses, sharpened by pain, drink in the
loveliness, as if the last my eyes should look upon. Two
chimneys at the end of a roof, between them the golden
rind of the moon, now near, but reeling to what beckoning
horizons, what unknown seas. The dark forms of the chestnuts are still, where the tall candles stand erect by day but are
now only a frill between the trees and the canopy of sky.
From the trees the dreamlike song of birds half awake.
Beyond the still house, occupants asleep, the three poplars,
their slender boughs moving like feathers from side to side,
in rhythm, against the East. A sign to youth of the spring of
life, leading men to quiet sleep on alien soil under the stars:
our brothers who went away in such summer dawns, and
died.

Now, in the house nearby, someone stirs in his sleep, and
coughs. A bat comes from nowhere, turns a somersault

before the open window, and with a little moan of ecstasy, passes on to nowhere. The day, encroaching on the night, drains the world of tenderness and shadow. I draw back and slowly shut the shutters to, until only a seam of light in the dark well of the room remains of the loveliness stolen from the land of sleep.

Perhaps it would be possible to sleep now, after the hours of pain: I still remember that bewitching hour of dawn. Dear Lionel disapproved of my cult of pain as sharpening the senses, and making the brain more acute. But what was I to do about it? I didn't know how to stop the ulcer from constantly breaking out again, or how to deal with it—I had had enough of doctors and their incompetence: I might as well make the best of pain when it caught me, turn it to some good purpose.

A day or two later I had to dash down to Cornwall to be the prize exhibit at the Cornwall Education Week which the County Education Authority was putting on to advertise its good work. They put out an excellent Handbook, which I am afraid I have never studied till now. There are all my old patrons and friends, who made their appearance in *A Cornish Childhood*: Quiller-Couch; John Charles Williams, the formidable Lord Lieutenant; R. G. Rows of Helston, the blind philosopher and enthusiast for education; F. R. Pascoe, the Secretary for the county, whose energy inspired it all. I was a prime favourite with him, and I see now a photograph of myself looking obstinate and fierce, and a tribute obviously written by him, which I never read, describing mine as 'the highest ascent on the County Educational ladder ... he began his climb from Carclaze Council School [his vocabulary] ... *given good health* a brilliant future ... etc.' I didn't know that they knew how much that mountain-climb, or obstacle race, had taken out of me. I had to make a speech, and this made me exceedingly nervous. In fact I was no good at speaking at all, until at the General Election a few years later I was thrown in, neck and crop, to sink or swim; and I learned how to, as usual, the hard way. It was practically the only useful thing to come out of my politicizing.

There is nothing whatever about it, Note-Book or Diary; the

real bent of my mind is witnessed by a scrap overheard in the dining-room on Reading station on the way down. Farmers were discussing the local shows. 'I used to think the Oxford Show the best around.' 'Well, it ain't now.' 'There used to be ten lords in a class sometimes!'—sufficiently revealing of a vanished society and state of mind. Talk proceeded about the coming Winchester Show, the colts, foals, and a prize mare whose picture was in the paper. 'Well, I haven't seen it, but if 'tis put in the paper, then it must be so'—an innocent state of mind. At this time I developed the habit of noting down the prize bits of nonsense I overheard humans exchanging. In Christ Church Meadows I passed two Roman monks: one of them, 'Did you kneel down?' The other, mumble-mumble. 'Did you kiss hands?' Mumble-mumble. 'For —Father Norbert is so scru-pu-lous.' Nothing I caught was as good as that which G. D. H. Cole's wife heard on top of a London bus: 'It was the *button-hook* that opened her eyes!'

Back at Oxford, along with my teaching, I was reading pell-mell Beard's *Rise of American Civilisation* and Parrington's *Main Currents of American Thought*, to confirm my Leftist bias, along with Mohr's *The Oil War*, which opened my eyes; I found it absorbing. Then Pavlov on 'The Cerebral Cortex' and Virginia Woolf's *Jacob's Room*—which I described as 'two great events'— and next day *To the Lighthouse*. The influence of Virginia Woolf was the more lasting; one can see it in the prose pieces I was writing and the way of looking at things which she induced. I owed Pavlov to Jimmy Crowther, Virginia Woolf to David Cecil; Leonard Woolf I came to know all too well, I could have dispensed with him for one glimpse of her. Well, I did have *one* glimpse of her in my London days, walking up Charing Cross Road where all the secondhand bookshops are, slowly and abstractedly with Leonard, followed by another such spaniel as 'Flush', whose biography she wrote. It was forty years before I wrote the biography of a cat, my Peter; but I got round to it.

Since I regarded myself, as a writer, as a member of the Irish School, I was reading Joyce and Liam O'Flaherty, along with Brandenburg's *From Bismarck to the World War*. A naïf Note draws, however, the sensible conclusion that the World War was the logical consequence of the German cult of the Absolute State as beyond morality; and that Bismarck's Machiavellian success in achieving German predominance in Europe, by the way of Blood and Iron, regardless of others, had naturally led to ultimate failure—for others were reduced to rallying together for self-protection against a bully. Germany's *Machtpolitik*, following direct from Bismarck to Hitler, produced an even greater catastrophe for Germany, with its permanent division in two. Even Meinecke, the author of *Die Idee der Staats-Räson*, saw that in the end with his tragic book, *Die Deutsche Katastrophe*.

When that second catastrophic attempt was over, and Germany lay in ruins, the first delegation of academics to be let out of the madhouse were brought to my rooms by Heinz Koepler. The foremost of them, the old head of the Münchener Technische Hochschule, still couldn't see the point: he thought that since everything had been all right for Germany under Bismarck, nothing was wrong with the course that Bismarck set: no idea of the consequences or what everybody else felt about his career of bullying aggression. Typical German obtuseness: there's a wall across their mind at a certain point, i.e. wherever the interests of others are concerned. Of all the shabby, down-at-heel poor brutes in my rooms that day there was only one who understood the point: he was from Hamburg, on the fringe of the barbarian mass, in touch with outer civilization. And he was afraid to speak up—he whispered to me at the tail-end of the delegation when they were passing out. Some years later, in the reception of my Bailey Lectures in Montreal on Germany in Modern Europe (I have still not published them), I met the same phenomenon.

However, the brutes met their match in Stalin: he understood what they were like well enough. He really wanted to exterminate the whole nuclei of this mentality among Germans: it would have meant eviscerating the nation.

I was constantly lunched and dined about the place by interesting people, in those days when it was possible for the intelligent class to entertain. The kind Bucklers kept open house at 1 Bardwell Road, a large hospitable establishment, admirably staffed by well-trained cook and parlourmaids. Georgina Buckler was a dragon, but a kind dragon; she was writing her book on the Empress Anna Comnena—I think she rather thought she was the Empress Anna Comnena herself. In fact she was the niece of Charles Kingsley's and J. A. Froude's wives, two Grenfell sisters; and her father, Walrond, had been a close friend of Matthew Arnold. So one met people with those fascinating Victorian associations: Arnold's own daughter, Lady Sandhurst; his American grandson, Arnold Whitridge, who looked exactly like him and carried on the Arnold passion for education as Head of a House at Yale. When I was writing my first research book, *Sir Richard Grenville of the 'Revenge'*, Mrs Buckler was most helpful with the Grenfell cousinage, with their Cornish provenance—took me over to the Field-Marshal's, introduced me to Lord St Just (they were all descended from Hercules Grenfell of St Just, near Land's End). I had no idea how lucky I was: I took it all for granted, casually enough. I wish I had made more of those opportunities *then*—I did make the effort to visit Froude's son at Kingsbridge (*his* son was killed in the war, the line extinguished). I was too much immersed in my own intellectual interests to regard social life as an end in itself—I found it rather a strain going out, unlike my contemporaries who lived for it.

Dining out in other colleges one could take in one's stride, with Emden at St Edmund Hall, or R. H. Hodgkin at Queen's. Later on I became a close friend of his eldest sister, Violet, at beautiful Bareppa near Falmouth. Daughter of Thomas Hodgkin, the Quaker banker—in those days when it was possible to make a fortune in banking and write *Italy and her Invaders* ('Gibbon for Schoolgirls') in a dozen volumes as a sideline—she was totally deaf, but could lip-read cleverly. She made an exquisite life for herself in that garden, making up by the sense of touch for the loss of hearing. The birds would pitch on her hand, would almost 'mob' one; the house was full of books, pictures, flowers, and at night one could hear the trickle of the spring in the trough outside as a background to sleep. Through her I came to know a number of that distinguished high-minded family, quite as many as I could make do with.

Douglas Woodruff would come to lunch and walk; Denzil Batchelor—it strikes me that that name is Cornish, from Denzil Downs near St Mawgan, and was that of Denzil Holles, the Parliamentarian opponent of Charles I—came to lunch, but not to walk. (Wystan: 'A walk! What *for*?') T. B. L. Webster, the classical scholar, would come to tea; I dined with G. N. Clark at

Oriel, and with his old friend G. D. H. Cole, who had returned to Oxford, with his Fellowship at University College. When Douglas Cole came eventually to All Souls I became fond of him, and we lived on terms of affection; but in these early days I was alarmed by him—alarmed by his reputation for brilliance, most of all by his brittle sophistication. I remember his asking me to lunch at his house in Holywell to meet Gilbert and Lady Mary Murray; the combination of Margaret with Douglas and them utterly *petrified* me. And when he talked of his fine collection of glass, Waterford and Bristol and what not, I was speechless: was this quite *right* for a Socialist?

The truth was that social sophistication aroused in me an inferiority complex; dining out was really a strain. The Buchans up at Elsfield, in spite of what was grandeur to me—the large house, the big library looking down the slope out over Otmoor—made up for it by exceptional sensitiveness and kindness to the raw youth, nerves on edge. All the same, I observed everything with an appraising eye. When I was asked to dine by Edward Thompson on Boar's Hill, in spite of his more Left sympathies, his books attacking the British record in India, I did not fall for *him*: a Nonconformist ex-missionary, too ethical and righteous, a soured and disappointed man, he was not my type.

It is evident that intuitive sympathies, Goethe's 'elective affinities', are more important than political affiliations. Mine, underneath my questing Socialism, were Conservative and Anglican. Edward Thompson was really a Nonconformist Liberal, and I never liked either. I once said to Douglas Cole, who had a Nonconformist background, how our original upbringing came through in subsequent life: he was always a nonconformist, always 'agin the Government'; as an old-time Anglican, my sympathies were really conformist and with authority, where possible.

At the end of June, after dining out: 'pain and awake at night'; next, 'broken night: awake with pain: 12,2,4 ... !' To duodenal experts this tells its precise tale, I now see; I didn't then, nor did they. Of course, I shouldn't have dined out—prolonged rest, until things came right. Instead of that, a mad rush of reading: I read the whole of Virginia Woolf that term, Helen Waddell, Frank Harris's *Oscar Wilde*, Gide's *La Porte étroite*—a key-book to him,

Belfort Bax on the Anabaptists, Croce's *Autobiography*, Vita Sackville-West's *The Land*, Jusserand on *The English Novel in the Time of Shakespeare*. What a diet! enough to give one indigestion in itself.

Then there are Notes, still on Swift: on 'the peculiar double character of his irony, a two-edged sword: it is at once a satire on his opponent's view, with a return upon his own. Is it an expression not only of disgust with the world but of contempt for himself? An uncertainty as to his own ultimate beliefs, I wonder? The root of this must be traced back to the psychological origins of the ironic spirit: make a whole section on Swift's predispositions to disgust and dissatisfaction with life.' Evidently I was still bent on that biography.

Not until mid-June did I resume my Diary.

> The innumerable activities that fill my life at Oxford do not call for comment: the thing is enough in itself, and so dissuades me from keeping a Diary. Or, rather, it isn't enough in itself: I am filled as much as ever with dissatisfaction. My real life is in the other, and however I am to bring about a fusion of the two and enable myself to live is hard to know. I'm tired out with the work of the term, and the irregularity of my way of life—too many people up [i.e. in Oxford] and about—and with the uncertainty of the outlook for me in the next few years. Today, Sunday June 11th, I have spent abroad in the air, reading in our little Common Room garden, and the afternoon walking up and down Woodward's lawn discussing steps for the future. I feel a good deal better. But it was a horrible sensation of sick fear that came on with my attack last night: no *great* pain, but I couldn't bear to have to go through months and months of illness again. However, the sun shines in on my desk and makes lattices on the carpet up to the darkest corner of the room.

A week later: 'A really happy day, among so many that are not happy; and happy, I believe, because it has been active. The night before last and all yesterday afternoon I spent in the throes of pain, some disturbance of my system through some cause I do not know. I wonder if pain is really a discipline; or an inducement to slackness, since it is a drain on one's energy.' It seems that there was a point in the latter suggestion, since pain represented the protest of my body against the over-driving I subjected it to: no wonder the young innocent considered it 'an inducement to slackness'— just what the body needed.

Yesterday, what with the pain and a crew of young men who dropped in—individually I should have welcomed any-one, but all together they were unbearable—I developed a rage and broke up the party in confusion. Tom was hurt by such fury, so I walked out to Bartlemas Road in the evening to apologise, sat on his lawn with the landlady's daughter [she had a predatory eye on him], and walked back down Headington Hill in the shadow of beeches and sycamores. To bed early.

After that, and abstinence from food, today has been most successful: three hours this morning in the Camera at Charles Beard's vast book, and two more in the afternoon. All the time ideas came into my head for my projected little book on Politics and the Younger Generation. So the con-nexion between illness and my state of mind is not, as I sometimes think, to the advantage of the latter. Yet I felt, as I looked up to the window and the changing appearance of All Souls beyond—it gives me a homely feeling to read at a window from which I can see the twin towers—Time passes, the clouds drift by, the days and years.

A week later I was welcoming the end of term, though I had to stay on for the examining I had undertaken. 'When one can live to oneself again, one experiences a relief like that after pain. Not that I dislike teaching, for I believe I am successful as a tutor; but the ordinariness of experience where other people are concerned makes me appreciate all the more the variety and richness of solitude.' How ordinary indeed they are! Fifty years later I am of the same opinion still—and find myself corroborated by a man of genius, Lacordaire: 'On ne fait rien qu'avec la solitude: un homme se fait en dedans de lui et non en dehors. Parler et écrire, vivre solitaire et dans l'étude, voilà mon âme tout entière.' As I have said, this is the best rule of life in an ill time. But *they* are without inner resources; that is why they cannot get along without direction and discipline. And since those have broken down, society is breaking apart.

Connolly, I remember, once objected to my 'moralizing'—but my view is merely a commonsense one, rational and secular, making no claims to anything beyond a sensible conducting of one's affairs. No moralist himself, but a complete hedonist, he died leaving a young family to provide for and an overdraft of £27,000. I do not approve of living one's life on those extravagant lines and then leaving the consequences to others.

Virginia Woolf wrote her book, *A Room of One's Own*; I made a cult of mine, all the more acute because of the terror of its ghost.

> As I sat by the open window reading *The Common Reader*, a transformation was going on in the sky over the garden: room and garden were filled with the white light that some-times comes before the burst of a summer raincloud. A wind was up, the trees tossing festoons like green feathers; the three poplars—that mean to me what the snapdragon grow-ing beneath the walls of Trinity meant to Newman—were caught all down one side, turned to a restless shower of silver ... I ought to have noted down every shadow as it passed across the face of things; now I remember only the curious gleam of unreality inside the room. The windows open on both sides, a wind came in and played about like a cat with the papers on the table, lifting the pages and making the covers flap. It was rather eerie.

> For some time I had not been to see remarkable old Joe Wright —the Yorkshire mill-hand who had taught himself Greek at the loom, made himself one of the leading philologists in the country, and edited, with the help of his wife, the great *English Dialect Dictionary*. 'He has been having slight strokes lately, altering the expression of the lower part of his face. Mentally he is as vigorous and rough-edged as ever. They are a lonely couple [his wife wrote a delightful book, *Rustic Speech and Folklore*]. I used to wonder whose was the portrait of the little girl above his chair in the ingle-nook, and of the boy above hers. Not long ago I heard that they were their two children, who died within a short time of each other.' Poor old couple: better to give no hostages to fortune, to

expose as little front as possible for fate to get a blow in at one—I always believed that, if it could, it would at me.

Coming back from North Oxford, passing in front of Wadham, I looked up at David Cecil's rooms—he must have been away. 'In one window was a pot of blue flowers, perhaps irises, in the other the parchment shade of his lamp and the polished letter-box close up against the window. I thought suddenly of the interior lit by the warm light, David sitting reading to me in the circle of brightness, with the light on his hair and glowing on his face as he looks up from reading out of the manuscript of his book [he was writing his first book, *The Stricken Deer*, the biography of Cowper]; and then of David away, anywhere, not there any longer: the room all shut up, the flowers fading in the sun.'

Over in Reading, where I had been to visit an old schoolfriend now at the University, there had been another such moment. Noreen and I were coming back along the riverside under the Abbey walls.

Along the Oxford Road the workpeople were pouring out in droves from Huntley and Palmer's: a squalid district, like the shabbier quarters in *Jude the Obscure*. The river walk was planted with trimmed sycamores under the heavy brick wall of Reading Gaol: I remembered the Prisoner, the sordidness of that story was turned into something strange, immaculate. For, while we pottered along under the trees, the rain dripping down drearily enough, suddenly, on the other side of the town, the bells of St Giles's burst out ringing a full peal. O magic moment: it was like Siegfried Sassoon's 'Everyone suddenly burst out singing'.

What I reflect on today is the sheer human idiocy of breaking that man of genius on the wheel, incarcerating him at all for his infantilism:

homo homini lupus!

Here is the room in which so much cerebration took place, photographed in words. 'At night the shaded blue light throws the bloom of a mirror on the dark panelled walls. A vase of red tulips stretching out their twisted stems to the light; within the glass bowls a multiplicity of white gleams. Upon the rows of tawny china, gold and orange reflexions; on one cup a straight line that burns with cold green fire: it holds my eyes till the world is but a breathing being that waits in suspense upon that steely slit of light ... But that way madness lies!'

I note some evidence of overstrain.

It was to be added to. Clearly my teaching was well thought of, for now Deane-Jones—friend of my ghost upstairs—invited me to take on a Lectureship at Merton. This gave me a regular assurance of teaching, with a modest salary and membership of the Senior Common Room, and access to that delightful garden, where Bradley walked always alone—as I came to do in my last years at Oxford. This was a good proposition, for them too: it meant that Merton had practically an extra tutor at less than half the cost, supported by All Souls.

There followed an interview with the miserly old bachelor, Warden Bowman, of the crabbed, spiderly handwriting, whom the college had relegated to his vast, monumental, tomb-like lodgings across the street. The story was that a Fellow had made a bet that he would make Bowman give him tea. So he arrived to transact business shortly before 4 p.m., when the Warden always had his tea. At four the latter rose, went out and had his tea, then came back, wiping his moustaches, to resume business. Today, I possess Warden Bowman's cutlery, for kitchen use at Trenarren.

For myself, the advantage was that I remained free. I never wanted to become a full-time tutorial don—which was partly why I was so furious with Christ Church for turning me down when I hadn't wished for their job. When they came back the year after with a suggestion of teaching half History, half English Literature —it would have given me complete financial security, trebled my income and ended my worries—I never considered it; but made my resentment doubly clear by slamming the door on them. And that was wrong of me.

Anyway, I was determined to keep all options open, and make whatever sacrifice was necessary.

6

Contrasts

After my long spell abroad I was not averse to going home for the vacation, though I did resent more and more the restrictedness of the small council-house we lived in, the constant exposure to demotic life, the insane noises of children shrieking in the road outside, the inanities heard indoors and out, wafted up to me as I worked away at my bedroom window. For I inhabited the front of the house to myself, up and down; my family lived contentedly at the back. I carried my meals on a tray into the front—as I still do—and ate by myself, reading the while: not very good for the digestion, but better for the temper.

For here is a sociological point of interest in the social revolution of our time. The generation I belonged to was the first generation to be carried upward from elementary and secondary school to the university. Thus we were borne up out of the ken, and the standards, of our parents. Several of my friends, whose parents were a bit better off than mine and enjoyed slightly better standards, suffered acute embarrassment from having to share their lives, eat at the same table, endure the unbearable boredom of their talk. I wasn't going to subject myself to that; in a way, I always had lived my own life, away from the family, even as a child.

Even worse was the case of those poor fellows who, impelled by sex, got caught in marriage to some female whom they could not possibly carry upwards with them, intellectually or socially. Such creatures should be left behind if they cannot make the grade—as many of them have been, their husbands finding more suitable partners on a second trial, having learned from the first. This was not going to be my trouble—at any rate, in that form.

The contrasts, however, were more glaring in my case. In Oxford the grandeur of All Souls in those days, changing every evening for dinner, silver candlesticks on polished tables, butler, servants—an upper-class way of life; at home, two rooms down, three up, in a working-class row. I wonder I stood it as long as I did. For one thing, I became tethered as a working-class candidate of the Labour Party—though it seems a mistake now, it was one whole side to my life, authentic and genuine; for another, I became so ill that I hadn't the strength to move. As soon as, after my final short-circuiting operations, I was recovering and free to move, I bought a charming house of my own, in its own acre of ground, away from people and with a wonderful view of the Bay—and transported thither my mother and a housekeeper (Father having died). My mother's first words on entering—it was beautifully decorated and furnished with things I had brought from Oxford—were 'This ed'n a bit like my 'ouse.' No, indeed; and she never did like it. However, I had had to give up hope of a normal active life, all thought of politics; and, for my part, had had quite enough of the life of the people.

But this was not yet: it was a dozen years ahead. Meanwhile, I endured.

On my way home at the beginning of August I was to stay with the Bishop of Exeter, old Lord William Cecil, and his wife, Lady Florence. I cannot remember how this was arranged—he was David's uncle, and all the Cecils were always extremely kind to me—but I may have met him at All Souls. The old boy wouldn't live in the ancient Palace at Exeter, draughty and huge and rambling; he merely kept a big room in it—with the armorial Courtenay fireplace—as an office, and chose to live in a charming Jane Austeny Regency house on the outer edge of the city, Barton Place, now owned by the University. It was by no means small, and very *gemütlich*. I was charmed by my 'upper room, looking west to the trees that fringe the Exe valley, the silver candlesticks on the tables, the bookcases within arm's reach of bed and hearth, the roses on the table by the window, the room so pleasant in lamplight, bed and curtains of apple-green, like Devon itself.'

The old couple had lost every one of their three sons, killed in the war. They couldn't have been kinder to their West Country 'peasant'-guest. (Mrs Curtis didn't know what company I kept—I never wasted much conversation on her.) Lord William had all the eccentricities of his famous family, and more than his share of their absent-mindedness; everyone knows the old chestnut about his having lost his ticket on the train, and without it, 'how do I know where I am going?'

He had also their distinction and charm; besides that, a rare intellectual openness of mind—utterly un-middle-class. He was reading Fülöp-Miller's vast tomes, *The Mind and Face of Bolshevism*; I was a bit surprised to find at dinner that all he wanted to talk about was Bolshevism, this venerable bearded figure, purple, silk cassock, gold pectoral cross—and without prejudice: he was intellectually interested. It was not the last time that I was to be taken by surprise by the Cecilian readiness to discuss anything on its merits; this was a general characteristic of that remarkable family.

The object of my visit was to explore the ground at Exeter—the project of researching into West Country history in the sixteenth century was slowly forming in my mind. I was extremely diffident about it; my reading and training, such as they were, were as much literary as historical. I had little idea how one set about historical research into manuscript material; there was no direction at All Souls, and there were no classes in palaeography, diplomatic and that sort of thing, at Oxford. What there was was excruciatingly medieval; Vinogradoff had had such a seminar and—unknown to me then, but to become my chief Cornish friend—Charles Henderson had attended it. Reading medieval documents was mother's milk to him—but he hadn't come near winning a Fellowship at All Souls, though he sat for it. (As had David, and his uncles, Hugh and Robert; the great Lord Salisbury, the Prime Minister, had been a Fellow. His noble forehead loomed down upon us at high table in Hall.) Charles Henderson, after going down from New College, was at this time attached to Exeter University as an extra-mural lecturer in Cornwall.

So I perambulated about the city, exploring for myself. I had never been there before, old ecclesiastical capital of the West Country as it was. Cruttwell one day commented that I had never been anywhere in England; nor had I: no money, no car, anywhere I went had to be within walking distance. I was fascinated by the historic city, before the cultivated Hitler's Baedeker raid had ruined it: direct hits on the Cathedral, the fifteenth-century hall of the Vicars Choral destroyed, so too beautiful Bedford Circus, eighteenth-century terraces damaged— and then all the rebuilding after the war, like anywhere else. 'All the morning I spent in the Cathedral. No such church is ever a museum to me: my imagination is too restless to find satisfaction in the present.' I saw it as it had been in the medieval world that created it, altars, lights, images, the saints, devotions. Oddly enough, the bombs—only fifteen years later—brought to light numerous cult-objects, wax figurines of the devotion of medieval folk, when a cathedral was a veritable spiritual factory. Even then I wrote, 'After all it doesn't much matter that what people worshipped was nonsense as that it gave rise to artistic achievement. Judge religions by their intellectual and artistic expressions —and what poor stuff Protestantism is!'

The northern tower was being repaired, 'a splendid masculine stump under a spider's web of scaffolding [a Muirhead Bone]. Men were pulling the long poles up the face and into position. Two men were at the bottom straining on the ropes, one, a thickset fair fellow of tremendous strength: muscles bulging, he threw himself on the rope with all his weight, then the two drew together in swinging rhythm. They were still at it late in the afternoon, when I was at tea in the hotel in the Close, from where the medieval wall encircling it must have been.' Here was my apprenticeship, piecing the past together in my mind: I noticed the line of roof of the vanished Treasurer's House, whence Henry VII had pardoned the Cornish rebels of 1497, halters round their necks. That evening I saw, appropriately, a Devon man's play, Galsworthy's *Escape*, and sighed—if only I had the dramatic technique and experience to put my Swift play into form!

Next day, instead, I made a further step in my apprenticeship to research, spending it in the Cathedral library and at the Guild-hall records. It was not until a later visit that I got down to manuscript research in the City Library, a beautiful building by a good traditional architect—fired and badly damaged in the

Baedeker raid. Equipped with a typescript of an Elizabethan
Survey of the Clergy in the diocese, I worked out for myself
how to read Elizabethan handwriting, by comparing it with the
original—all the training I had. When I eventually followed
Richard Pares to the Public Record Office, I recall my first days
of frustration when sometimes I could not make out a complete
sentence in a morning—learning the hard way again.

That vacation at home I was reading a good deal of history:
the interminable Beard and, better, Ranke and Lecky, and a
history of the diocese of Exeter, fruit of my first visit there. The
pleasures of home were simple ones, walks and talks with my
old schoolfriends, to favourite places like Carn Grey, Luxulyan,
Trenarren, Porthpean and over the cliffs to Charlestown, the little
harbour where Noël Coward used to spend his boyhood summers
before me.[1] Recently, when it fell to me to be patron of the fund
for completing the spire and putting in the bells at the pretty
Victorian church, Noël gave me £350 for a bell—the light tenor
one, which we have called Noël. He was born in Christmas week.
When he died, they rang a muffled peal for this former choirboy:
I hope he heard those sweet-toned bells ringing out over the
harbour and into the bay.

One evening on my walk there was a variation. A little German
ship, the *Conrad Euring*, was in harbour, nobody about but a
young German with immense shoulder-muscles washing on
deck, preparing to come on land. Nothing much doing for either
of us, he was only too pleased to find someone he could talk to,
and I was delighted to have some practice in German again. He
came on my walk and kept with me all the evening. At the old
Napoleonic fort at the top of the cliff, he announced, 'Ich hab'
warmes Blut.' What did he mean by that? (Wystan would have
known—and thereby came the wound.) I took no notice, though
I 'naturally wanted to be kind, since he was young like me, and
in return for the kindness I received in Germany.' I invited
him for a walk when he was free on Sunday, perhaps I would
take him to my adored Luxulyan, my idea of bliss. It was not
his.

[1] Carn Grey is 'the grey heap of rocks'; Luxulyan, pronounced 'Luxillion',
a name used by Hardy, is Locus Sulyan, 'the place of St Sulyan', a Celtic saint
whose well is in the village.

He told me about his life, his dislike of any occupation on land, of a fight he had had with his friend over a girl he was engaged to; his chum had taken out a knife and given him a nasty cut over the bridge of his nose. 'What a rum life!' I commented: I was fascinated, living inside my ivory tower, but longing to make contact. 'L'homme moyen sensuel': what is the German for that? He must have found me a disappointment, for of course he never turned up for that walk.

Another evening a longish steamboat, the *Jolly Susan*, was coming into harbour.

> The men came trooping down to open the dock gates, one or two recognised me and spoke. On board a sharp look-out was kept for the sides of the diminutive entrance, the harbour men letting down wads of cordage to prevent the vessel from scraping. The setting moon was looking on, as it went down the sky above the hill towards Porthpean: at one moment its worn curve set perpendicularly upon the Coast-guard flagstaff, a sickle fixed on top of a pole. There was the *Conrad Euring* moored; in the house behind, music, a woman's voice singing, an aria broadcast from London. Gradually the bustle in the harbour died down, the harbour men disappeared, the steamboat swung close into the opposite quayside. The three masts of the German boat swung gently to one side and back; then the lamps were lit one by one.

My young German had passed irrevocably out of my life, I decided. But the next evening there he was again, in his natural environment: with his pals on the wall enjoying the spectacle of the young females of the village bathing vociferously and to admiration in the harbour. Had I come to look at 'die Weiber'? he asked. No, I had not come to look at *die Weiber*, and went on my way alone.

'Everything was already autumnal. Two vessels were at anchor in the bay, with high riding-lights, a small rowing boat between these and the land, indistinct and soundless upon the water. A moment's horror as I looked over the edge of the cliff from the oak thicket; getting very near the edge I tempted myself with a direct look down a hundred and fifty feet. All the rocks under water are quite clear for some distance out, and inshore is lapped by the crawling sea:

> The alternate lapse and spill of the unquiet sea
> Upon the patient shore.'

Next day I struck inland from the coast at Crinnis—now 'Carlyon Bay', God save the mark—stopping to throw stones down the echoing shafts horribly near the cliff's edge.

The moon was over the bay before I left the coast, and followed me up the Garker[1] valley with hardening bright stare. At the sharp turn in the road by Murder Cottage, I stopped and looked down the tin-streamed brakes to the sandy bottom of the gully. The unseeing eye of the moon was upon all, the broad bowl of the bay in the cleft of the hills gleaming like silver. I waited there, though the place alone at that hour gives me a shudder. 'Est-ce toi, Jérome; est-ce toi?' I was tempting myself again.

Why should I always think of that bleak disused house, with the broken wall and blocked windows, as a house of murder? [There had been murder, nearer home, in the village, but that is a separate story in itself.] It is a gaunt place, standing on the shoulder of the hill, making a sinister silhouette against the sky at night. By day the deserted house looks merely pathetic. It is of granite, with stone steps going up to a second storey; grass grows between it and the outhouses. Nothing more desolate. Perhaps it never was a dwelling-house as in the story I invented tonight, but a lodge for the tin-streamers, or a blacksmith's forge.

Sometimes after supper I would join in in the kitchen to listen to talk of old days and customs, folk-lore, and folk-speech—what I really liked, an observer again. August 4th—date of ill-omen:

The best part of the day was after supper when Father and Mother told stories of Tregonissey village in their young days—full of life and enjoyment. Father said that people made happier families in those days. Things are

---

[1] Garker means 'the garden beneath the caer (prehistoric round camp)'.

different now, when there are different standards of education and manners in a good many homes. Then, with no regular sports or cinemas or wireless [let alone TV, the real opium of the people today], the family had to provide amusement for itself. Practical jokes, bonfires, frightening people, riddles and stories were the order of the day. When old Tommy Harvey married a spinster of advanced years, they thought to do it on the quiet in the town. But when they returned in the evening all the long lane to Tregonissey was lit by candles, with two big torches at the entrance to the village, where a crowd awaited them with a band to accompany them home, the musical Rowses to the fore. Jollifications were kept up while the couple went indoors to enjoy each other. When the crowd got bored with Tommy's concentration indoors, somebody shouted in that he ought to be castrated, 'an ole man like 'e'. Tommy, aroused, came out to know who said he should be galvanised, and danced over a broomstick to prove he'd got a good deal of go in him yet. There was then beer all round—till Mary, cross at spending her first married evening alone, came out and laid about her with her umbrella, dispersing the company.

A good deal more about village life follows: this was the origination of *A Cornish Childhood*. At first I did not intend to write an autobiography, but a biography of a working man, my father, with the background of village life. To this the earlier chapters of the book are devoted, and I remember a feeling of dismay when I had to start on myself; however, there were far more materials on that subject than the exiguous records of Rowses in the village. Afterwards that evening he told me 'as much about the clayworks and the secretive china-clay families as would make matter for a good scoriating novel.' Alas, I don't think I could write a novel, but some of these stories appear, not much altered, in my *Cornish Stories*—many years later: the point of them to me is that they are the authentic stories of the parish, town or country, family or individual, the historian finding the true stories of life far more strange and riveting than people's inferior imaginings of them.

They are like the true stories Hardy wrote up in *A Group of Noble Dames*, only he got his from Hutchins's history of Dorset, while mine come from authentic local lore and memory, verbal tradition. I still haven't written some of them up. For example, the squire and wife of nearby Trevanson: he with a short leg and cork heel and no great potency; she handsome and sexy, a combination of aristocratic pride with being no better than she should be. She consoled herself with the steward; a neighbouring young gentleman of family drowned himself in a pond—ass that he was—all for the love of her. When the squire died, he left the estate—rhododendron plantations, camellias, mimosas—in flourishing condition. The wild widow wasted his substance in horse-racing and betting, so too the son and heir. Now the place is going to rack and ruin, drives overgrown, timber sheared off to pay the debts of both. Not long ago a magnificent larch, as wide across as the window-frame, was cut down—it would break the old squire's heart to see it. There was Ned Bartlett, too, a professed Methodist, who used to help himself to the coal and was caught by the police—summarily dismissed after thirty years' service (and helping himself to coal). Mother added knowingly that the other servants had probably informed—if I wrote up the story I should add, one who had a grudge against him, unrequited love perhaps.

September 8th: A disturbed night after so much activity right up to getting into bed. I woke up the others in the house by shouting in my dreams. Apparently I am liable to talk and shout in my sleep, a thing I never used to do until these late years of so much strain and illness. Last night's nightmare was of snakes, in bed and covering the ceiling. Revealing from the Freudian point of view, I believe, like the women of the family dreaming of being chased by a bull; mine didn't seem erotic, more of visual hallucination. The Cornish folklore is, if you dream of snakes you have many enemies—and I probably have; if you kill the snakes, which I did not, you conquer your enemies.

Katherine Mansfield noted at Looe that if the fire burns brightly, your man is in good temper. Mother added that if your apron unties, your man is thinking of you:

> If your apron untie,
> Your lover is nigh;
> If your apron undo,
> Your lover is true.

O sancta simplicitas! the simple sexuality stands revealed. My brother told me, of a handsome miner in the family, that the sight of a woman's bloomers blowing out on a clothes-line gave him an erection. These excitements were denied to me, but I heard and noted them all, with Swiftian fascination and distaste at the human condition.

And here was Swift again—I found the *Journal to Stella* 'even more exciting than I had thought: all the unused ideas about Swift for a play, a biography and an essay go on and on in my head. Apart from the first two, already planned, what an opportunity to connect up with the development of one's own ideas!' This was ultimately carried out, nearly fifty years later.

A last walk with Noreen, before going back to our respective universities, to Trenarren and out on the Black Head, the rare cone-shaped headland—like Rame Head and St Ives—turned into a primitive cliff-fort by ditch and vallum across the narrow neck. 'We sat on one of the outcrops of felspar at the very end. It gives one a sense of exultation to be thrust right out into the sea, miles of heaving grey water on every side. No very rough sea seems to break there, only the sense of the tide running past one, with soothing heave and fall, for miles inland to Porthpean and the farther beaches. One might be on an island, or the earth itself might be crumbling away in all those leagues of sea.'

There follows the idea for another story, a reflexion of fear, yet another with which to frighten myself—the *culte de sensations*. On the way home Noreen told me the story of the house that would one day be mine, bought by the china-clay worker's son. It had been built for a china-clay magnate's alcoholic offspring, with all the best materials, timber, tiles, roofs, from the clayworks. This lucky fellow was killing himself with bouts at all the pubs in the district (I never entered one); his father got the innkeepers to deny him, so off the fool would go, having a car of course, to Plymouth, returning at dead of night. A nurse had married him, to look after him; they had also a housekeeper, but there was no restraining him. He died in the house, no age; when we got there, after an interval and a successor, we used to wonder, with some trepidation, in which room.

Before returning to Oxford a new experience came my way, a portent to the horrid future.

A stump orator of the Unionist Association appeared at the corner of our avenue to hold a meeting. After ten minutes, with my heart thumping wildly, I ventured an inarticulate interjection at some rubbish I couldn't stand. So then I had to go on, and surpassed myself and the orator at obstruction and abuse. It really was beneath me; but the people expected me to speak up for them and backed me up manfully. For the first time in my life I directed my words to what would appeal to the audience. He was holding forth on Wages [my father got £2 2s. od. a week in the claypits]: I asked how much more he got as a paid speaker of the Unionist Association. He said he got his living by his brains. One or two of the crowd backed me up with 'He's got more brains than you have.'

I'm afraid we gave him a rough house, and I felt, ominously,

If only I were given the chance by the effete Labour Party in the division, I should make a good demagogue. If it hadn't been for his disgraceful references to the men who died for us at the front, while Socialists skulked at home, I should never have got over my awful nervousness. But a crowd certainly has a debasing influence. At one moment I thought of the crowd scenes in Franz Werfel's *Paulus unter den Juden*; I should never have believed there was such simplicity of mind in general among people, even though my prime conviction is the stupidity of the human race. I suppose it is possible to have a certain pity and love for them all the same.

This was followed up by a Labour meeting I attended at Truro, addressed by Philip Snowden and Margaret Bondfield. She was a good woman, devoted to the cause and of sensible judgment. Snowden was a wizened little man with a twisted face, hard gem-like eyes and an intermittent sweetness of expression; he had been crippled by an early accident and walked on sticks. I noticed that he compensated for the weakness of his voice by accentuating the consonants; this carried his words, but gave them a hissing sound, an edge of bitterness which went with his personality. He was really an old Gladstonian radical. Either then or later I was presented to this eminent politician—his eminence 'due to the flatness of the surrounding country', as Marx said of Mill (wrongly)—but I have no record of what was said. A few years later, in 1931, he made any reasonable solution of the financial crisis, small enough in itself, impossible for the Labour Party; the consequences, not only for Labour but for Britain, were disastrous.

My unsympathetic observations were corroborated by my companions in the railway compartment on my way back to Oxford.

The first two, agents of the Trade: a wizened one, beaked nose and thin nostrils, I guessed to be a traveller in spirits; the other a low-class barman, so fascinatingly ugly I couldn't but keep looking at him: yellow, leathery and liverish, bilious sardonic creases running from nose to mouth, a ridiculous moustache, full at the corners, non-existent in the middle. From Exeter to Oxford, two North Oxford types: a gaunt fellow, self-consciously playing the gentleman, stirring his tea with a scroll of paper for lack of a spoon, with 'Well, Necessity is the mother, etcetera'. The wife, furtively severe, eyed with disapproval every move her husband made towards the luggage on the rack. The corner occupant on my side complained of the draught; no sooner was the window up than everybody complained of the stuffiness; opened once more, a stream of smuts and soot blew in on my book and me. Coming into Oxford, an enormous poster informed us: OXFORD, THE PLACE WHERE MORRIS CARS ARE MADE.

Lionel Curtis, whom no millionaires could resist, once entertained Ford himself at Oxford—but found no response whatever to its beauties, no wish to see any historic building, university or college, cathedral or gallery or library. At the suggestion of a visit to Cowley—of which Oxford was but the Latin Quarter—and Morris's motor-car works, Mr Ford came alive at once, and off they went. (Myself I have driven an old Morris Oxford for years; but I take it for granted, like the plumbing: I have never been to Morris-Cowley.)

On another occasion I witnessed Lionel's frustration, though he kept his temper admirably. We were only four at dinner, on a fine summer evening of vacation, with Woodward presiding. Lionel had as his guest Mr ffenell of Wytham, a philanthropic millionaire of South African extraction, his father a Schumacher. He was benevolently inclined to the university, and Lionel was bent on milking him to some good purpose. Woodward embarked on a diatribe against rich men expecting honorary degrees from the university by using their money, etc. Even I blushed for him; Lionel behaved with absolute self-control. Woodward once had a discussion with Pares about whether I was a 'gentleman'; in the end it was decided that I was (myself, I think not). But was the Abbé altogether?

On that earlier evening, after my filthy journey and the 'wasted vac., it was overwhelming to rush down to the Common Room for dinner, a cheerful fire on the grand fan-shaped hearth, candles, lit high up above gleaming table. I felt stupefied by my journey and the contrast; it was quite a strain to take part in the Woodward–Pares conversation.' Indeed, I often felt a pang of inferiority complex on first coming back from the simplicities of the other side of my life. Today, both the one and the other over, I have a more sophisticated reflexion: clever academic talk—what does it all add up to?

However, at the time,

There is an unmistakable sense of the graciousness of life in coming back again. This afternoon I sat with all the new Paul Valéry and Péguy books on one side, tea-tray on the other. Whenever there was a break in the sky, strange lights came floating into my room; once, a steely gleam like a mirror, on the wall above the sofa, something new and eerie to see light there, as if the sun were travelling in northern skies. When the rain stopped, the sky was fresh and blue; the bright red clusters on the crab-apple in the Warden's garden shone ardent in the sun. So I went for a walk round Magdalen, and thought of gleaning a small harvest from the ruined holidays.

I had never yet been to Cambridge; before term set in with its now accustomed severity Jimmy Crowther invited me for the week-end to his own old college, Trinity, from which he had gone down early without completing the course. Kind as he was, he was also encouraging my progress in Marxism. He lent me regularly *Plebs*, the organ of the Leftist Marxists in opposition to the W.E.A.; they had an independent Labour College, and their star was R. Palme-Dutt, the Communist editor of the *Labour Monthly*. Dutifully I read the claptrap, complete with jargon, which he poured out month by month all his life. A clever Balliol man, he was perhaps the worst type of Left intellectual; if Neville Chamberlain 'saw world affairs through the wrong end of the municipal drainpipe', Palme-Dutt saw them through the ocular distortion of his origin. His father was Indian, his mother Swedish; so the perspective was that of Swedish India. In other words, he inhabited a Never-Never Land. I read religiously what he said, but it never made any impact on this commonsense peasant mind.

I took the opportunity to go up to London and resume my Viennese pursuit of culture, hearing my first Promenade Concert at the old Queen's Hall—destroyed by the Germans—of which the acoustics were perfect: Beethoven's *Leonora* Overtures, Eighth Symphony and a Bach Concerto for two pianos. Next morning to the National Gallery to see Van Eyck's 'Jan Arnolfini and his Wife'. Van der Goes was known to me from the so expressive fragment, a 'Lamentation', at Christ Church; now I was struck by his 'Death of the Virgin', with its inset of the town square, a knight riding in from the country, the radiant colouring of the angels' wings. I thought the Velasquez 'Cupid and Venus' 'amazing in its modernity'—one saw where Ingres and Courbet derived inspiration from. I fell too for Zurbarán, whom I have always liked; I have continued all my life to respond to Latin painting—French and Spanish, let alone Italian—far more than Dutch, let alone German.

And so to Cambridge, where I dined in the Hall of Trinity, Monty Butler presiding, silvery and smiling old person, a figure from the Victorian age, looking (I thought) like my grandmother. Next morning I spent inspecting the splendid manuscripts good old Archbishop Parker had saved out of the maw of the Reformation; and if he hadn't given them to Corpus Christi, no doubt they would have disappeared into the maw of the Puritan Revolution. Here were early Celtic Gospels from the eighth century, illuminated with the crane motif with interlaced necks; Thomas Becket's own Psalter, beautifully decorated from the School of Tours; and Chaucer's *Troilus* with traditional portrait of the poet, a hunched-up man with red cap and rapt gaze, hands clenched under skin, blue eyes and thin yellow beard.

The chime from Great St Mary's kept reminding me of Truro, where the Cathedral has a similar chime; this created a comfortable atmosphere, 'which is almost inexplicable, though all this Diary is an attempt, if not to explain it, to weave again the illusion of its presence.' But a cold wind, blowing down the streets and around the corners, reminded me that this was an eastern town. 'I was too tired and too much in company for a good crop of thoughts: it was only one or two odd moments when I was really moved by things. One was when I was alone in Jimmy's room at the corner of Great Court, looking out on the charming brick building that connects itself in my mind with Newton, perhaps because Jimmy said, for effect, that it was built in his time.'

As for the company, I have no memory of it. It was on a later visit that we hobnobbed with Maurice Dobb and went punting on the Cam, dined with him at the college at which he was Lecturer: the custom of dabbing behind one's ears with scented water from a silver ewer impressed me, especially having to follow the lead of a notorious Marxist. An acquaintance with Piero Sraffa at King's, sympathetic as he was, did not go far. Jimmy was mesmerized by the eminent scientists who were the stars of Trinity. He was a friend of Kapitza, the leading Russian researcher into low-temperature energy, for whom Trinity did great things: made him a Fellow of the Royal Society, and arranged a large grant for his research. On a subsequent return to Russia, the authorities clamped down on him and wouldn't allow him out again—his research was to be for the benefit of Mother Russia. I understand that, for some years, it rather broke his spirit for research—for which one needs the breath of freedom after all. Kapitza and I were the sole witnesses of Jimmy's second, and happier, marriage; and I provided the lunch.

On this or a subsequent visit to Trinity we had the honour to play bowls with the great Eddington—at any rate, he was a great name in those days, venerated by Jimmy, for whom these scientists were the stars in heaven. I had no such veneration, but I duly read their books, Eddington and Jeans, Sir Charles Darwin and R. A. Fisher, as much of them as I could understand. A scientist who came to speak immeasurably more to me than these was Sir Charles Sherrington, a man of genius, whose book, *Man on his Nature*, is one of the cardinal books of our time; it expresses exactly my own beliefs, no more and no less.

At the time, what was I looking for?—History and Poetry, the sense of the past and the sense of the present *sub specie aeternitatis*. This meant, not Eddington let alone Jeans, but G. M. Trevelyan and T. S. Eliot; these were my real fellows in spirit, towards whom I instinctively gravitated, both of whom took me under their wing and made me a friend.

One other magical moment at Cambridge remained with me all my life; I was alone, when all the best things happen. An inveterate sight-seer, I was finding my way about Cambridge in the Vacation—should I write an essay, like Lamb's on Oxford? —through Caius and into the Chapel, dismantled, a few surplices and hoods hanging dingily outside the screen; into Trinity Hall, where I dawdled in the front court to look at a trellis of canes upon a sunny wall. My footsteps led me out—and suddenly I found myself in a secret garden, overwhelmed by its magical atmosphere. 'An open gateway led into dewy morning shade, autumnal and cobwebby; tall trees hung over the lawn, the dewdrops not yet dried from the blades of grass, even the birds not awake. Only the silk threads of the spiders barred the gate; as I passed through, a light touch of filament on my eyelids.' I was in an enchantment, like that of *le grand Meaulnes* when he penetrated through the forest to the lonely *château* in Berry. 'But no! It was prosaic enough: a modern girl was in possession: no

extraordinary sun shone here over the trees.' *Le grand Meaulnes*
had found romance awaiting him at the end of his penetration;
for me the spell was shattered.

I returned to All Souls to find roses awaiting me in my room,
along with a poem; since this is a portrait of its domestic interior,
a way of life, I reproduce the exchange of not bad verses. The
Common Room possesses a series of betting books, which have
their historic interest, for they go back to before Waterloo, with
Fellows betting about Napoleon's whereabouts at the time; and
later about the likelihood of bomb-attempts on Napoleon III—
and there followed the Orsini attempt. Oman has edited two of
the earlier volumes: only he could. I was a frequent better, led
on by Woodward, who invariably won: not a way of endearing
himself, either. (There came a day, however, when I would never
again enter a bet in that historic record.) The warmer-hearted
E. F. Jacob had lost his bet to me, and paid it with roses, and
verses:

To A.L.R.—with some poor conceits

The furtive hand that plucked this secret rose
Fingered a white, and now a scarlet, petal;
But flame it picked. And why? The loser knows:
The winner needs but search his heart to settle.

And as it droops again it shall respire
In a fresh close, the more selective garden,
Where is no Church to castigate desire
Nor need to ask a holy sleeper's pardon.

Goodness—as I transcribe it, I see how frankly Freudian it is!
At the time, youthful head in air, I considered 'what a lovely
thought of E.F.J. that was', and repaid him for his 'kindness and
friendship' with this:

Into a room I came and found these flowers,
Three roses that were stars, but one a flame:
Now will they light the dim and ghostly hours
When difficult life is an uncertain game.

175

And when they come to die, as roses must,
They will bequeath their memories to this place,
Mingling the scent of gardens in their dust,
And in their death the shadow of your face.

Polite, but I see now that that did not meet the point. Alas, as the years went on, what a deterioration our relations—and characters —suffered from 'the world's slow stain'! However, I am glad that when he died I gave him a good send-off in the cathedral at Christ Church, erring deliberately on the generous side.

'Difficult life': that meant that I paid the penalty of my jaunt to town and my week-end at Cambridge

by a fearful time last night. From three till eight I was tossed about, half awake and half dreaming, in pain. It gives the mind a peculiar overheated clarity to be awake at night: one sees and even understands things visually. When shall I come to the end of it all? At night, in the interminable hours, I fear there may be nothing for it but to give up struggling: to live the life of no endeavour. Then this morning, from eight till half past nine, there came the most blessed sleep: just an awareness, except that one's eyes are heavy-lidded, and one's body full of an exquisite lassitude that holds but a memory of pain. So that I would not be entirely without pain; though perhaps now I have had enough.

Life is sweet, after all, to a valetudinarian. The days of recovery are so pleasant. I have been reading quietly all day, on a fairly low level of attention, but with no great strain. And there is the compensation I have come to regard as a positive thing: the pleasure of pain that has passed away. In the evening, when day draws in, there is even a comfortable glow in existence once more. I am justified by the morning's application at Greek Political Thought, and the evening's reading of Gide's *Corydon*. I shut the window to, for it is cold; the fire gets warmer, the room full of shadows. As I came over to my desk, there was a quick dark flash of a swallow across the window pane; the other side of the quadrangle and the spire of St Mary's, with grey waste of sky behind, like the embattlements of a dead world.

Later, I began to put the experience of pain, and its curious associations, into my poetry. From the first, I had been interested in expressing the stranger sensations, the magical and ecstatic. the atmospherical, especially the feeling of fear, the edges of experience—without quite toppling over. I agree with that writer of genius, Flannery O'Connor, that the real writer is much more inspired by the strange and extraordinary, than by the everyday and ordinary. 'Ah, que la vie est quotidienne!' This is why the kitchen-sink school of contemporary writers—Pinter, Sillitoe and the rest—haven't got the marrow of inspiration in them and are not likely to last; and also perhaps why, when such writing is what is popular, my poetry has always been overlooked and dis-considered. However, no inexperienced critic myself, it will last longer than they. An early poem, 'Animal Afraid', in *Poems of a Decade*, expresses the simple exhaustion from pain; later poems, 'Night-Piece in Pain' and 'Pain Receding', in *Poems of Deliverance*, express the curious dissociation of mind from body as I progressed further into this region, almost a *Doppelgänger* theme.

A more commonplace reaction was less surprising. I had been prepared to work like a horse to get to Oxford, and then on to All Souls; now that I had got there, was I never to be able to enjoy myself like other people, lead a normal life? (If I had been able to, I might have got caught by life—in marriage; and that would have been a disaster.) I was resentful enough at my origins —so inappropriate for an aesthete; my resentment was now doubled by what I had to put up with. Was it any wonder?

On a cosier level, here was the domestic interior.

At dinner we were a happy equable group to begin with, but with the usual cross-currents. I sat next to Eric Beckett [of the Foreign Office, later a gallant anti-Appeaser], with the fire blazing up on the other side. He was entirely charming; we talked of Germany and German beds, the difficulty of sleeping under a square bag of feathers not one's shape, and with an enormous pillow that takes up half the bed. Next to Beckett was Reggie Harris, holding forth about Reparations and Foreign Loans, quite oblivious of the ragging which was being worked up by Woodward and Pares. They are amusing to hear, as they are the cleverest of the bunch; but still more amusing to watch, for—though they make a league against anybody taking more part in the conversation than themselves—they are not quite at ease about each other. Usually R.P. makes provoking remarks for Woodward's benefit, which he doesn't much appreciate for he loves to have it all his own way, conversationally as in everything else. He's a clever, complex, ambitious man.

Ultimately, I found that his mind was commonplace, supercilious but pedestrian.

'Tonight, for some reason, R.P. held with him, and together they ragged Reggie. It was a fascinating spectacle. They got him on the subject of ecclesiastical vestments, about which he knows a great deal, and of which he is very fond [he possessed a fine Portuguese chasuble, purple silk, of the seventeenth century]; everybody else professed scorn for the subject.' *Ich nicht.* I remembered that Woodward too had had his papistical leanings, popping in and out of Pusey House with his biretta on his head. Once, when attending service in Nôtre Dame, he had been caught in the middle of a pew when procession was being formed and candles handed out. He had made an assignation with an unbelieving Oxford friend to meet him there, who was surprised to find the Abbé marching round with a lighted candle to testify to his faith. He was living in the house of some Modernist priests, of the stamp of Loisy; but was saved from that fate by meeting the Abbess, gentle and kind and vague, whom I remember always with a wisp of floating flaxen hair in her mouth.

Reggie rose, as usual, to the bait and rattled on and on, telling us as a climax that the Habsburg cope in the Hofburg represented the fact that the Holy Roman Emperor was, as such, a sub-deacon. Everybody laughed. 'A poor show on the whole, I thought; though I laughed too, it was so comic. Poor Reggie! I expect he's miserable tonight, when he at length realized.' But perhaps not: he had had his moment, and for the rest, naïf and sweet, was totally without malice or resentment.

R.P. had never seen the Founder's jewels, which we possess, and they were brought in during dessert for us to look at. They are in a beautiful box, covered with faded Elizabethan damask, gold-threaded and flowered. The box was placed at the upper end of the table in the candlelight; it gave me a feeling of the pathos of things to see Pollard open it [A. F. Pollard, the Tudor historian] and take out the intimate relics of a man dead now five hundred years. Little of Archbishop Chichele remains, but there were his fragmentary possessions being handled by ordinary folk: the gold ornament of his mitre, like hazel-nuts cupped in leaves, the clasp of his cope, the pectoral cross of rock-crystal set in gold. Just these few things left high and dry by time, when all the rest—except indeed his college—has perished with him; we handled the little treasures carefully and put them back—those things that a dead man inconceivably far away had cherished. It made the clever game that had been going on seem small.

And now, fifty years later—in the days of a mob of unknown Visiting Fellows—one of those treasures, preserved so carefully for centuries, is missing: a small medieval hanap, the jewelled and enamelled top of a goblet. Gone for ever: I can see it still. Autumn was advancing.

Coming back late from Common Room, Beckett and I stayed in the dark well of the quad, looking up at the unimaginable whiteness of the spire of St Mary's gleaming in the lamplight and starlight. The stars had the clear brilliance of autumn cold. The days are becoming more bountiful. There has been a restless joy in sitting by the window and looking up now and then to observe the day's progress. The first hint of winter has turned the trees to dead greens and greys; still and unruffled they are like tapestries in a Van Eyck, or in the travelling altar-piece of Charles V, of which I am having a print framed for this room [now in the attics at Trenarren]. Richard calls it 'the tapestry time of the year'.

Sometimes his father, Sir Bernard Pares, came to stay. Possessed of extraordinary charm, a magnetic lecturer, he was really in love with Russia and should never have married. No wonder 'Lady P.', as Richard called her, was a feminist and marched with the Suffragettes. Once when the children were young and Sir

Bernard proposed to leave her yet once more for Holy Russia, the young wife revolted. After a quarrel, it was decided that the Professor should pray for guidance; which he did, and God told him that he should go. Not to be outdone, his wife went upstairs and prayed: God told her that he should not go. Their family life racketed along with increasing disaccord, until the pair ceased to speak to each other and would communicate only through their clever eldest boy. Richard told me he could hardly remember the time when he didn't think all adults dolts.

So there really were some positive advantages in having illiterate parents, who couldn't anyway interfere. All the same, I couldn't help a little smart of jealousy when Sir Bernard would encourage the brilliant *boutades* of his son, which I could not compete with. I had no intention of adding Russian to my burdens, but, a fanatic for his subject, Sir Bernard arrived on me to give me an hour's tuition in Russian, which I had not asked for. He was a most gifted simplifier, practically reducing it to Basic Russian. After lunch, he arrived to give me another hour — just like him: I saw something of what Lady P. had had to put up with. However, he recited a poem of Pushkin, to show me how euphonious Russian could be, the consonants got round so that it sounded like Italian. (There was another fool! fancy throwing such transcendent genius away in a duel over a bitch.)

One, more relevant, thing I learned. Sir Bernard had given G. M. Trevelyan for a wedding present the Garibaldi book which started him off on his series of books about the Risorgimento, which made his name and proved best-sellers.

One night I had an extraordinary dream about Richard, a pursuit dream which turned to terror — and in a ghastly way, it proved prophetic:

> not the sort of pursuit the psychologues desiderate, there wasn't the faintest suggestion of the erotic in it. It began as a sort of wager that Richard wouldn't be able to overtake or trap me in flight, and was full of the sense of physical motion, flight [like one of Simon Forman's dreams].[1] It began on a high down, with other figures gradually drawing in upon me among the bushes: I escaped by flying, feeling the scrape

[1] Cf. *Simon Forman: Sex and Society in Shakespeare's Age.*

of the furze as I skimmed over the top. This shook off all the pursuers but Richard. I found myself in a deep valley by a cross-roads: an Italian-looking house with high walls and no windows, no way to get in for shelter. At last I discovered a stable door, with wooden steps up to a loft, with a pile of boxes and rugs under which I could hide. But the pursuit was getting grim and dangerous; I heard footsteps below, and leaped magnificently through the upper window, to find myself on a lonely road farther down the valley. White roads climbed the brake on either side, a bridge crossed here, just as the road at St Blazey turns off for Luxulyan. The pursuer was close on me now, and for a time we doubled up and across the hillside.

With incredible swiftness the scene changed to the interior of a great dome like St Paul's, with winding stairs spiralling up its interior. The chase was desperate now; I leaped whole groups of steps for life's sake, and then took great jumps across the interior to escape. For some seconds my pursuer and I leaped across the well like apes, going up and up, with all the rings of stairs in a dizzy perspective beneath. At the last moment, just when I might have been caught, Richard failed in his leap and crashed down the dome. I watched him bump horribly down and down, until he lay still at the bottom, a flattened mass on the floor. I was there too in a second, and saw his left hand move in a convulsive spasm above his head, his face one with the stone. The horror of it woke me up, and it was day.

But what a terrible dream!

Richard was back in college, getting on with his research, and a congenial Lectureship had been found for him at neighbouring New College: all very convenient since he was a Wykehamist— no doubt found for him by Woodward, who was also a Lecturer there. So they became colleagues, working together, and Richard's feet were on the ladder that led him to a professorship in the end. When I admitted once that I had no wish to be a professor, he was rather chagrined: 'Now, my withers really are wrung.' I was surprised in turn at anyone of his brilliance setting his sights on becoming just a professor; but at the bottom of the

naughty boy of the Hypocrites Club, friend of Evelyn Waugh
and the rest, there was a *fond* of conventionalism. He even made
a dynastic marriage, to the daughter of another professor, niece
of A. D. Lindsay, Master of Balliol. I wasn't going to settle down;
I didn't want to be a full-time tutor, either. When G. N. Clark
suggested that I succeed him at Oriel, I never even considered it.

But I became very fond of Richard. A year or so senior to me,
he was my mentor in matters and ways of historical research; I
his, to some extent, about politics, though he had been a member
of the Labour Club before me. I learned from him a great deal;
he never would learn from me about writing. Scintillating as he
was in conversation, this never came through. Partly by way of
reaction against his father, Richard was obstinately, perversely
academic: he deliberately chose to exclude what was *living* from
his work. He would say that that was not history, when I protested at the unreadability of his vast *War and Trade in the West
Indies*. He worked and worked, wrote and wrote, and emerged
with half a million words of 'history'. But it wasn't an organic
whole, as a book should be. G. N. Clark and Namier set to work
and excavated out of the mass two books: the first, and a second,
Neutral Trade and the War against French Commerce, and a couple
of hefty articles besides for the *English Historical Review*.

When he eventually wrote the story of the Pinney family,
A West India Fortune, he said, 'Here is a book that you really
will approve of.' When I asked why, he said, 'Because it has a
beginning, a middle, and an end.' Form is the foundation, but
that is not all there is to historical writing; it is but the beginning.
When Richard died, a close friend of his told me that he would
have given anything to write a book that appealed like mine to
a wide public. He never said so, and why wouldn't he learn from
me? People are very odd.

We walked and talked together constantly, until he got
married. (I never liked my friends marrying.) 'The trees are at
their best now, Richard and I went a special walk last week to see
them, and were best rewarded up by Wadham. Sunlight played
down the avenue; myriads of leaves, as they fell slanting into the
road, were caught in the live rays of light. A car passed by: they
were stirred and whirled after it, gleaming again in the yellow bars.'

Sometimes I retired from Common Room in a spasm of sup-

pressed anger. Old Spenser Wilkinson was a good-hearted sentimentalist, but he had a trick of putting a series of questions to lead
one into a political argument. As a Labour man, my views were
held to be heterodox; he came from a Manchester family, right
back in Victorian days when shopkeepers lived over their own
shops. 'I would never let myself in for a political argument with
a conventional old fool, except as a duty, to show them that their
commonplace views can be met from the other side.' But Uncle
Spenny was insistent upon knowing what I really thought. 'Tonight when he went nagging on and on, I thought how much the
opposite of solicitous he was, dear old thing as he is underneath:
I was being shaken with anger, though I believe I controlled it:
if he were really considerate, he would know that it isn't hard to
raise a storm of nervous indignation in me [Woodward often
did], that ruins my peace of mind for the rest of the evening. It
will be interesting to see if I pay the penalty by another sleepless
and painful night.'

I go on to excuse the old boy. 'One can't expect the old people
to be always the same, any more than oneself: to turn up always
pleasant and kindly. They must have their off-evenings like us,
though they don't ever seem to be afflicted with pain as I often
am. It's a difficult business, old and young living together. I
found many illusions about people dispelled in that way this
summer, though I love them no less for it. Some time ago I
started compiling reminders, like Swift's, for when I come to be
old; I wonder as they occur to me, if I shan't become the same
nuisance myself—should I live to be old.'

I cite this not so much to show that it was not all beer and
skittles—or claret and bowls—living in college with the elderly;
for the most part I was intensely grateful, for I learned and learned
all the time from them: the greatest boon in my life. Since an
autobiography should authentically portray one's character, warts
and all, something more peculiar is involved, something I do not
wholly understand now.

What was the source of the trouble?

People complain that they do not understand me—and here
I am working my fingers to the bones (in longhand) to try and
make myself as clear as possible. In college I always needed an
interpreter, and Richard gallantly interpreted for me—I suppose

now that he put my more original thoughts, or Marxist thoughts, or whatever, into conventional bourgeois language they were all used to. It is obvious enough that I was neither bourgeois nor conventional, and I really needed an interpreter: I was often enough misunderstood. There was something more subtle. I have always thought of myself as all too communicative, too unreserved, forthright and rude. But people find me reticent. It was made a strong point against me at the Wardenship election (when John Sparrow was, more suitably, elected), expressed quite candidly by Goronwy Rees, on behalf of the Junior Fellows at that time: 'People feel that they don't know you.' This surprised me, I considered myself all too obvious and open with people—though it is clearly indelicate and inaesthetic to expose oneself like a fat old woman without any clothes.

Other people must have a point, however. For again and again they have found me exceedingly difficult to cross-examine. When dear Peter Wright—to whom I owe my life—examined me before my final operations, he said he had never met a patient more elusive. I *wanted* to co-operate, I didn't want to head him off—only I was so sensitive about my ghastly insides, I didn't want to bore him too much about it, I thought he would know already. Other people have had a similar experience. I suppose the technique with me is instinctive: talkative as I am, talk can be a form of defence—and really people are very obtuse. Now, after a lifetime of their obtuseness, one way and another, I don't care whether they understand or not. In fact, I prefer now—like Wystan at the end of his life—that they should *not* know me; and I don't wish to be written about—he did. When people write to me for information—even for a thesis!—I give no help: I put obstacles in their way.

A Junior Fellow, whose qualities I admire, at last put his finger on the issue only the other day. He thought I was open and unreserved enough about the things I meant to be unreserved about; reticent about those I wished to be reserved about. But isn't this understandable, with the strangeness of my family background, and the different inflexion of my own nature? Wystan had early come to terms with his; I hadn't, and I realize now that strenuous repression only increased ulceration. In fact, I owed everything to my difference: there was far too much heterosexuality in my family already—if I had been one of *them*, *I* should have been a fool like the rest of the family. To that difference I owed everything, taste for things of beauty above all, fastidiousness, the feeling for quality in life, intelligence—not, as many have supposed, to any putative upper class descent (again showing the commonness of *their* minds).

Quite early on I celebrated this difference with a poem—one can say anything in verse, since people won't understand it:

> Nature I hate, and what's unnatural choose
> For rule of life, rather than hourly lose
>
> The sense of separateness from the common world,
> Admit a likeness which I never willed
>
> To all that's human, similar and mean ...

lines which shocked some pukka Anglo-Indians when Penderel Moon recited them in his club at Simla. (He always laughs at recalling it.) Naturally, I don't suppose these lines to represent the makings of a popular poet; but they are authentic, as sincerely meant as anything of Swift's.

To the difference I owed also an over-sensitized nature: coming back to my room I often found 'a little frightening [but I was not giving up: the room meant too much to me], especially in the evenings when one's sensibilities are all alert. On opening the door into this or into my bedroom, I think I catch the vanishing impression of somebody's presence, just the leap of a shadow or the illusion of a face. Last night, when I went up to change for dinner, a curious gleam of light in the mirror caught me, on turning on the light at the door. It is a game I play, not without its terrors.' There then follows a poem:

> I came into my room to find
>   Somebody waiting for me there:
> Who it can be I may not know
>   That stands so quietly by the chair.
>
> Some face I have not seen in life,
>   Nor ever comes to me in dream;
> And yet I know him who he is,
>   Though all the sentient world should seem

185

Dust of an iridescent Time,
  And all the castles of the mind
Should crumble into nothingness
  Like motes behind a faded blind:

Still would he be and I not know,
  Still would he wait until I came;
And, gazing in unfathomed space,
  I meet his eyes and know his name.

Anyone with a religious frame of mind would have given this
a mystical turn and meant Christ—the Hound of Heaven and all
that; this way was barred to me, for, though I was churchy,
religious belief never meant anything to me intellectually.

David Cecil, with his family background, always had the consolation—and the support—of religion; Wystan came back to it
after the death of his mother. (He, too, a victim—or a creation—
which ever way you chose to look at it: the two are complementary.)

> Nov. 30th: A disturbed day again, because D.C. came to see
> me late last night and stayed talking till nearly two this
> morning. In a kind of waking sleep I listened; and the night
> passed with pain in a cold dream. The day after, horrible.
> But really, I oughtn't to blame David: he told me fascinating
> things about Mary Queen of Scots and some ghostly stories
> that disturbed my sleep. And one wonderful phrase that
> somebody found in an old manuscript at Ludlow: some
> Parliamentarian inquisition after Charles I. 'Tell us, was it
> the face of Charles Stuart you saw?' 'No; for the candles
> were not yet lit.'

This was the kind of thing I owed to David, our real mutual
interests of mind. After fifty years I recall one of the things about
Mary Queen of Scots, little known, which came from his mother,
Lady Salisbury: one of Mary Stuart's nostrils was larger than the
other, a characteristic of the Guise family. On a lighter note,
here was one of his family dreams. A relative dreamed that
his aunt was blown up by a bomb, and the cook said, 'Pouf!
There goes her ladyship!' That night David told me the story
of *The Turn of the Screw*—not a good recipe for sleep; I hadn't

read it, and for years Henry James meant nothing much to me.

Mary McCarthy has a title, *The Company She Keeps*; here was mine. The Frau Pastor came over from Hagen, and I gave her a good time; she lunched in my rooms twice, and I took her to the theatre to see *Juno and the Paycock*. (I never met Sean O'Casey, but later when he came to live in Devon he used to cheer me on with fan-mail.) One Sunday in mid December,

> tired out with all the pain and sleeplessness of the last few days, I woke up thinking I was in Germany again. I thought of Sunday in Hagen with an acute sense of actuality, with pleasure and regret at the same moment: *Nostalgie für Hagen*, who would have thought it? I heard the soft deep rumble of the three bells in the Catholic church ... how well they sounded from the high *Wald* on a Sunday last winter. Last year already, my twenty-third year gone by. Only my health is the same, and that's bad wherever I am. How often I found myself up in the *Sauerland* restlessly prowling about with that gnawing pain inside me. Still it may have given things their unique savour, the way of looking at the world, as if for the last time: when one is ill, the world is too beautiful.

Richard and I walked into Christ Church Meadow and looked up at 'the large window upon St Aldate's from which Father Ronnie Knox surveys the world. There, sure enough, was his light burning—right at the end, like looking up an avenue of the Prater: the beacon of the Church. Richard, who thought the day so dreary as to be almost ingenious, suggested we might call on him, offering ourselves as intending Papists to be given tea.' I wanted to get back in mind to Germany,

> to Sunday quietness in that ugly town with its own charm for me, groups of young men leading up the paths into the woods. In January the stillness and snow along the forest ways, in the evenings going up alone through the trees, with the lights of the town receding farther and farther. Then to come out on the hard parade-ground of the Bismarck Turm, with all the valley spread below stretching

away to the mass of Hohenziburg, where Charlemagne
fought a great battle, they say. It is the sense of adventure
in one's blood; now that it is constantly denied, it becomes
an adventure of the mind. A rarer thing it is to be on the
track of ultimate experience in this way, and to have
glimpses of things in return which, if they came to one in
the flesh, one would never see or know.

There was the cult of repression, and its fruits.

With Rudler[1] I lunched to meet Paul Valéry, for the first time,
whose work I much admired: more about him later. Maurice
Bowra came for walks; Bruce McFarlane too, our friendship
formed in distress, for he was ill too, 'a comrade in misfortune'.
I lunched with Wystan in his rooms at Peck V. 5, I see: nothing
more. Norman Ault, scholar and anthologist, came to tea, and
Ronald Bottrall from Cambridge, the Cornish poet whose
laudation by Leavis did him no good. Letters to C. K. Ogden
and T. S. Eliot, those mutual exclusives, are mentioned in the
same breath. I dined with Cole and gave a little lunch-party for
him to meet Richard Pares: we became faithful followers and
recruits to his Society for Socialist Inquiry and Propaganda,
with which he sought to make up for the damage he had done
by breaking away from the Fabian Society. I gave another
little lunch to A. H. M. Jones and his bride, to celebrate their
wedding, both Labour Club members, he on his way to become
the finest Roman historian of his generation. Maurice Dobb
came over for the week-end from Cambridge, so also Ogden,
that quintessential Cambridge type, of *The Meaning of Meaning*
(—and why not *The Meaning of Meaning of Meaning?*).

I was teaching far too much: here is a typical mid-week day,
for the record. 'Morning: teaching 9.45 to 1.15 p.m. Afternoon,
walk, reading in the Camera. At tea, reading Margaret Kennedy,
and Aubry's Life of Conrad. 5–7 tutorials again [five on one day!].
At night, finished Morley's *Machiavelli*, began *Simplicissimus*
[greatest of German novels, a parallel to Swift], and read an
essay for tomorrow's tutorial.' Phew! At the end of term there
were still '3 hours and more teaching; Reports afternoon and
evening. Ill all night, and next day.' But I went out that morning

---

[1] Professor of French Literature, leading authority on Benjamin Constant.

to wire some of the money I had earned to my brother down on his luck in Australia.

Before going home I had a few days in London, stopping with Roger Makins, invited by his mother who was always exceedingly sweet to me. After all Roger and I hadn't much in common, though we had been taught together at Christ Church and elected together at All Souls: he was on his way to a very different life, a career of public service and many honours. Theirs was a vast Norman Shaw house in Kensington, where my courage would have failed me if it had not been for his mother's sensitive solicitude. Staying in such luxury 'gave one a vivid sense of wellbeing. An enormous house with lovely things all about: pictures mainly English and Pre-Raphaelite, a large collection of jades of all colours, green, pink, white, and pieces of semi-precious stone, coral and cornelian, jasper and lapis lazuli. My room was so *gemütlich*, blue and orange colours, dove-grey walls, and—of all inconceivable luxuries—a fire at night. Going to sleep was so pleasant, it was like having someone to say one's prayers to at night, in childhood.'

I took my opportunity to hear *Samson and Delilah* at Golders Green, and *Messiah* at the Albert Hall under Beecham.

London is always a foreign place to me, more so than Munich or Paris or Vienna—after all I know them better. The Park might really have been the country, for an icy mist blotted out all the houses round. I spent all my working day in the Tate Gallery, meeting my friend David Low for lunch there. I gave a quizzical look into the House of Commons Yard as I went by, and wondered a little ... What a typically English foundation the Tate Gallery was—given as a thank-offering for sixty-five years of a prosperous business career: Sugar, and how often have I seen the Tate label on boxes of sugar in our little stores, when we kept shop in the village at Tregonissey!

7

Friends and Acquaintances

I do not apologize for the detail of this book, for it is precisely the detail that is revealing and what the historian most values. As Macaulay wrote about his History: 'With a person of my turn of mind the minute touches are of as great interest, and perhaps greater, than the most important events.' Having established the routine of my life as a don, the rhythm of term and vacation, tutorials and reading, examining and committees, I shall not go further into that. The reader must assume it as the background to more interesting things going forward: a far more active social life than I had remembered—I am surprised at the number of my friends and acquaintances—and, underneath, there was the inner life I treasured most.

At the beginning and at the end of 1928 I made two of the closest and dearest friends of my Oxford life, Bruce McFarlane and Charles Henderson; and through me they became friends. Each of them sought me out and made me his friend; for, curiously enough, though I have had a large circle of friends, I have always been rather passive about friendship. Hardly a single person have I gone out of my way to make my friend, and only one person whose acquaintance I deliberately sought—Sir Winston Churchill; and that was because, in writing the family history of the Churchills, I needed his help to gain access to the archives at Blenheim, which had been denied to G. M. Trevelyan.

I had hardly known Bruce and his friend John Garrett, and *his*, Evans-Pritchard, as an undergraduate. They formed a little group of sub-aesthetes, whom I regarded with rather a doubtful eye—Evans-Pritchard, indeed, slightly shocked me, with his velvet dinner-jacket and exotic tastes. Each of them, however, achieved distinction and made a valuable contribution to the life of the country. Evans-Pritchard became our leading anthropologist, thought the world of in America; after years of life with the natives in the Sudan, with the Senussi in Cyrenaica, and in Egypt, he came back to Oxford and to All Souls as a professor. Thus in later years we became warm friends—he was a warm-hearted Celt; though I never fully shared the high intellectual regard in which anthropologists held him.

I reserved that for Geoffrey Hudson, for whose qualities of mind I have always had the highest admiration. If 'disinterested curiosity is the life-blood of civilisation', as H. A. L. Fisher observed, Geoffrey was the most civilized of men—an extremely cultivated man, and a great gentleman, in any case. His range of interest was astonishing, and it was a passionate intellectual curiosity that inspired him. Geoffrey was half-Cornish; his father's was an interesting mining family, his mother left a young widow, who reared him at Plymouth. At his school there, in the General Intelligence test, Geoffrey was the only boy in the school who knew who the conqueror of Adrianople was in the Balkan War, and the only boy who did not know who the current Lord Mayor of Plymouth was. This was characteristic of him all through life—esoteric knowledge, natural distinction of mind, with an absence of practical sense, indeed an absent-mindedness that exposed him to mortifying experiences, led him to be taken advantage of, and helped to frustrate one of the most remarkable minds I have known of its full fruition. He suffered too from an extraordinary paralysis of the will: it is like what Wordsworth said of Coleridge, if you knew what an effort it cost him to get his work done, his book written ... ! The result is that little enough was accomplished to show his powers of mind— though, again, what he did write is written with fine distinction.

When quite young he wrote his book on *The Relations between Europe and China*. He was no linguist, but had immense knowledge, a searching historical sense, and an exquisite cultural discrimination. Asked to contribute a Note to the first volume of Toynbee's *A Study of History*, Geoffrey contributed three-quarters of a page, which concisely and cogently overthrow the whole 'Challenge and Response' thesis of the book. Toynbee was too imperceptive to notice—Pares used to refer to him as a 'man of rubber'. I thought of him as more woolly; and there always was a wobble in his focus. No historian thinks as highly of Toynbee's *Study of History* as non-historians and simple-minded Americans do: it is really an attempt to put history into a sociological strait-jacket, like Spengler, from whom the impulse originally came. Hudson could have written the book much better himself—if only he had had the will-power to write it at all.

He was always going to write a big book on the Tokugawa dynasty of Japan: it never materialized. He promised to write a brief 'Marco Polo' for the series I edit, *Men and their Times*: he never got round to it. Then he was to do a 'Stalin' for me; but I knew he wouldn't get it done. He was one of those, *unus ex istibus*. But he did write, towards the end, a masterly and concise *Fifty Years of Communism*, which never received the recognition it deserved; that was in part his own fault, the price he paid for not getting forward with his work. He had an ecumenical grasp of civilizations, not only of China and Japan, but of the Middle East; he knew what was going on in Tibet, as well as in the ramshackle states of South America, or for that matter of New York, the domestic interior of Tammany Hall. He was fascinated by the goings on behind the Iron Curtain, none of the infantile illusions of Left Intellectuals about Stalin or the Communist leadership (though he had become a Labour man, largely under my aegis).

His absent-mindedness—at least, in the not so important matters of life—was rather endearing. He is known to have travelled up to London by train in his carpet slippers. At Shrewsbury, where he rowed, the crew were kept waiting on the river, while Geoffrey, having gone up to change and taken off his clothes, put himself logically to bed (he was probably thinking of Tibet). Often, coming back by the late night train to Oxford, he found himself at Worcester or Banbury in the early hours of the morning, waiting on the draughty platform for the early milk-train to bring him back. I took him to see his childhood's Plymouth, utterly flattened by the Germans, all landmarks gone. To all right-thinking Plymouthians Derry's Cross is the centre of the universe; I was much amused to hear Geoffrey, hesitating on a pavement, say to himself, 'If only I could find Derry's Cross I should know where I am.'

I used to wonder what could account for such a degree of

absent-mindedness: what could be the psychological explanation? He regarded me as very 'present-minded'. Dear Geoffrey, I have so many amusing memories of him in all kinds of odd circumstances.

There was nothing in the least absent-minded about Bruce McFarlane: he was very much on the mark. But he was a psychological and physical casualty, too, like the rest of us: it is not natural to the human species to be too intelligent, something abnormal about it, it takes too much strain out of one's physical constitution. Bruce had had a terrible time as an undergraduate, with his mother dying of cancer. He had hoped to come up to New College, but had to content himself with a scholarship at Exeter. From the first he was a professional historian, winning a University prize for an essay on Cardinal Pole, very chaste and good; but he made no impression when he competed for the Fellowship at All Souls. This left him with a bit of a complex against the college, like a number of dons at Oxford (an open competition by examination, fair enough) — one notorious example in particular, an ulcerated enemy for that reason.

So Bruce had to content himself again with a *pis aller*, a University scholarship to support himself while researching and waiting for a better prospect. This came with a Research Fellowship at Magdalen; when the opportunity arose of becoming a tutor there on a permanent footing, he did not fail to take it. I was a little innocently surprised — but there was a canny Scot on one side of Bruce, a warm-hearted sentimental Devonian on his mother's side. He went on to become the best History tutor at Oxford, with a faithful following of distinguished pupils who muscled in, after his death, to edit and publish what he had been unable to produce in his own lifetime. For Bruce was another — there was some psychological obstruction that prevented him from completing his work and bringing it to the boil. It was very odd, for he made himself the best authority anywhere on fifteenth-century England. Another psychotic consequence was that it gave him an acute complex about my ability to get on with my books — he was quite incapable of doing justice to them or even hearing about them; though I understood perfectly the psychological *Ursprung*, it was hard to put up with in one's closest and most intimate friend.

For I owed my life to him. It was he who found the surgeon who performed the ultimate operations that enabled me to live—I never forgot that, and made more allowance for Bruce's complex than I would have done with anyone else. (I don't put up with that sort of thing from ordinary people—Bruce, though a first-class historian, was no genius.) This surgeon was 'Peter' Wright, husband of the well-known sex-consultant, Helena Wright, to whom Bruce in turn owed his life, or at least his sanity, for by the early 1930s he had a nervous breakdown. Bruce had met the Wrights at All Souls, at a lunch given by the ever-hospitable Lionel Curtis, who by this time was on to China, which they knew, and was writing *The Capital Question of China*. This Capital Question was being attended to by a number of eminent worthies, All Souls men among others—the great Lionel himself, Sir Arthur Salter, Warden W. G. S. Adams—let alone the impeccable Tawney; the more they attended to it the more it fell apart, I observed with some amusement: for weren't they portentous about it!

When I first came to know Bruce he was living up a number of flights of stairs above Boffin's cake-shop in Cornmarket, very convenient for buying chocolates: he was then addicted to chocolate liqueurs, with a puffy, pasty-faced complexion in consequence. It was heaven for him to move to the fleshpots of Magdalen, where he was treated by sentimental old C. R. L. Fletcher as the baby of the college and, more cautious than I, Bruce did not inflict his increasingly Labour views (under my influence) on those old reactionaries. They were a rum lot, the Fellows of Magdalen, their urbanity hardly increased when—under pressure from me—Bruce later recruited another Leftist, A. J. P. Taylor, as History tutor. Bruce once said to me that each Fellow there lived inside his separate cage, glaring out at the others.

In those early days Sir Herbert Warren was just retiring as President—he had done everything for Magdalen, and the Fellows made it hell for him. Of course he was a Victorian snob; but what did that matter? Rather naïf, and endearing. When Annie Besant tried to get Warden Spooner of New College (and Spoonerisms) to take Krishnamurti, an Incarnation of Our Lord, as an undergraduate, that fly old bird said: 'I did not think we could take an Incarnation of Our Lord as an undergraduate at New College, so I suggested that she send him to the President of Magdalen.' Lionel told me that Spooner denied ever having said 'any of those silly things [Spoonerisms]. All that happened was—I was in the High Street and my hat blew off, and I found I was chasing a little dawg.'

Herbert Warren's grand *coup* was to get the then Prince of Wales—subsequently Duke of Windsor—as an undergraduate at Magdalen; though whether that much redounded to its credit is rather doubtful (the precedent was not followed). The eminent talents of All Souls were drafted to teach this young man, the sainted Warden Anson and the genial Grant Robertson; but they do not seem to have made much impression. Robertson once told me that the Prince's devotion to tutorials at All Souls was much impeded by constant interruptions from Father to meet visiting personages officially, Kaiser or various German relations—they were numerous. His parents had not, however, drafted the Regius Professor of Divinity and a bevy of canons of Christ Church, as in the case of Albert Edward, later Edward VII, when at Oxford. That young spark once escaped their surveillance and made an assignation to meet a girl at Abingdon, going down incognito on one of the blameless Salter's steamers for the purpose. His tutors found out just in time to arrange for him to be met off the boat, by a brass band playing 'God Save the Queen'.

Bruce was in clover at Magdalen, the river, the grove with the deer, those shady walks, the bridge across the Cher to the private Fellows' Garden where we often walked—hardly anybody else did. He was much attached to the flowers and shrubs, introduced me to the catalpa and others; he was the first to show me the fritillaries growing thick in the enclosed meadow—to me they had been but a name in an Arnold poem:

> I know what white, what purple fritillaries
> The grassy harvest of the river-fields

practically extinct now as wild flowers along the Thames. Bruce liked comic names (he used to call old Sir Charles Oman, of All Souls, Sir Raffle Buffle), and I remember the chuckle with which he identified a rarity growing in a chalk-stream at Ewelme as mimulus. He was full of mischief. When he was Vice-President, A. J. P. Taylor woke up one morning to find himself nominated Curator of the Taylorian, and C. S. Lewis as a curator of the Warneford Lunatic Asylum. He was highly critical of both. With me he had to arrange everything, always be top dog; I didn't mind, he was a good organizer and organized our walks and trips everywhere.

Once he arranged an Easter vacation visit to Pugin's hotel at draughty Ramsgate in honour of that worthy. He often spent his own vacations at candle-lit Llanthony priory under the Black Mountain, to which he took me. Further afield were Helmsley, Rievaulx and Byland Abbeys and the Vale of Pickering; in Derbyshire Tideswell, Haddon Hall and Hardwick, from the 'Peacock' at Rowsley, where we both went down with flu. He introduced me to Lincoln, to which we pilgrimaged up the escarpment of the Cliffe, with those towers rising and sinking as we approached—an English Chartres, I thought, and how marvellous it must have been when each lofty tower had its spire—to stay at the delightful 'Angel' in those days when English hotels still kept their charm. We explored in his mother's native Devon, where we infiltrated into the unspoiled interiors of Ipplepen and Torbryan, rood-screens, bench-ends, candles, everything. I once heard him breathe as we marched up the churchyard of Cobham, 'Seven brasses in the chancel, think of it!'

Nearer Oxford we walked or went by bus. In Combe Wood near Wheatley he had a gamekeeper's cottage; a squat toad who lived at the foot of a tree he named after Sir Arthur Salter. The three Miss Briggses, last of their line, of Holton Park—now some sort of educational institution—did not much approve of the bachelor occupant of the cottage, where he entertained his undergraduates. We walked all round those beloved haunts in the spirit in which Matthew Arnold walked the Cumnor Hills:

Runs it not here, the track by Childsworth Farm,
Up past the wood, to where the elm-tree crowns
The hill behind whose ridge the sunset flames?
The signal-elm, that looks on Ilsley Downs,
The Vale, the three lone weirs, the youthful Thames?

Once, walking up the Cher valley to Tackley, I saw him bend over the marble effigy of some warrior of the Hundred Years War, whom he knew all about, and print a kiss upon the cold brow. That was what Bruce felt about the past, but he could not, or would not, express it. When I think of all the places we walked to when we were young—Waterperry and Waterstock, Shabbington and Thame and Rycote, Long Crendon and Brill and Lower Winchendon, Christmas Common, lonely Fingest and down through the beechwoods of Stonor—it gives me still a sad ache at heart to think that he is gone.

Charles Henderson was a very different personality, a more integrated one than Bruce; they did not always hit it off together, for both were medievalists and each an organizer, wanting the lead. In Cornwall Charles was king. Once in a Cornish church Charles was flatly contradicted about the dating of a font by the vicar, who appealed to the authority of the great Mr Henderson, not knowing that here he was—who waited for Bruce to tell the poor parson. Not a bit of it: Bruce kept a malicious silence, and chuckled over Charles's irritation and feeling that he couldn't go back to that church again without embarrassment. Bruce had an instinct for pin-pricking. Charles was totally without malice, the kindest of men, made on a large scale—he was six feet six inches, pink and boyish and vastly learned about Cornwall, particularly medieval Cornwall. Fortunately, he did not like the sixteenth century and allowed me to take up Tudor Cornwall, was generously willing to help and take me under his wing.

From the time he was a boy he had been crazy about documents, transcribing, translating, collecting wherever he went: country houses, to which he had the entry for he belonged to the cousinage of county families, lawyers' offices, estate agents, churches, cathedrals, libraries—all was grist that came to his mill. He was thus immensely overdeveloped on this side, underdeveloped in general reading, both in history and literature; though he was already contributing prolifically to the local newspapers from his vast stores of knowledge, he did not really know how to write: he just strung the simple sentences together.

So we were complementary: when he came back to Oxford as a tutor at Corpus, I gave him tips about general history for his

reading and teaching, introduced him to contemporary literature—my passion for D. H. Lawrence and Virginia Woolf. In
return, he took me all round Cornwall—he was three years older
and socially more at ease, altogether more sophisticated, besides
being well connected—and used to have me to stay at draughty
Penmount, the Georgian house on an exposed hill outside Truro
(never have I been so cold in winter). One would be warmer now:
the place is a crematorium.

So Charles and I walked or bussed or were driven by his sister
Chrys all around Cornwall. What a marvellous education that
was—lucky I to be taken under wing by these patrons of scholarship! I learned from each of them the whole time: from Richard
Pares about the eighteenth century—he didn't want me to tell
him anything about writing; from Bruce about the fifteenth
century—he didn't want to learn anything from me about the
sixteenth; from Charles Henderson about all times and places in
Cornwall.

It all worked out in the end providentially for my own work.
When Charles died, only thirty-three, on his honeymoon, I
was heart-broken—it took me years to recover from his loss.
Of course, I had not wanted him to marry, and could not believe
but that the catastrophe would not have happened if he had not
been run off his feet, overtaxing his strength (with a weak heart),
chasing round Spain and Italy on his honeymoon. He died at
Monte Gargano in 1933: I shall never forget the tremor that went
through Cornwall at his unexpected loss, or my own misery and
desolation for years. I determined to do everything to keep his
memory green—weighed in to forward the Memorial, the
collection of manuscripts, at the Royal Institution at Truro;
helped his widow, Isobel Munro—he had made a dynastic
marriage to the daughter of the Rector of Lincoln; wrote poems
in his memory, wrote him up, and dedicated my *Tudor Cornwall*,
when it ultimately came, to his shade.

There is a cult of him in Cornwall, naturally enough—he
started so many things, he was in at the beginnings, and in his
short life he collected so much material. Again, he did not finish
much in the way of books: a couple of parish histories, many
short essays and newspaper articles, a voluminous mass of notes.
He was really an antiquary—an honourable title—rather than an

historian. Simple-minded folk in Cornwall do not know that; nor that, when he died, he was actually turning away from his intense, rather parochial, concentration on Cornwall, perhaps in process of development towards becoming an historian. He knew Italy and Italian, and now was turning towards Spain, thinking of writing about Charles III, who rehabilitated Spain in the eighteenth century.

I had met him for the first time only this year, when he was brought to dine at All Souls, and couldn't believe it was he. I thought I had seen him once before at a seminar of Sir Charles Firth's; but that must have been Hamilton Jenkin, between whom and Charles not much love was lost: they were rival Cornish authorities. In Cornish matters I did not count, their junior anyway: I was no rival. My interests were as much literary as historical; I thought of Q as my model and mentor. In the event, it fell to me to fulfil myself as an historian and, in the unexpected way in which things work out, to become the inheritor of much of Charlie's knowledge, of all that he told me (I have forgotten nothing of it), and what I learned from others: the repository of so much of Cornish folklore and tradition, verbal memories and characters, along with so much history.

Such were these closest friends of mine; not a day passes but I think of one or other of them, Geoffrey and Richard, Charles and Bruce, with love and grief.

My Diary shows as busy a social life as ever, and an extraordinarily varied acquaintance, widening into politics. I had Arthur Greenwood to stay: not much fruit of the spirit in that. Greenwood was a good old war-horse of the Labour Movement and in the terrible 'thirties was Deputy Leader of the Parliamentary Party — to whom Amery addressed the famous adjuration, 'Speak for England', in the decisive debate in 1940 which overthrew the disastrous Chamberlain. Indeed, Greenwood was no anti-patriot, and had far more sensible judgment than the Intellectuals of the party — Harold Laski, for instance. Greenwood had a charming, good-looking son at Oxford, Tony; promising, too, though I have rather lost sight of his ascent.

In November of this year, 1928, I gave a lunch for younger Labour people to meet: Michael Stewart, Richard Hare, E. H. P.

Brown, the economist, and Evan Durbin. This last I did not much care for: too much of the Nonconformist preacher about him, smugness shone in his moonlike face. All the same it was a loss to the Party when he was drowned at Crackington Haven; he would have made a moderate and sensible Cabinet Minister. A far greater loss in that group was Hugh Gaitskell, whom I just knew, but not well. At this time he had a richer and more varied spectrum than these for background, rather naughtier, I am glad to say: aesthetes like John Betjeman—frivolous, I thought them. It did not go well with the rather prim, pursy look he had; he was a tremendous favourite with Cole, who confessed he loved him (platonically, of course). We can all see now that Gaitskell's early death gravely harmed the Labour Party. What ill luck it has had!

Closer to me in spirit were the literary folk. I had Wystan Auden to lunch to meet Bruce McFarlane; in July Wystan came to tea, then to dine on a Sunday night. Odd and disreputable as his clothing was, he always togged himself up decently to dine at All Souls—in later years too, when he came as the guest of his publisher, Monteith of Faber's, though Archie Campbell and I were far older, pre-war friends. Maurice Bowra, too, continued to come and collect me for walks and to dine; he liked dining at All Souls, though he was jealous of the college and affected to disapprove of it. (Wadham was poor: it was as simple as that.)

Since Maurice has been so much written about, a whole book devoted to the public figure,[1] I should say something about a side to his personality not very well known to those writers, who knew him less well than I did. They knew him on the public side, the public performer, the leader of a salon, a social luminary; I was not at all interested in that side to him, after all I had something of a following of my own, which I took more seriously—a bit of a fanatic, I wasn't interested in social life, let alone *panache*. I knew the private side to Maurice: it was very different from the public side, which everybody knew. Everybody knew the ebullient exhibitionist, the natural wit, the jokes—Queen Juliana, 'every ounce a queen'; Enid Starkie, 'in all the colours of the Rimbaud'; or the belated marriage of Sir William Beveridge to his secretary, Mrs Mair, 'Purification of the Blessed Virgin Mair',

[1] Edited by Hugh Lloyd-Jones.

etc. Maurice was a perpetual fountain of such *boutades*; as David Cecil said, he should have been made an earl for his jokes.

Inside the rumbustious public performer—I didn't like the noise—underneath the over-exuberant vulgarity shouting people down, there was a shrinking spirit lacking complete confidence in himself. It is a not unusual case; in Maurice's it had something to do with his shortness of stature. There was an awkward law case about some mechanic having a Wadham undergraduate on the canal-bank; Maurice, as Dean, had to appear in court. 'Stand up, Mr Bowra,' said the judge; 'I am standing up,' said Maurice. Everybody laughed—and Maurice was terrified of being laughed at.

I understood this instinctively, though the younger, and always set myself to support Maurice's inner confidence. So we met privately; I never attended his salon, and rarely went to see him; he came to take me for walks and occasionally to dine. I was not competent to judge of his classical scholarship, though I gathered it was not of the first class. When his first, and best, book of modern literary criticism came out, *The Heritage of Symbolism*, he was on tenterhooks lest it be attacked by the clever boys. Fancy anybody being afraid of what John Sparrow, Goronwy Rees and Isaiah Berlin might say! I wouldn't have cared tuppence. So I wrote a review of Maurice's book, giving it the serious praise it deserved—the main point of it was the advantage there was to have difficult works like Valéry's 'La Jeune Parque' explicated by a trained classical scholar. Actually Maurice made more sense of that absurdly obscure poem than anybody else has ever done.

After that I could do no wrong with Maurice: he trusted me, and confided in me, as he never could the clever boys, much more as he saw of them. I didn't have time for that sort of thing, or much time for them, amusing as they were. One of the clever *claque* queried what literary future there could be for Maurice, when his printed works were unreadable, his unprinted works unpublishable. Maurice went on to become a first class Vice-Chancellor of the University, and—a good friend to me—wanted me for either Warden of All Souls or Regius Professor of Modern History: neither of which jobs I wanted, wasting my life on committees to decide who should cook, or cook up, what. My deepest wish was to fulfil myself as a writer. He told me, what I never knew, that Halifax, then Chancellor of the University, had wanted me to become Warden. Isn't that just like life—the man I so deeply disapproved of as an arch-Appeaser, who had come to Chamberlain's rescue and taken Eden's place as Foreign Secretary! (Perfectly clear as I was about my own best interests, I naturally did not relish being rejected by the third-rate, for the benefit of the second-rate.)

Acquaintances were all too numerous; some of them I appreciated. Most of all, perhaps, André Maurois, of whom I became a friend over the years. I met him at lunch at Trinity, and took him and his two ladies on to Christ Church, where they wanted to see Hall and kitchen. His second wife was the daughter of the famous Madame Caillavet, Anatole France's Egeria. In the kitchen the novelist was tickled by a notice which said: 'The Dean: gooseberry tart and ½ pint of cream'. The ladies wanted to know what we were laughing about: 'C'est le repas pour le Doyen du Collège, le vieux Monsieur!' That night Richard considered half a pint of cream a lot for a Dean; at that rate, how much would be proper for an Archbishop? Maurois told me a typical story of dear Q at Cambridge, who had produced a selection from the Bible as Literature. Q was in his bath, when his bedmaker woman opened the outer door and shouted in, 'You're wanted on the telephone, sir.' Q asked what was it that was so urgent. 'It's the *Daily Express* wants to know what you've done with the Bible.'

Maurois had been initiated into English life by his service at the front as an interpreter, upon which he wrote *Les Silences du Colonel Bramble*; that made his name. He followed it up with *Ariel: ou la Vie de Shelley*, and brief but very successful biographies of Disraeli and Edward VII. Extremely kind to me always, he devoted a couple of pages to my tiny little book *On History* in his Cambridge lectures, *Aspects de la biographie*. Transported, I felt it was like having my name inscribed on the dome of St Paul's. There came an awkward passage in New York after the fall of France in 1940, when Maurois blotted his copybook badly about Britain. Churchill launched one of his transfixing phrases: 'We thought we had a friend; we found we had only a customer.' It took years for Maurois to work his passage back. During this period our publisher, Cass Canfield of Harper's, gave us both a delicious Founder's Day lunch in his pretty house on Thirty-Third Street. Maurois told me that he had written the Queen Mother's (then Queen's) speech to the women of France in 1940, and that she had given him a pair of platinum cuff-links he treasured. Nothing whatever was breathed of the awkward episode: I often wondered whether he knew that I knew.

When he came back to lecture at Oxford years after, I welcomed him at dinner at All Souls—in spite of a reproof I received from Lady Waverley, through Isaiah (as if I was going to take any notice of that). Jean Seznec, my fellow Breton, was grateful that I had helped to make things easy, and later I had a pleasant visit with Maurois at his opulent apartment in the Boulevard Maurice Barrès. He told me all about his acquaintance with Kipling—always pro-French and anti-German—who had encouraged his work; as well as about himself. Half-Jewish, he had succeeded to the family cotton mill in Normandy, and had begun with considerable independent means, his writing merely an accessory. As cotton declined, his independent income vanished; his earnings from writing (which were very considerable) took its place. I regret only that—passive and unenterprising as I am socially—I never bothered to accept his warm invitation to stay with him on his farm at Saint Médard in the lovely country of the Dordogne. But I am not much for staying with anybody.

On Maurois' last visit to Oxford, at over eighty, he had an enthusiastic ovation. It was thoroughly deserved: a remarkably sympathetic survey of trends among younger writers in France whom he can hardly have liked much. However, he was essentially a sympathetic interpreter, rather than a creative spirit; as a novelist, an intelligent observer of character and mœurs. I preferred his later biographies, his best work, of Victor Hugo, George Sand, Dumas and Proust: solidly researched, full of information, intelligent and just.

Lionel Curtis brought his friend, Abel Chevalley, over; whom I was glad to meet, for he was the leading authority on Thomas Deloney, the Elizabethan novelist, whose biography he had written. Alessandro d'Entrèves was a research student at this time, working for his book on Richard Hooker, a far greater Elizabethan spirit. D'Entrèves came for walks, as Douglas Woodruff continued to do. So, too, G. W. Stonier, who became a regular writer for the *New Statesman*: I rather liked his personal prose-pieces, though they had not much strength or vitality—sub-Logan Pearsall Smith.

Stanley Casson made himself an acquaintance, though I did not much like him. A friend of Woodward, he was an archaeologist don at New College: a curious mixture, for he was a brash vulgarian, with a dash of adventurer about him, and yet perhaps a touch, no more, of aesthetic appreciation. Casson directed an excavation of the Hippodrome at Constantinople, to which he recruited A. H. M. Jones and Geoffrey Hudson. This led to Geoffrey's first female entanglement and a son—a millstone round his neck up to the Second War; there followed a second, and another son; since both were publicly recognized in his will, there can be no objection to my mentioning these obstacles to fulfilment of *himself* and his own talents, rather than the purposes of Nature. There followed yet a third feminine imbroglio, more deleterious than any: I should have thought he had been sufficiently warned, but he went on to make yet another—incomprehensible! He once said to me that life was like a track through jungle, with lions ready to leap out on one on either side. No doubt, if you take that path—better to keep out of the jungle! I always believed, fatalistically, that if external circumstances could get in a blow at one, they would: better to give no hostages to fortune.

Casson was the subject of an authentic Spoonerism upon his election as Fellow of New College. Meeting him in the quad old Spooner said, 'I hope you dine tonight to meet our new Fellow—Mr Casson.' Casson, who was not wanting in self-confidence, was rather taken aback, and protested, 'But I *am* Casson.' Old Spooner, equal to anything, replied sweetly, 'Never mind. Come all the same.'

Casson had published a book on the archaeology of Macedonia, where he managed to be a millennium out in his dating. That did not prevent him from putting up for the professorship against Beazley, the most indubitable genius of my time at Oxford, along with Gilbert Murray and Sir Charles Sherrington. I remember being surprised. And he told the Abbé Woodward an unspeakably vulgar story, which he then related across the Sunday night table at All Souls to shock me—but succeeded in shocking Coupland (W. P. Ker: 'Coupland, ma non copulando'), who made the Abbé apologize for such ungentlemanly language. I sat back, much amused. The only redeeming feature in my eyes was Casson's devotion to Boscastle, on the north coast of Cornwall, where he had a cottage. He perished in the Second War, when his plane went down setting off on a mission to Greece. Alas, the losses from the two wars inflicted on Europe by the Germans! Casson, though not a first-class scholar, was a personality, as brave as he was brash.

C. R. Cruttwell, tutor at Hertford and a leading figure in the History School, was in part a casualty of the First War, wounded, afflicted with arthritis, invalided out. An All Souls man, he came into college every day for lunch, a relief from incessant tutorials, examining, lecturing, his round as Dean at Hertford. Since he was Evelyn Waugh's tutor and since Evelyn has left a caricature of him in his autobiography, it is my duty to put it right in mine. The novelist's eye for externals is just enough in its rendering: there was something awesomely comic about Cruttwell's appearance—Richard described him as 'the Dong with the Luminous Nose'—and his table manners were not of the best. His voice was a ferocious bark, and he had a choice vocabulary which Richard—with his Wykehamist background of 'Notions' —thought of codifying. Male dons were 'hacks'; female dons 'drabs', unless they were emotional, then they were 'breast-heavers'—I cannot remember them all.

Underneath this rebarbative exterior, there was a Christian gentleman, a far better practising Christian, let alone gentleman, than the naughty Evelyn. Cruttwell had kindness of heart and surreptitiously, unknown to the recipient, helped many a poor scholar; he was devoted to his Christian duty. His nature was 'homo-erotic', as he once described it to me—like Evelyn's, for that matter; but Cruttwell sternly repressed it, and grievously he suffered, psychologically (as I did physically), from repression. As an undergraduate of Hertford, Evelyn was a waster and a drunk, self-confessed. When he went down, he put the name of Cruttwell into novel after novel, as a lunatic nurse, a club bore, or crazy army officer—I forget the various avatars. I suppose Cruttwell could have had him for libel; all he said to me was, without malice, 'I suppose I should have sent him down.' Evelyn admits that the letter he received on his Third in the Schools was a score for Cruttwell.

Cruttwell had bought a Queen Anne house, The Vinnicks, near Newbury out in then empty North Hampshire; he was much attached to it but found it lonely. At the end of the summer term he invited me for the week-end and drove me out in his car, an excursion as staccato and explosive as his speech: *that* really was an alarming experience. As the 'thirties wore on, each of us became more and more ill, comrades in pain. A comment of his I appreciated: he told me quite early on that he could recognize my style in my writing, it was so very like my talk. A characteristic personal style, as Matthew Arnold diagnosed, is the attribute of the real writer, 'the born man of letters'. Geoffrey Faber once questioned whether I was a writer; he was not a very perceptive man—and what the hell else was I but a writer? In re-reading those early Diaries for this book—I hadn't looked at them for years—I notice two others of Arnold's tests borne out: 'the *devouring* eye and the portraying hand'. Faber, however, had not had the advantage of reading those: he might have come upon some revealing things about himself if he had! After Cruttwell's death, when I asked for the books I had lent him—a volume of Motherlant's *Pitié pour les femmes* never came back; did he disapprove? I wondered—I learned to my surprise that he had left me £500. That seemed a large sum to me then; it made his death sadder still, to think he had cared that much for me.

In those days I was lending everybody books, I notice: some in improbable quarters, for example Katherine Mansfield to Swinton, a General (but a writer of talent); French novels to Spenser Wilkinson, less inappropriate, since he was willing to have it supposed that he had enjoyed the favours of Sarah Bernhardt; catalogues of the Munich and Viennese art galleries to cultivated Warden Pember. One of these loans I have never ceased to regret: I was one of the subscribers to the tiny edition of Wystan Auden's first volume of poems, hand-printed by Stephen Spender, orange paper covers. I lent it to a young acquaintance whose name I still remember, Malcolm Davies: if he still exists and should light upon this reminder, he might return it—but I don't suppose that that copy has survived. And I long ago learned my lesson.

To my senior acquaintance was added the Omans, Sir Charles and his Lady, a Maclagan: there was Oman, away out on the right wing, and I right out on the left—it made no difference. I was regularly asked to their rather grand lunch-parties—I can't think why they were so angelically kind, except that my table manners were better than Cruttwell's and, though nervous, I did my best and always had something to say for myself. The Omans lived in considerable style in Frewin Hall, behind the Oxford Union: an ancient gateway which Erasmus knew, the house that had been taken for the cloistered residence of Albert Edward as an undergraduate. It was a large barn of an historic house, endless corridors, plenty of parlourmaids, and I was always appreciative of the beautiful china in which it abounded. Oman himself told us of the improbable event which made the garden memorable. In those early days of flights over Oxford a toilet-roll dropped from an aeroplane, unrolling and unrolling until the whole garden was draped in its toils.

In June I went to stay with Oman's contemporary at New College and All Souls, Headlam, then Bishop of Gloucester, at the Palace in the Close. (Headlam: 'I like a *large* house.') He had another, in Durham, on the upper Tees, where he was a country squire and cultivated his garden. In Gloucester he terrorized his clergymen. A large gorilla of a man, with a habit of gnawing his knuckles—he was said to have the blood of both Oliver Cromwell and Peter the Great in his veins—he was a formidable figure, but not to us in college who knew and loved him. As a young man a fortune-teller had diagnosed that he was a man of strong passions, but added that they were well under control. Hence the grimaces and facial twitchings. With his physique he should have been the father of fifteen, but his wife was invalidish and he had no children. As a diocesan he was a disciplinarian; Dermot Morrah used to say that Headlam was neither High Church nor Low Church nor Broad Church, but *Hard* Church. I dare say he had reason to be. Up in the Cotswold hill parishes parsons mouldered away with too little to do. In one place where the clergyman was at loggerheads with the parish, who refused to come to church, Headlam was at pains to bring them back again. The parson, having got them safely inside, went down the aisle, locked them all in, and grinned in through the windows at them.

O dear old C. of E., where alone such entertaining eccentricities were possible! No wonder Headlam asked a Junior Fellow to stay, to accompany him on his round of confirmations, that 'you may see what fools my clergy are.' Actually the reactionary bishop was a reformer: by joining parishes together and giving his clergy more work to do—it often involved knocking heads as well as parishes together—he managed to double the stipends. Himself a man of independent means, he spent more on the Church than he ever received. Once he went to visit one of his clergy in retirement at the Warneford, and had a perfectly sane conversation with him. When he was leaving, the clergyman said, 'You see that man over there? He thinks he is God!'; and then added, 'But how can that be when I am He!' The clergyman remained in the establishment. Headlam consented to preach in the Chapel: 'You have to be careful what you say: you see there are so many authorities on theology there.'

Beneath all this, there was a simple believing Christian—none of the complexities and subtleties of Lang, the Archbishop; who should have been a cardinal *in curia*, and thought himself more than one, *alterius orbis papa*, 'through whom God chiefly speaks to his English people.' (He was a Scot, by birth Presbyterian. Q.E.D.) Headlam had a love of animals and flowers, as a countryman was a great one for preventing the populace from rooting up wild flowers in the countryside. He had noticed that where, in Victorian days, the flowers grew right up to the towns, today—with easy access by car—plants and flowers are scuppered within miles of urban areas. (What does anything matter in our filthy society?) As a Canon of Christ Church he had kept an eye on the trees in the Meadows; today one sees patches of the river choked, the ivy everywhere crawling up the trunks. One understands the difficulties: impossible to get anybody to do any work—as if ordinary people were good for anything else. What would one want them for? Their conversation? Their opinions? Possibly for their looks, if good-looking and responsive; I quite see the point of the old squires' *droit de seigneur*: it improved the stock.

During the war Headlam shared rooms with me. I well remember the alarm he occasioned G. M. Trevelyan's daughter, when the door opened behind her and out came this episcopal gorilla.

I was fond of him, however, and he of me. He had a nephew and niece, the Headlam-Morleys, who, half-German by blood, were wholly pro-German in sympathies, in spite of everything. Headlam, to his credit, was too intelligent to fall for that; but I could not forgive them for it, when one considers what Europe has gone through at the hands of the Germans.

8

Paris in the Spring

The chores of term over, I was off to Paris in the spring: so
much more congenial to me than London, with its mercurial
grace (London is a masculine city), and actually more familiar.
Meeting Mrs Pember in the quad, she said:

'We're just off!'

'Where to? Going abroad, or to Shropshire?'—where they
had Broncroft Castle, in those fortunate days.

'Only to Shropshire. Where are you going?'

'To Bourges, and places on the Loire.'

'I'm sorry you won't see the dark red roses in the Bishop's
garden. But it's a dream of a place. Do stand at the north-west
corner and look at the forest of silver birches.'

The Warden comes up with a bunch of keys in his hand. She
continues:

'He's going to see our old friends, the French cathedrals.'

'Oh, is he? Which?'

'Bourges.'

'Delightful old place. And while you are there, do look at
Autun and Nevers.'

'I must get a map. Are they near?'

'Yes. You can get a train from Bourges to Autun, that runs ...
Well, goodbye and good luck!'

My calendar tells me, for March 29th: 'To Paris indeed: sea-
sick all the way from Folkestone to Boulogne.' My first two
mornings I spent dutifully in the Louvre; my second afternoon
sheltering from the rain in the arcades of the Opéra, and along
the Boulevards. I was reading Mauriac's *Destins*, Gide's *Isabelle*,
Sée's *Philosophie de l'histoire*, and a book on Georges Sorel in
the Tuileries Gardens. *Réflexions sur la violence* indeed! One had

only to look up the avenue at the vast gap between the Pavillon de Flore and the Pavillon de Marsan where the Palace had been, destroyed by the violence of the Communards in 1871. To me it left an aching void: I tried to imagine how it had been, with its columned façade and long lines of windows—built by Catherine de Medici, burned down by the cultivated people, the hope of our time.

On this visit I stayed at the Hôtel du Quai Voltaire, for its literary associations; either it or a neighbouring house was where Voltaire died on his last visit to Paris, this was the hotel where Baudelaire and Wagner, Wilde, Arthur Symons and Rilke all stayed. From my room high up on the sixth floor I could see the whole length of the Louvre and imagine the Empress Eugénie escaping, after Sedan, down those galleries from the Tuileries to the old Louvre at the other end, where her American dentist had a cab waiting for her, unrecognized by the mob. Just like Louis Philippe after all, and before him Charles X.—As their successor, Charles de Gaulle, said, 'How is it possible to govern a country which has three hundred and fifty cheeses?' But how much the most lovable of countries, after all, everybody's second country.

In after years Eugénie returned to stay at the Hôtel Continental, again looking out on the Tuileries Gardens, but looking south, instead of west and up to the Arc de Triomphe. She said once how sad a fate it was that all three of their favourite residences should have been burned down—this, enchanting St Cloud, and the Villa Eugénie at Biarritz. Years later, her great-nephew, the Duke of Alba, showed me in Madrid—where his Palacio de Lirias had been burned down in the Civil War—a charming picture of the Empress's boudoir in the Tuileries: looking out on a summer parterre ablaze with flowers, within, her bureau surmounted by the bust of Marie Antoinette—of whom she had a cult, and feared that one day she would be trapped in the Tuileries like her. Alba had also a picture of Napoleon III's study at St Cloud, dusky, littered with papers, a candle guttering into the dawn. Think of the ruin and destruction wrought by the people, capable of creating nothing—except under direction! And the direction has gone.

Here was my Paris, and here was Cyril Connolly's—both of

us Left-Bankers, where he was spending 'a blissful winter' in 1929, 'at last living within my own and other people's income'. Oddly enough, Eliot told him that 'one should see Paris for the place, not the people, as their activities got in the way of the appreciation of the city itself.' This corroborated my own tastes and, since I knew hardly anyone there, there was no temptation to waste time on people. Cyril was differently constituted. We did share, however, a passion for Flaubert and Baudelaire, and he too was reading Paul Morand, his books 'blueprints of what a young man might then hope to find in the sleepers, river steamers, bars and night-clubs of post-war Europe.' This was not my world, and I have no detailed memory of his books.

Cyril, too, stayed in the Hôtel du Quai Voltaire, but could not resist the Ritz, of which he has a nostalgic account, with its English *habitués*, Michael Arlen and Evan Morgan, Lord Tredegar, whom I was not to meet, greatly disapproving, till many years later in Rome. It was years later still before I penetrated the Ritz, then only once, but with Proust's acquaintance Princess (Marthe) Bibesco, become a close friend.

Relations with Cyril were not unfriendly, but in suspense. I never forgave him for rejecting the best of my longer poems, 'The Old Cemetery at St Austell'; true, with my usual defeatism, I put the words of rejection in his mouth, citing Yeats and Valéry's 'Cimetière Marin' as having influenced it. In fact, it was a totally different poem, with its own character, my own idiom, and worked out more closely to Gray's reflective, nostalgic 'Elegy'—which also had a frosty reception from silly critics on its appearance.

Then Cyril wanted me to contribute a political article to *Horizon*—like Eliot, always wanting something political—and I was too busy to bother. He may be said to have made amends with his generous review of my *William Shakespeare*, saying that it was the most interesting book he had read for years. But it was obvious that he hadn't taken in the scholarly conclusions of the research in it, for he went on repeating the old confused nonsense about the Sonnets remaining a problem. Here is the difference between the scholar and the literary journalist: Cyril had never been one for doing his homework, merely skimming the cream. I used to call it 'living off chocolate éclairs'.

We always retained a link, however, in our close friendship with Richard Pares, about whom we corresponded. Cyril had moved on, responding to the husky voice of a rich American girl, which 'seemed to promise the ultimate alleviation of the heart's hunger.' He married her; the marriage 'took care of the next ten years': when she grew fat, he fell out of love with her. I do not entirely disrespect a welcoming attitude towards the chances of life, though it was not mine. I see now that I was strenuously engaged—in spite of a highly sexed temperament—in always holding life at bay: in order to impose my own discipline upon it, fulfil my own intentions—not the intentions of nature—not let it carry me where it would. (Actually Henry James's attitude, clean contrary to Shakespeare's.)

All the same, I am grateful to Cyril for his passion for literature, especially for collecting his *Evening Colonnade*. Virginia Woolf was wrong to call him a 'cocktail critic': he was at once discriminating and had a capacity for enthusiasm. (He was much too enthusiastic about Hemingway, with his un-adult point of view.) His judgments are almost always right, all in all the best critic of contemporary literature, or perhaps, rather, writers. Cyril had a touch of genius after all, and I suspect he couldn't have done any other than he did.

In Paris I was at it again—churches, museums, galleries, opera, concerts, reading, observing, note-taking. Beecham was conducting the orchestra of the Conservatoire at the Opéra; I noticed how impressed they were by his waving away the music stand and conducting without a score: it put them on their mettle. Patriotically he included a work of Elgar I rarely hear, the 'Cockaigne' Overture; the musically minded ladies in the boxes above fluttered their programmes down like a snowstorm, to my annoyance. Next night I heard Honegger's 'King David' and 'Psalm XVII' at the Grande Salle Pleyel, where I had heard Debussy's 'Ode à la France', another work I have never heard again in my laborious life.

At the Opéra, suddenly the image of John Clark, my boyhood friend at school, came vividly before me, the smile, the deprecatory gesture, the whaleskin mackintosh over his shoulders.[1] I

---

[1] Cf. *A Cornish Childhood.*

came up against the pronouncement of the Archbishop of Paris, Cardinal Dubois, against Communism: 'L'Église fut toujours à l'avant-garde des réformes sociales utile au peuple'—was it, I queried, in the eighteenth century? He was following the lead of the reactionary Pius XI, who is not to be pardoned for riveting Fascism on the necks of the Italian people by giving Mussolini the triumph of the Lateran Treaty, which the Papacy had always denied to Parliamentary governments. After the liberal-minded Benedict XV, the *petit-bourgeois* Pius XI exhorted the heads of states 'to unite their efforts to deliver themselves and their populations from the terrible ravages with which they are ineluctably menaced by Socialism and Communism.'

What a world away from the accommodating sentiments issuing from those portals today! The Revolution has intervened.

I went nostalgically down to Chartres again—

> Nous sommes nés au bord de votre plate Beauce
> Et nous avons connus dès nos plus jeunes ans
> Le portail de la ferme et les durs paysans
> Et l'enclos dans le bourg et la bêche et la fosse

—to concentrate on the architecture, that marvellous creation of medieval faith. I looked long at the sculpture of the north portal, the Judgment of Solomon: the woman falsely claiming the child, brazen and glad; the true mother full of grief; an attendant already drawing the sword. On the central pillar of the western entrance, Nôtre Dame de Chartres: this, the gate of honour, decorated with incredible richness of plastic imagination, luxuriating foliation inside the canopies, leaf designs at the base of the capitals.

What an expression of the human spirit—the loving exfoliation of childlike belief: compare it with a characteristic expression of today, even at the best, the Unilever or Seagram Building in New York, Dulles Airport at Washington. As for the People's Republic, think of the vapid giantism with which Moscow has been disgraced—with the ancient Kremlin for comparison next door!

As I moved round the great shrine the chatter of jackdaws—always present around French cathedrals—mingled with the steady drone of an aeroplane, ancient with modern. A group of children looked out from a window high up under the gable of the Cloître Nôtre Dame, while the silvery chime of a clock pealed behind the Ancienne Évêché on its terrace. Moving round to the south side, beyond the transept, I came to the little chapel of St Pyat beyond the apse, its slender and aspiring lines bright with sunlight cutting the silver stone with grey shadow. Buttresses led the eye up the steep slope of the roof, red tiles speckled with golden lichen gleaming. Above, the clear blue sky of the corn-growing Beauce in spring, all the sharper through the fresh green foliage of the beeches on the terrace.

There was M. Houvet, the sacristan, in his little den by the chapel, who cared only for the twelfth and thirteenth centuries and could not abide the florid composition of the eighteenth-century altar in the choir: 'Mais, c'est ignoble!' He held forth on altars in general, and a new one going up, to his indignation: 'C'est du vingtième siècle. L'autel, c'est une table; ce n'est pas un monument.'

How many English vergers would entertain such archaeological enthusiasm, or express themselves so epigrammatically? Again and again I have noticed the ordinary Frenchman's precision over language compared with the slipshodness of the English—and the Americans! In that country where democracy is a fetish, and nobody must stand out from the rest, it is the thing to speak the language as badly as everybody else. Once, on a motor-bus in Provence, when we were going over the Durance, the conductor said, 'C'est une rivière assez capricieuse.' Can one imagine an English or American bus-conductor saying that the river was 'somewhat capricious'?

Back in Paris, to hear *Siegfried*, I was struck by the trumpet-tone of the Sword motif: it seemed to me expressive, or prophetic, of the revived German Empire; I thought of old Wilhelm I and his paladins, Moltke, Bismarck and the rest, as they appear in stone on Charlemagne's heights at Hohenziburg. A woman in a box drew my attention, for she was fashionably dressed for about 1909 or 1910: whatever caused her to stop dead just then? A high-necked blouse, hair drawn up at the back to a pile on top of the head, a projecting wave on her forehead. Her very gestures were straight out of the pre-war fashion books: a slow turning of head to shoulder, a downward glance of the eyes that mingled

condescension with modesty. Mesmerized, I couldn't keep *my*
eyes off her. I fear that every moment of the day, all my life, I
have offended against the Catholic concept of 'custody of the
eyes'. But what is the world for, if not to look at?

Left on my own, I constantly wrote Notes. On the history of
Dragons, for example. 'Are they the result of a dim race-memory
of the human struggle for existence with saurians and such
vanished reptiles? Or a composite creation of the mind, agreeing
remarkably in detail at different times and places?—in China as
in the West, the Dark Ages (Beowulf and the Sagas) as in the
Middle Ages or Renaissance. The one thing they certainly are
not is a deliberately conceived image of the idea of Evil in the
world.' Here was the constant urge of my mind against
the religious tendency to take fancy for fact, my bias against the
insistence upon concepts as truth when it was sufficient to accept
them as beautiful, my preference for the aesthetic as against the
metaphysical. I suppose now that the reason why people do not
find aesthetic experience sufficient is their inability to experience
it—so they prefer bogus concepts, metaphysical nonsense. To
the aesthete, the beauty of the world is enough.

I continued: 'It is curious to think how far man is dominated
in his mechanical inventions by the forms of the natural world;
or, rather, how his inventions tend to approximate to natural
forms and patterns of construction. Motor-cars going slow, seen
from a high place, are like heavy purposeful beetles, especially at
night, their dark shapes lumbering along, with their antennae
reaching out into the darkness. And how like gnats small aero-
planes are, seen flying afar or at great height.' Or there was the
obvious imitation of nature in the forms of art: the transformation
of palm trees into the columns of Egyptian temples, that of
northern forests into the aisles of Gothic cathedrals.

An unexpected Note appears on 'the parallelism of patterns in
astronomy and mathematics: the elliptical orbits of comets, the
paraboloidal form of some comet-tails, etc., a kind of objective
universal picture of concepts fundamental to mathematical
thought. What is the nature of their relations? Why this dualism
of form in thought, objective and subjective? Is it that the genesis
of mathematics is to be found in observations of the universe,
and that, even now, the mental framework for mathematics

depends upon these pattern-concepts of external derivation?'
This thought would not be very agreeable to G. H. Hardy with
his view of pure mathematics, in *Mathematics for Philosophers*,
and his detestation of externalist 'Hogbenian' mathematics.

If so, does this throw light on the old debate of intuitional
as against environmental origin of ideas? The dualism of
the thing-in-itself and the environment seems to run through
all forms of thought, the evolutionary conception of science,
history, etc. Is a compromise possible between externalists
and subjectivists? Namely: the thing-in-itself is no passive,
unanalysable object, but fluctuating and capable of movements (at present incalculable, unpredictable) — but all within
determined limits. As with the atom, or cosmic ray, so in the
case of the individual unit in history. Even the exceptions—
quantum-phenomena in physics or negation of survival
purposes in the individual person — may they not relate to the
general deterministic laws, perhaps their variation follow
discoverable laws of their own?

These reflections which bothered my mind were set off by
my attempting to square Marxist determinism with commonsense
experience. I was not going to swallow any preconceived dog-
matism of Marx, let alone Lenin, but try to think things out for
myself. There are arguments devoted to theologians and theo-
logical discussions — taken more seriously then and occupying
more of a place in the thought of the time — which I spare the
reader. A Note questions,

How far is thought — or art — connected with masturba-
tion? Thought (and art) seem to depend upon exploiting the
interval between the nervous excitement, the original
stimulus, and its resolution in an orgasm. Thought and art
then would be built up upon prolonging the interval, post-
poning the orgasm. [Here was the Manichee strain again,
victimising the body.] It is curious to think that our mental
world should be built upon such physiological foundations.
It may be significant, then, that those thinkers whose achievement depends upon so manœuvring that the orgasm never
comes off become increasingly incapacitated from action,
towards which thought aims as its natural end.

That this reflection was not so far-fetched was borne out by a large book which shortly appeared from the University Press, by one J. D. Unwin, on *Sex and the Sexual Origins of Artistic Creation*.

'There is a sense too in which a highly specialised thinker—a Bradley or Santayana, a Bergson or Paul Valéry—thinks for himself alone: an audience, a listener, or a partner in speculation is superfluous. He speculates because he must, for his own satisfaction, and is his own best critic. He hardly needs the outside world, except for background. The solitariness of Bradley's thought and life, the narcissistic character of Valéry's poetry and thought, have here their explanation.'

> Mais moi, Narcisse aimé, je ne suis curieux
> Que de ma seule essence;
> Tout autre n'a pour moi qu'un cœur mystérieux,
> Tout autre n'est qu'absence.

Perhaps Narcissism was my own religion, incapable of making a junction with any other in the world outside me?

A Note on Obsessions cited Virginia Woolf's in her work: that of a falling tree in *Jacob's Room*; of journeying out to a lighthouse, in *Night and Day* and *To the Lighthouse*, of which this was the germ, that of being the lighthouse itself, a light shining in the waste of waters. Later, I was surprised that no one noticed the obsession of being under water in her last book, *Between the Acts*: shortly after, she drowned herself. An obsession of my own was connected with windows, particularly at night with the light on, no blind drawn, myself exposed: of someone observing from without, with evil intent, perhaps to shoot. (I still have it: *absit omen*.) Or again, when playing the piano late at night in the unfrequented room high up in the roof in college: feeling that the improvisation awakened memories in the room. 'Something stirs in the inner room: whom does the music awaken? whose chords are those that I have broken in upon?'

A story formed itself in my mind—why did I not write it? Why was everything held up, postponed, waiting? Was the impulse to create being frustrated by the insatiable desire for more and more knowledge? Perhaps the two impulses were at war for years—one reason why people could not understand my work, when it appeared, let alone me. Some people, my

Cornish friends, thought that I was a poet who had strayed into history, and that my real self was there, in poetry. Commonplace historians, and not they alone—professional historians—both without imagination, thought of my historical writing as 'literary'. Of course it is: so was Macaulay's, Froude's or Gibbon's: history has always been a most important part of literature. Why not enjoy both worlds? If only literary folk had a proper sense of history, and historians knew how to write! I am all in favour of the virtues, as well as the rewards, of ambivalence. Both were taken aback at my embarking on Shakespeare; they should not have been surprised, for both disciplines are necessary to understand the most historically minded of dramatists.

How much I loved Paris then!—the first great city I had ever stayed in. The Pont Royal glowed in a shower of warm spring rain, the purple paving-stones alight with heat, shining with the wear of traffic. While sheltering in a doorway of Mazarin's Library, a car came swiftly round the wing of the building that projects out towards the *quai*. As it happened, I had never seen a prison-van before. I looked inside: four policemen, an usher dressed like a parish beadle, and the prisoner, a middle-aged, hearty-looking fellow, close-cropped, with a splendid brush of beard. 'I felt that the morning was put out by it, and, quite irrationally, it roused one's gorge. There's no rational case for doing away with punishment, but the apparatus is so ghastly. Immediately after, there came a respectable-looking young fellow, poorly dressed and with thin shoes in all that rain, who said he had had nothing to eat that day.' In those days, sensitive and young, I often gave money to people who begged. At that moment, I hadn't anything to spare, for a comic reason. Stopping as I always did on the Left Bank, I assumed that restaurants there were reasonable, and wandered by mistake into one of the most expensive, Lapérouse. Flabbergasted at the prices, and too shy to go out again, I settled for a wing of chicken and nothing else: it had cost the earth. 'In the evening I made it up with my conscience by contributing to the support of an alcoholic old woman, who was begging by the Café des Deux Magots, across from St Germain des Prés.'

One afternoon I spent in the past, in the sombre historic church of St Roch, another of those enormous baroque churches of the *grand siècle*: grey stone interior with wide vaulting, sculptures and monuments by Lemoyne and Coysevox. I concluded from the monuments that it must have been in the fashionable quarter in the seventeenth and eighteenth centuries. Bossuet died near by in the Rue Sainte Anne in 1704, his body brought to rest in the church before being taken to Meaux—'the Eagle of Meaux'—to be buried. Here, too, was Le Nôtre, gardener of the King, Louis XIV: 'Il répondit, en quelque sorte, par l'excellence de ses ouvrages, à la grandeur et à la magnificence du monarque qu'il a servi et dont il a été comblé de bienfaits.' What a career! What could be more satisfying than laying out the gardens of Versailles, the Tuileries and St Cloud, setting the fashion to be followed all over Europe, in those days when monarchs and aristocracies set the standards, and taste prevailed. Corneille was here too, and the Abbé de L'Épée, inventor of the deaf-and-dumb alphabet.

Many of the monuments were of grandees of the reign of Louis XIV: Claude François Bidal, Marquis D'Arfeld, Maréchal de France, 1667–1743; François de Blanchfort de Créquy, Maréchal de France, Gouverneur de Lorraine, né en 1625, mort à Paris le 3 février 1687. How the dates themselves spoke to one, had a pathos of their own!—born the year of our James I's death, died the year before James II was sent packing. Here was the naughty Cardinal Dubois, minister of Louis XV, a suppliant kneeling on a heavy tasselled cushion, robes trailing grandly, biretta laid aside. In an attitude of graceful and conscious abasement, he nevertheless looked more like a suppliant for some lady's favours than someone seeking the remission of his sins.

Coming up the Boulevard St Michel a young couple provoked the repressed narcissist: a lad no older than a *lycéen*, student's beret, raincoat like an artist's work jacket, with his arm around the waist of his girl. He was but a beginner, drawing her to him with a flush of bashfulness; she was leading him on. What was so provoking was that he was so handsome, dark, mobile features, with attractive grace and free movements of body. I started a story, an idyll in my mind—naïf as a child, yet already seeing through the disillusionments of life. A curious paradox: no wonder I was not ready, or willing, to begin.

O well—hell!—tomorrow to Bourges: yet another cathedral.

Inside the Cathedral I was taken by a woman who wouldn't let go pestering God with her prayers: a spare, vigorous type, elderly, in the fashion of 1903, wasp-like waist and hat perched on top of her knob of hair. Taking her praying-stool with her she comes down the aisle from the Chapel of the Host to St Joseph, from St Joseph to St Anne, then on to the Sacred Heart and back to the Blessed Sacrament. Here was the kind of human fool the clever old birds in the Vatican (I had not read Gide's *Les Caves du Vatican*) have to cater for. Spinsterlike, she was very insistent. The last I saw of her was nailing a verger at the door of the sacristy, who was trying in vain to edge out of the range of her tongue for a full quarter of an hour. Her case was evident: it wasn't God she wanted so much as a man.

Meanwhile, I studied the architecture, though not with the textbook precision with which Bruce would attend to the plan of a cathedral, each bay, triforium, clerestory, complicated patterns of vaulting, fan or lierne or what not. I was not so precise, or so dedicated; but I appreciated the splendid originality of the design, the vast ship-like *nef*, the dominating unity with scarcely any projection beyond the ambulatory for eastern chapels —none of the mystery of Chartres. The general effect—with double aisles on either side, the inner higher than the outer—was that of a vast casket of three tiers leading up to the central ridge. And indeed one saw the inspiration common to medieval chests, caskets, reliquaries, like miniature versions of Gothic churches. Bourges is of a prodigious height, the sense of it increased by the columns soaring straight up without break to the height of the ambulatory, and above that still triforium and clerestory, a little dwarfed by the inhuman height of the arches.

It was borne in upon me, what I have often thought of since, the far greater ambition, intensity and originality of the French in art (excepting always the Elizabethan drama): one sees it not only in their architecture and painting, but in their furniture, simple details of design in their stuffs and materials. There is an aesthetic audacity in the French genius: no one has ever equalled their eighteenth-century interior decoration, in their furniture the imaginative use of wood with every variety of stone and gilded bronze. Consuelo Vanderbilt—who had graduated from Duchess of Marlborough to Madame Balsan, and spoke English with a marked French accent—said to me once in New York, surrounded as she was by Pissarros and Segonzacs, Marie Antoinette's own console-tables: 'Everrything French is best.' She evidently expected the usual English rise to the bait, a patriotic protest. I agreed with enthusiasm: 'But, of course.' She didn't quite know how to go on from there.

Indeed, the boldness of imagination in the French cathedrals *is* beyond that of the English, fine as some of these are, Lincoln, Durham, Canterbury, York, Wells. These do not reach the heights, however, that *essor* of the spirit, of Amiens, Bourges, Chartres, Notre Dame; it is not surprising that the French over-reached themselves with Beauvais, so tremendous an effort that the centre toppled in—like Louis XIV and Napoleon.

Outside the west door of Bourges was a woman equipped with two crutches, her face open and honest, burnt by sun and wind to a crust of brown. A cold day, nobody comes to the door. An hour later, while I am studying a curious motif at the base of a capital—the head of a man with a bird on each side pulling his ear with its beak—there are shuffling painful steps; the old woman comes in to rest against the many-fluted pillar and say a prayer. When I go out, I give her some of my small change: no believer, I am the first by whom her prayer is answered. After that, many pass in and out, and from across the square I notice that many give, almost always men. The young women without exception give nothing, with rather an insolent air. I was about to cross and give her a five-franc note, when a whole crowd went by, and I saw greedy hands plunge frequently into her well-filled pocket. Her prayer was answered.

A Note reminded me to remember the arrangement of the apse at the east end, with alternating bays and buttresses, the latter towering and disengaged, the bays little hexagonal chapels springing like projecting turrets from low piers. At the summit of the three-tiered apse, the uppermost tier looked so slender in its height as to appear a corona of stone—no doubt the designed effect. What geometrical complexity within the overriding unity, the integration of design! I was to remember, too, in the Hôtel Lallemant, where I stopped overnight, the parquet flooring of original pattern, like a spider's web. In fact I still recall the Archbishop's garden, outside his palace, all secularized, a little public park; and, at night, returning once more to the façade of the Cathedral, the silence and desertion of the streets. In the church hall, the choir was practising—do they still, I wonder, or is all dead?

My last impression of Bourges next morning was of 'a wedding in a half-ruined church, in the square behind La Boule d'Or. The west end in the hand of restorers, one entered through a temporary wall of brick. Suddenly, a bell rang out loud and slow, very near: enclosed in a little penthouse on the ground outside. While it swung to and fro carriages drew up in the sunlit square; the bride descended. As I went up the street, a schoolboy swung his satchel to and fro in long slow strokes, in rhythm with the bell.' For me, a moment in time was fixed.

I was going on to Orléans next morning. Spring floods were out; from the train I watched the west front of the Cathedral to the last moment, keeping its watch over the waste of waters. The main ribs of the structure stood out in a blue haze of sunlight, which caught the high roof of the barracks, once the seminary, and soon all the roofs of the town on its mound were gleaming. At La Ferté Saint Aubin the low-lying fields with their ditches of water reached out towards the passing train with the curious perspective of lines on a sundial. All this Sologne region—celebrated in Balzac's novels—appeared marsh and forest, mainly birch and fir, with clearings for cultivation; occasionally apple blossom flashed across the window pane. Here, a large cat stalking in the fields; there, workmen sitting on the railway embankment, having their lunch under the spruce.

At Orléans I was enabled to appreciate at first hand the horrors of Protestant iconoclasm, what made the religious wars of the sixteenth century so ulcerated. One saw the damage wrought upon the churches, the fury of the mob, destructive as always, launched against unoffending sculpture, decapitated figures, angels obliterated, whole areas defaced, flattened, chiselled away. The south porch of the church of St Paul had been terribly mauled. At St Étienne de Montfort only choir and transepts remained, the nave having been destroyed by the Protestants. Some beautiful detail remained, so long as it was not figure sculpture, vineleaves at the base of capitals and around the porch, for example.

But was present-day Catholic taste any better? The Cathedral was full of atrocities, which it gave one almost a perverse pleasure to see the Chapter keeping up. A new statue to Sœur Thérèse of Lisieux, as sentimental and sickly as all renderings everywhere of the Little Flower, patron of sentimentality in our time, the kind of thing to pander to the taste of the people. Averting my eyes, I went out to look at the more congenial monuments of the past: the charming names of the old streets, Rue de la Chèvre qui danse, Rue de l'Écu d'Or; and along the Quai Cypierre the eighteenth-century houses looking out over the Loire, wide here, sullen and swift with the floods, and the fine bridges spanning the favourite river of the Valois.

Back in Paris, after the constant *va-et-vient* of Oxford, I felt 'too lonely, though I kept myself busy with concerts and reading'. I was now reading François Mauriac, whom I was to meet after the Second War: to me a sympathetic writer, in spite of his simple heterosexual obsession. His poetic sentiment, combined with his passion for his own provincial *pays*, the Bordelais and Les Landes, were what appealed to me; and I have never ceased to regret giving away his rare little *Vie de province* to Lady Warwick — Edward VII's old flame — who mesmerized me for a moment in the 'thirties with her violet eyes and that expanse of pneumatic bliss, which often enough had pillowed Albert Edward. Here, too, was the kind of thing that spoke to me in Mauriac: 'Il éprouvait cette même fureur dont sont la proie certains hommes vierges et condamnés à la virginité, lorsqu'ils envisagent l'horreur de mourir avant d'avoir connu la joie charnelle.'

But I was self-condemned, by an exorbitant will.

While waiting for my old schoolfriend to arrive I resumed my round. I heard Mgr Baudrillart, a celebrated preacher of the day, preach at Nôtre Dame; a Note for 'Swift' says, 'Preaching is after all a bastard art, like all oratory.' (Actually, Swift's are very unlike sermons, more like *Spectator* or *Examiner* essays, not without humour, especially that 'On Sleeping in Church'.) Perhaps this was why I never liked Paul Claudel, whose play *L'Ôtage* I saw at the Odéon; he represented the rhetorical side in French literature, which the English dislike. I revisited my favourite haunts, Saint Sulpice, Renan's Seminary next door, also turned into a

barracks; Saint Germain l'Auxerrois with its memory of the
tocsin that announced the Massacre of St Bartholomew. Every
street in Paris, every alley, was filled for me with historic memories that I could share in, every turning led to something exciting; one never knew what might turn up.

Saint Gervais was new to me: there follows a provoked, and
provoking, Note about the direct hit the Germans had achieved
on it, during Good Friday devotions in the war, when numbers
of people had been killed. I reflected that, if they had not been
there at their devotions, they would not have been killed. 'It
gave me some satisfaction as an unbeliever to contribute some
coins for a chapel in their memory'; and I was intrigued that the
Church had found a text to cover, if not excuse, the case: 'This
day shalt thou be with me in Paradise.'

Bent on educating myself I spent half an hour contemplating
the Venus de Milo, 'instinctively walking on tiptoe up to the
statue, waking from marble into life: perhaps it is for fear of
surprising that moment of re-birth that one holds oneself so
quietly, unconsciously, without thinking.' I imagined the still
figure in the watches of the night, 'dans les intermittences du
cœur', with occasional gleams from night lights upon the white
body—until dawn gave semblance of life to the stone. A more
acute thrill was, as usual, connected with fear. One afternoon, at
the hour of closing, I was caught in a basement room of horrible
Egyptian eyeless birds—were they eared owls? At the cult of
sensations again, I fancied myself shut in for the night with all
those menacing sockets without eyes closing in on me.

At the Café des Deux Magots a young German had taken my
corner and was engaged at my own occupation of writing notes
while still under the impression of the thing observed: I saw it was
his 'Parises Tagebuch', and thought of Rilke a generation before
in these haunts, and his *Aufzeichnungen des Malte Laurids Brigge*.
There was still a lingering impression in those days of Paris as the
literary capital of Europe, as it certainly was in painting and the
arts. (Whatever were Auden, Isherwood, Spender doing in
Berlin?—Wystan was positively anti-French, precisely the culture
he needed, not more of the Nordic.)

The moment my friend Len Tippett turned up I had to take
him to a doctor, 'new ground broken'. It gave me the chance to

crack a modest little joke in French; Len had got wax in his ear, the doctor wanted to know if this impeded conversation: I said, 'Ce n'est pas qu'il est ordinairement loquace.' The doctor at any rate laughed, and extracted the wax, but it put out my plan of spending the day at Versailles. Instead, a hurried visit to the Louvre, to look at the casts of male figures from Delphi, the Venus and the Leonardos. Thus I encountered my first Courbets, woodland landscapes, and his masterpiece, the 'Burial at Ornans', like a fresco in its lateral composition, the long-drawn-out line of mourners on one side of the grave; on the other, the bearers with white scarves, the priest in black cope with acolyte at the nodus of the scene. Two or three Delacroix full of drama and movement (he has never specially spoken to me): one a street scene during the July Revolution, the figure of Liberty leading the populace. I thought of Alfred de Vigny's reproaches on the feeble way in which Charles X gave up: 'O race des Stuarts!' Another Delacroix portrayed the shipwreck scene from Byron's *Don Juan*—a kindred spirit, and what prodigious *luck* Byron had as a writer, what *réclame*! Whistler's 'Portrait of the Artist's Mother' hung there secure in its perfect poise and serenity; though I was amused to see this creation of French Impressionism labelled 'École Américaine'.

At last we got to Versailles in a crowded train; I was tired, but had to stand up, with a young fellow pressed up against us by the crush, while I held on to the rack overhead. He was utterly charming, curly brown hair, a strong square jaw with a most attractive cleft in his chin. He tried to follow the conversation Len and I carried on, though he understood very little English. He was Italian, and wanted to know if we were with the young women to whom we had given up our seats. I dissociated ourselves with a look which amused him; I said they were 'bourgeoises anglaises', he said, not getting the point, 'anglaises bourgeoises'. One of them gave me a perch on the arm of the seat; uncomfortable as it was, I was too tired to stand any longer. He led me on, observing that 'elles seraient contentes'; I replied that they would like him a good deal better. He raised his eyebrows to know if they would do, and came closer to hear the reply. I sheered off into 'the kind of conversation about languages and peoples, when the participants don't know the language they are talking very well. But my young friend kept his charming smile and the interested brown eyes on me till the end. When the train drew up at the station I held out my hand, gave him a hearty handshake and said goodbye. He seemed to find this somewhat unexpected.' Oh, well, all good things come to an end, I reflected; but I have still not forgotten his charm.

Really, I must have been too difficult for anything or anyone. For shortly, 'I long for solitude again after a very few days being with anybody.' Once before, on a visit to Paris, I had given the slip to an Oxford friend who thought to spend his time with me. This time, I decided, 'to be forewarned is to be forearmed'; I didn't run away, I just sent the accommodating Len off on his own, while I stayed behind and read.

And, really, it has been much nicer up here, sitting at the window high up overlooking the Seine and the Louvre opposite. Just now an enormous blue thundercloud, with white billows, sprang up behind the Champs Élysées; I watched it loom like a giant over the long length of the Louvre and pass away to the east, over St Gervais. For a moment a strange green light hung over the buildings and bridges; the water, by contrast with the delicate spring foliage of the trees overhanging, showed a dull oily sheen. Lights were turned on in the rooms near the Pavillon de Flore. This afternoon, going over the Pont Royal, I was thinking of the little Prince Impérial, in the boredom of exile at Farnborough: 'Oh, if I could see now the omnibus Grenelle–Porte St Martin debouching from the Rue de Bac!'

Now, after a half-hearted sunset through mist and rain, it is dark. The street lamps are being lit, and many lights in the Palace, both in the Pavillon and the south gallery. What can be happening—a fête of the Second Empire? Even the *bouquinistes* have been driven away from their boxes by the quays. Only one poor old soul holds out: I passed her stall just now on the pavement, herself wrapped in a shawl, woollen slippers on her feet. She didn't seem to notice the rain or intending customers, her nose, surmounted by old horn spectacles, was far too deep in a book. Her devotion to literature is impressive, but not likely to bring her much profit. One last look before shutting up shop myself, I see the old lady has gone too; over the river pass the swift diverging lines in the wake of a steamer, already out of sight under the western bridges.

Such were the consolations of solitude. However, I did act as Len's guide to Chartres.

After his brief visit was over I had a final week to myself. On Low Sunday I went off to St Cloud, almost by accident:

I jumped into a tram at St Sulpice, quite simply. I spent the afternoon in a dazed sort of way, with my head full of Napoleon III and Eugénie. [I had been reading the *Souvenirs* of Augustin Filon, the Prince Imperial's tutor.] It is a stiff climb, to anyone as out of condition as I am, to get up those terraces and diagonal drives across the hillside. Plenty of time to appreciate all the fountains and basins, stepped down the slopes, and to imagine the noise of falling waters in the stillness at night, before the Court left St Cloud for ever. I couldn't decide, among the several platforms, where the site of the palace was; this led me on and right up to the top of the avenue, half way to Marnes. So I came back and asked, then looked at the view from their balustrade —much changed: across the river an enormous building rearing up in the foreground, *Matériel de Téléphone* sprawling across its ugly forehead. One can only be sure of the dome of the Panthéon—Péguy's St Geneviève—which lifts itself up with elegant exactitude in the vista of trees, as seen from the upper terraces. That is how *they* must have seen it.

At a restaurant just within the palace gates, a sudden rush took place from the crowded tables into the more crowded square outside. I asked my waiter who it was: 'Costes et le Brix', touring round to receive the plaudits of the people after their air-trip. I said it would be more interesting if it were the Empress Eugénie. This dumbfounded him. I said, hadn't she lived in the old palace? 'That was Napoleon,' he said hesitantly. Then, brightening at the word 'Impératrice', he thought I meant the 'Impérial' and pointed to the enormous garish restaurant across the road: a string of electric bulbs announced 'Dancing IMPERIAL *Restaurant*'. Through the open windows one could see innumerable couples jigging to and fro to jazz.

For the people are what they are at all times and in all places, in every country, everywhere. It is a subsidiary theme of this book, as against the self-education of the educable, the very few. as it is of all my work: a salutary emphasis against all the democratic humbug of today—even more lie than humbug. The only consolation of living in such a society is that one can at least tell the truth—in Communist society one cannot, though they know it very well—but for how long?

9

Term and Vacation

To my Diary, irregularly kept, I was now adding a series of pocket-books, in which I could catch everything, as it were, on the wing. I had taken the tip originally from Stevenson, but it was corroborated by Macaulay, who had the habit of writing down the look of places while they were under his eye: hence the vividness of his descriptions. To these I added other motives: there was the feeling of being outside life, an observer as it passed me by; and, as time went on and illness became more pressing, I was afraid that I might die before my time, with nothing accomplished. The little pocket-books were intended to pinpoint life itself as it passed, an *ersatz*; in fact, to myself I called them 'Das Buch des Lebens'. Some half a hundred of them, they now add up to a life!

Here was the kind of thing. 'A night of wakefulness and pain, as morning came in with gusty showers that shook the trees in the garden and filled the building with the sound of running water—

> The thirsty land drinks up the rain,
> And I my pain ...'

It had the advantage that one could snapshot a scene, an incident, or wing a phrase: 'in Addison's Walk, a rat all rounded and hunched up, as rats are'; at another time, a snake 'gliding its slow length along', as I watched. My journey back from France has these snapshots. 'A black and white cat sitting in the fields between Picquigny and Pont Rémy'—the names themselves echoing the Hundred Years War, Edward IV's Treaty of Picquigny. 'Two blackbirds standing in water on the edge of a swamp of the Somme'—of a more recent and terrible memory. I had evidently visited André Siegfried at his house in the Rue de Courty, around the corner from the Chambre des Députés—a convenient listening-post for him. There is a note about his story of a face at the window, but not, alas, the story; and another of 'Mme Siegfried's duck: a duck at the general Resurrection [they were a Protestant family: hence their Anglophile sympathies], regarding its Creator with questioning, if submissive, eye.' Their daughter, Claire, I had entertained at Oxford, to which I was returning for term. 'Coming into port at Dover, two precise seagulls stand upon the station parapet watching the proceedings on the water with practised eye.'

Immediately on coming back I find a Note towards *A Cornish Anthology*, another work which I did not carry out until forty years after. Having had the idea and collected a few items, I wrote to Q suggesting that he undertake it: he was a practised anthologist, a steady part of whose income came from his series of Oxford Books of Verse. I once said to the old boy, who never made much money by his books—a number of them were simply pirated in America without payment, before it subscribed honestly to international copyright: 'You never expected you would find a little gold-mine in your own back garden, did you?' He was pleased at this sally, and lit up. 'No, I didn't, did I?' Over the idea of a Cornish anthology, he passed the buck back to me: 'Why don't you do it?' The truth was that it was another of those books that I simply could not do—yet.

When I went over to Cambridge this term I did not dare to call on my revered mentor: far too eminent, and I was absurdly modest and shy of imposing myself on anyone. I skulked about with my Marxist friends and, better, on my own. The familiar, slow cross-country railway journey via Bletchley was famous in its time, so many celebrities traversed it one way or the other. I always approved of the interchanges between Oxford and Cambridge, the more cross-fertilization the better—as between history and literature. Q and A. E. Housman were very much Oxford men, transplanted into Cambridge soil. It was many years before Q acclimatized himself: he always meant Oxford when he said 'we', not until his last years did he include Cambridge in the term. Myself, I have always adored going over to Cambridge; and great was my pleasure only the other day when the kind lady in Deighton and Bell's bookshop invited me to sit down on the creaky chair upon which dear Q and Housman used to sit, when they came into the shop.

G. M. Trevelyan once said to me that, when he got into the train for Oxford, he always felt that he was going Somewhere. When young, he had tried for a scholarship at Oriel and, not getting it, had to content himself with the family college, grandest of all academic institutions: Trinity, Cambridge. (There were Trevelyans at Oxford, of the original West Country line, one of them a Fellow of All Souls.) It is curious to speculate if it would have made much difference to Trevelyan as an historian, if he had been an Oxford man. I rather doubt it, since he was in any case more of an Oxford type of historian; conversely, I think of G. N. Clark—Balliol, All Souls, Oriel—as a Cambridge type. Something high and dry about that, more precise and academic, certainly nothing romantic. Now Newman—what would have happened to him if he had gone to Cambridge? The imagination boggles at the thought of it: one cannot conceive of him at Cambridge, he was so much the essence of Oxford. The railway in its day brought men of genius in the reverse direction to us: notably Sherrington and G. H. Hardy.

Since that railway line is now discontinued, along with so many charming others, here are snapshots of it. 'Just out of Oxford I glimpsed a swan, on an island among willows, engaged in turning the eggs in her nest.' Today, I think of a painter friend, Felix Kelly, photographing in his mind a similar image for future use: a swan on her nest of gathered sticks and straws, islanded in the River Camel, just beyond the most historic bridge in Cornwall, fifteenth-century Wadebridge—ruined since the Second War by being doubled. (Why couldn't they have built a second bridge, for traffic the other way, instead of destroying something irreplaceable?)

'At Fenny Stratford, on an escarpment overlooking the railway, a little group watches the train: an old woman, grey hair and ash-white face, holds an excited little boy, who is attended by a rather larger shaggy dog.' Bletchley: 'a depression between railway banks, filled with water; two dogs, accompanied by their mistresses, enjoy themselves noisily; the younger swimming about in the pond, waiting for the older and fatter to come in. A swan sails up, like a ship with sails spread in the breeze; it looks for a moment like attacking but is evidently only on guard. In the distance a wooded ridge with church tower perched half-way up. At Old North Road, lilacs out already; bushes in the little station garden cut into fantastic shapes.' Would anybody bother to shape them now? Station gardens are few and far between, a relic of a society which cared for things.

Nothing in my Diary about the human side of my visit— Maurice Dobb and Jimmy Crowther punted us all day on the Cam—but plenty about the pictures in the Fitzwilliam, adorable gallery.The Gainsborough of a Fitzwilliam held my eye: 'a massive pale face, of soft opaque texture, like powdered silk, keen hazel eyes, a fine candid forehead. The tight wig cunningly stroked in with light browns amid the grey, thus carrying on the predominant brown of the cloth suit, and the ribboned cane he is holding. All full of luminous serenity, like the best Gains-boroughs.' I noted the Highmore series on subjects from Rich-ardson's *Pamela*: 'full of life and colour, but none of Hogarth's quality of transcending the immediate subject.' A couple of Hogarths showed up: George Arnold, 'a cheery red-faced man, with tear-glazed eyes from too much English ale: a study almost wholly in silver-grey. The daughter, in lemon-coloured satin, not so successful.' A rarity was a Thornhill portrait of Handel: in bright green coat and red cloth headgear, seated at a clavier with his fingers on the black keys (sharps in white): a very German face, open and self-confident.

Evidently it was the portraits that caught me on this visit. Sargent had painted a Sicilian peasant, splendid and virile—I thought of Giovanni Verga, whom D. H. Lawrence was then translating—hair and moustaches in vivid, glowing black, face and coat in tawny and sand colour. And, indeed, how much finer were Sargent's Italian pictures, his Impressionist sketches of Venice, which he painted for love, than the grand Society por-traits which he painted for so much money! Shortly I was to have a private view into his interior, being taken along to dine at his sister's, Mrs Ormond, in their house in Chelsea. Her son, Guillaume, was all his life organist of Truro Cathedral— or 'disorganist', as Charles Henderson called him, he was so absent minded. His family on him: 'Il se fourrait dans la prêtraille de la Cornouaille.' He inherited a large number of those enviable sketches and watercolours, to decorate first his flat in the Old Manor House by Boscawen Bridge there, then his villa 'Tranquillity' at Penryn.

A recent portrait by Gerald Kelly of J. N. Keynes, Registrar of the University and father of Maynard and Geoffrey, both of whom I came to know, displeased me: 'too vivid and garish, photographic; all brilliant scarlet, in bright lights'. Though Gerald Kelly was friendly later, asked me to lecture at the Royal Academy, and read my books, I could not reciprocate with any enthusiasm for his painting: not my cup of tea. Not Gerald, but Felix, Kelly spoke to me: the latter's fantasy-view of the world, the rare imagination inspired by nostalgia (like all the best art), the subdued refinement and elegance of execution. And the subjects so much appealed to my own imagination, like the picture I own: the Alcázar at Segovia, a Castle of Otranto threatened by a storm cloud, a gaggle of priests walking below the battlements, putting up their bat-like umbrellas—the fine line between the sinister and the exquisite, the line I liked to tread. Or indeed his renderings of old disused railway lines, the antiquated steam engines, the plantation houses of the Deep South, tapestried with Spanish moss; steamboats of the time of Mark Twain and Huck Finn on the Mississippi. Or to come near home, the combination he glimpsed one day with me at Truro—and carried away in his head—of a Victorian gasometer, decorated with circus ironwork, and J. L. Pearson's Gothic Cathedral in the background. How much I should like to have *that* picture; how much I love his work, cool, distant, refined, a world of colour, form, feeling, all its own!

On my way back, 'Old North Road again: the lilac bush in morning light and wind. The train halts in open fields: a lark sings in ecstasy above the ploughed land. My dreams in the early morning were filled with birdsong from the gardens of Cambridge. Bletchley: the train is drawn up at a platform for an express to pass on the line ahead. It passes, one doesn't see it, but the rhythm of its speed pulses through our waiting train—the tremor in the body of a swift hound.'

· · · · ·

Richard used to take me to the Musical Club, which met on Tuesday evenings in the Holywell Music Room. It was a dons' club, and here they were in their rows,

> the middle-aged, and the young ones pretending middle age—the quirks of academic relations exposed. The window high up is festooned with summer leaves like a vine hanging over, a pattern of square panes making it formal: a painted scene for a stage. A bat hooks uncertainly up into the picture, hangs for a moment like a leaf, and is gone into the hurrying dusk. There sits a subdued, submissive Canon of Christ Church. The second violinist, a face of Chinese creases, obscene gestures of a Greek phallic dance, contortions of assumed ecstasy. A young man has a cruel mouth, discontent, or at least unsatisfaction, in his eyes: the usual human dilemma.

One is described as 'God's idea of a don: a youngish man in his late thirties with a girl's expectant face, but a bald domed cranium of prodigious exaltation'. Bobby Longden's beautiful peroxidized hair made its appearance—actually it wasn't peroxidized, but merely looked it, of such a coppery gold, naturally curled too. Bobby was a great friend of Richard, and a still closer one of Cyril; I faintly disapproved, as I did of all the 'Sligger' set, and of Sligger Urquhart himself. I thought he had a deleterious softening effect upon the young men he surrounded himself with, but I may have been wrong. The only thing that interested me in that old Catholic pussy-cat was that his father, an idiosyncratic figure, had known Karl Marx. Sligger inherited his papers, which didn't interest him in the least; he handed them over to the Catholic Workers' College, where they slept. He had no intellectual interests whatever; his were snobbery and, I suppose, religion. I can hear his creaky, unctuous voice even now, see the pink creased features of an old boy, tired blue eyes, and loose blue lips.

Bobby, however, must have been a great dear; everybody loved him—Cyril and he were supposed to have been united in an embrace on a sofa for fourteen hours. Talented, charming and kind, not too clever, he was already beginning to have a civilizing influence as Headmaster of Wellington—which Charles

Henderson had found so austere and barrack-like (in spite of producing Harold Nicolson)—when a bomb descended on the school and, selectively, obliterated the Headmaster.

A familiar figure at the Musical Club was 'an intelligent but fleshly Etonian, who sits and listens elegantly, self-contained; a shining rim of white collar appears, rather clerically, above his dinner-jacket.' This was Dundas; the dons of Christ Church, and the grander colleges, changed for dinner. It was odd that, as time went on, I resented the cat-and-mouse game he had played with me at the House, more and more. I never ceased to play it back on him; the game gathered momentum, and I teased him. He resented my turning my back on my old college, of which I had been so proud; shortly I began to reject their invitations—I think genuinely enough: they were not the kind of people I wanted to know, and I was not sorry for opportunities of bringing that home. Some young Scottish peer at New College, I think an Elgin, was anxious to make my acquaintance; Dundas wrote to me on his behalf. That settled the matter; however, I teased Dundas with a correspondence holding out hopes before closing down. He won the round with his argument that it was a duty, one should do one's best for the young men, etc.; he was right, but I didn't let his young peer make my acquaintance.

When, later on, he was occasionally brought to dine at All Souls and I happened to be presiding, I never bade him up or talked to him, but left him modestly at the bottom of the board. Once I embarked on a torment which gave me delicious pleasure, all the more because my companion was quite oblivious of what was happening. Crossing the bridge in Blenheim Park with Salter, then Sir Arthur, I spied a figure in a shabby raincoat surrounded by a crowd of under-age schoolboys. Dundas was in his element, but catching sight of me shrunk into the shelter of the parapet, to avoid notice. So I led Salter across the bridge, straight through the witnessing group, under Dundas's nose; Salter, with the imperceptiveness of the great civil servant and hopelessly heterosexual, having no idea of what naughtiness I was up to.

The window in the Music Room fascinated me, I do not now know why; I called it the Magic Window—it opened a casement of the imagination, I suppose, while the music was playing.

While a little fugal movement of Beethoven's was in constant transition between major and minor, the window was 'fading as evening advanced, while we have been wandering in the fields of the morning'. Later, 'while the muscles rippled over the arms of the woman at the piano, the heavy laden branches waved across the window like plumes. As the window darkens it becomes more and more unreal, the trees leaving a purple shadow in the oncoming dark.'

I fear my attention cannot have been given wholly to the music: I was easily distractable, then. I remember being put off by the feminine affectation of Beatrice Harrison, a good cellist—but she distracted from the music with her fripperies, calling attention to herself. Harriet Cohen, for whom Vaughan Williams wrote his difficult Piano Concerto, was a more serious artist; so too Myra Hess, whose playing of the Brahms Intermezzi always moved me. One of the regulars was Vere Somerset of Worcester College, who came up to us with a silly riddle I have not forgotten. Indeed, he had a streak of silliness—though nothing like the falsetto silliness of Garrod. I never much liked mere donnish silliness, of which John Sparrow made a perverse cult: I used to call his pet cronies among his seniors, Garrod, Farquie (Farquharson of University College), and Geoffrey Madden, talented, clever, excellent scholar, who never made anything of any of it, his 'Old Sillies'. Vere Somerset, however, made something of his talents; not very good as a history tutor, I fancy, he at least wrote an opera. Today I think of him every time I pass through the archway, with his name inscribed, into the further garden beyond the lake at Worcester—the garden he loved, which has given me some of my intensest moments of happy solitude in my last years at Oxford.

That lake—with its backward look at the noble front of the Provost's Lodgings, a country house in the middle of the city, the forward view dominated by the Italianate tower of St Barnabas, Hardy's 'ritualistic church of St Silas'—has its own unforgettable memory: Nevill Coghill's production of *The Tempest*, the most breath-taking production I have ever seen. As Prospero's barge was rowed away into the darkening distance and Ariel ran out across the water to say farewell, the moon rose upon the scene. The young men were just coming back from the anguish of the

Second War. One's heart turned over at the beauty and poignancy of it all: I unashamedly wept.

Once some association—sound or smell, as with Proust—aroused

an unexpected memory after more than fifteen years: the unforgettable rancid smell of the saddler's shop at the bottom of East Hill at home, to which Father sent me on rare errands with bridle or bit, a belt or a whip to be repaired. The tutelary deity of this dark hole was old Sam Clymo, with his slow deliberate way of quizzing a small boy, his grey eyes opening wide and fixed in a glassy stare through old-fashioned pince-nez, perched precariously on the end of his nose, shaking them to and fro so that I wondered when they would fall off. They never did, but it was a fascination to watch him shuffle about behind the counter; a never-ending subject of wonder was his breathing apparatus, he wheezed and queazed through thick bubbling lips and porpoise mouth, the breath whistled in and out, with scraps of gruff remarks and mumbled questions. 'You can't ride a horse? Then what do you want a bridle for?' 'D'your father give you the whip? That's what little boys ought to have.' Or he would tease me with, 'Ee ed'n your father', and this annoyed me: I would answer him back. 'Get along 'ome now!'

Outside was the sound of the rattling, white-coated china-clay wagons, the jangle of harness as an empty cart came down the hill. Inside was the dark haunt of a mystery, the saddler's trade. Behind the counter were rows and rows of drawers and boxes: whatever was in them all? Nails and studs and brass heads and bits of every size and description, festoons of reins hanging at the side, saddles and spurs, whips and leggings. From the doorway at the back of the crowded shop came the noise of hammering and tapping, the beating of leather: the suggestion of the mysterious masculine world into which I was never initiated.

What a curious association for the Musical Club at Oxford—anything might come into one's mind at any moment, whenever the active will was suspended. As if that were not enough, there were odd psychic experiences, to which I have been accustomed all my life, frequent if irregular examples of telepathy—as to which there need be no doubt, considering the fact of wireless communication; and an active dream-life, to fill up any vacant spaces. Letters, for example. Often someone I hadn't thought of for months or years would come into my mind just before the post arrived—a letter from him or her had arrived at the lodge and was just on its way over to my room. I dare say many people have similar experiences. This was odder: while I was in Cambridge I kept thinking that I had received a letter from my old headmaster during a tutorial, so that I put it by unread under the books on my table. So strong was the feeling that I had received this unread letter that I looked for it on my return, under the books and everywhere. Almost immediately 'the letter arrived, in substance as well as in mind.'

These unaccountable, subliminal coincidences—about which Arthur Koestler has written—continue. While writing the passage in an earlier chapter about Richard Pares's dynastic marriage to Janet Powicke, I had not thought of her for a great long while, I shortly heard that—unexpectedly, for she was years younger— she died just at that time: she must have sent a thought in my direction at the end.

Somewhere I have accounts of strongly visual dreams; there was one of 'Professor Gilbert Murray living at the North Pole', another of 'Colonel Lawrence in the Garden of Eden'—not surprisingly, the gardener turned out to be Lionel Curtis. Now here was a nightmare. Someone had been murdered: it was found to be Professor Walter Raleigh, whom I had never seen. No one could tell who had done it, and we all went in terror of more murders being committed. There was a shadowy episode of a ride home late at night to a strange place on the outskirts of a town, where roads and houses were unfinished, with vacant plots. We were next rushed back to a grim building in the town, for the murderer had been found: a pallid puffy girl with lank black hair, bobbed but unkempt. The trial was going on, onlookers frightened, while the girl showed no interest at all, just the despair in her eyes of someone faced with hanging (unlike a Myra Hindley). I was taken to see the body, the impress of the figure on the bed, streaming with sweat and some stains of blood.

At the end I saw the wound on his body, a knife-stab in the stomach, very neat and swift, a hole clotted with congealed blood like jelly.

This may have been a reflection of one or other of my horrid operations—'like a stuck pig' was my schoolboy observation upon the first of them. Shortly after, I ran into my (recent) surgeon.

On the way down St Aldate's I passed Ronnie Knox on the other side, carrying an attaché case, on which I imagined I saw the initials, R.A.K. I must have invented them. Then to the School of Art to see an exhibition of paintings, chiefly of Cornwall. Homesickness took me there … and who should come in but Mr Bevers, my surgeon. A curious sensation at seeing, for the first time after my operation, the man who saved my life then. Only a few feet off he stood, and I standing by with his handiwork all down my stomach. I wondered if he would recognise me; the doubt put me into too uneasy a frame of mind to talk to him when he did. He gave me the opportunity, but I thought it a hard life for a surgeon of his standing if all the people whose lives he had saved came up and addressed him familiarly. [Again, I see the young man: too sensitive, both proud and modest, only too much aware, one skin too few.]

So I left, and consoled myself with a rare walk, which I save up over long periods to go alone: into the old part of the town around St Ebbe's, which might never exist so far as the university is concerned. There it is, much as it was in the eighteenth century, some streets wide, others narrow and deep like canyons, following the same lines as they have since the Middle Ages. Paradise Square was at its best today, with the wind in the trees of the enclosed gardens: in return I wrote a poem on it.[1]

This area was much to the fore in medieval times, for here were the Blackfriars, and the Greyfriars, to whose truly great philosophers Oxford owed its European reputation.[2] Paradise Square was a monastic or, rather, friars' paradise or garden, today the

[1] Published in *Poems of a Decade*.
[2] Cf. *Oxford in the History of the Nation*.

whole area obliterated by a mammoth shopping centre. Why couldn't the shopping centre have been placed a little farther out, on the site of the disused Bletchley line railway? Plenty of room there, for approaches too. I used to reconstruct Paradise Square in my mind as it ought to be—as it once was: decent eighteenth-century houses like a modest London square, the garden re-integrated and replanted in the middle. Instead of that, Paradise Square and London squares are alike destroyed for the shopping centres of a hideous demotic society. Any aesthete must *hate* its guts—as in fact all the men of genius of our time have done and do: Eliot and Trevelyan, Housman and Bridges and Yeats, Evelyn Waugh and the Sitwells, John Betjeman and his friends, John Piper, and Osbert Lancaster who has caricatured it so truthfully. To these I add my modest name.

From St Ebbe's into Christ Church Meadows: 'There was Ronnie Knox again, where I usually meet him, for we take our walks at the same hour. He was reading his breviary as he walked; so I took out my pass book and read in that, as I went down the avenue in front of him. I found that I had a balance of about £70 in my earthly treasury, the Midland Bank.'

Longer tramps I took in company. Here was a summer one, in high wind, with Bruce McFarlane and Douglas Woodruff. Up to Headington, down the valley and up again to Elsfield; over the high country from which one sees Brill and the Chilterns. Thence, instead of the high Roman road, along the level and down the dip to Beckley: we stopped at a gateway to look out over Ot-moor (shortly to be drowned for a reservoir, to accommodate the insane population explosion, proliferating like hell). In the fore-ground a sloping field of waving grasses, at the bottom a long line of lichened red roofs, the barns of the farm.

We had a grand tea—lettuce, radishes, home-made apricot jam—in the inn. High tea was laid in the sitting-room for a cricket team; shortly the team arrived, a gathering of red-faced country youths. How few fine grown-up men one finds in these country places round Oxford: where have they all gone? The only one I saw during the afternoon was the innkeeper himself, a large strong-armed man, but with a paunch and a wooden leg. The war, I take it, our Enemy: one constantly sees in these houses a photograph of a young man of ten years ago in uniform, beneath it a sprig of leaf to keep his memory green.

Today there are their names and their sons' on the memorials of both wars in the churches—at Hinton Waldrist, for example, the whole family of the squire, Loder-Symonds, wiped out, the mother dying in the midst of these griefs, before they were even over.

A group of people whom Woodruff knows, among them Evelyn Waugh, come to stay a while at the inn in summer. They had left their photos on top of the piano; the landlady, who had a redder face and a larger bosom than I have ever seen (a redder face than Steel-Maitland and a larger bosom than Bishop Temple), was proud of her *clientèle*. She had been promised a copy of the book on Rossetti [!] which Evelyn Waugh was writing there last summer. We came home through the wooded part of Woodeaton. We stood a long time on the crest of Beckley Hill, looking out over Otmoor, while the wind raged in the trees, tearing their sprays. It was like the thunder of the sea running into the bay at home, under a strong sou'wester; walking under the elms with the wind in their upper branches was like walking undersea, with the noise of the breakers above one's head.

In an autumn storm I tempted myself with a dangerous wind-walk.

October 16th: A tremendous wind is raging through Oxford; in the gardens the trees are tearing about, branches being ripped off, the tops thrashing about like the sea. Inside, the rooms are full of noises, the panelling creaks, panes of glass rattle, doors bang, in the chimney there is a hollow roar. At the height of it I went for a wind-walk, and struggled round Addison's Walk: a superb sensation beating up against the wind, leaning on it, being buffeted by it and having to run. I kept hoping and fearing a tree would fall across the path; at the corner, where the duck-pond is, such a gust of wind and rain came together that I was frightened by the dangerously swaying trees. Down the Walk behind me not a soul was out in it, nor anyone ahead: everybody was safely indoors, only I foolhardy enough to go out tempting the wind ...

[A few days later] Cruttwell and I went round the Meadows to view the devastation: a score of big trees felled, three of them in the Broad Walk ripping up railings and hollowing out enormous pits. It gave one a strange sense of satisfaction to see the destruction. Some of the larger trees have fallen right across the river and block it completely. Cruttwell has a countryman's knowledge of trees and how they fall. In front of the Physick Garden a poplar had gone; apparently they break off a few feet above ground, for their roots hold strong while their trunks are hollow and liable to snap off. He pointed out a hornbeam, a splendid creature at the turn of the Cherwell: I've often wondered what it was, for its bark is like a beech, but the trunk splits into several a short way up. (A playing-ground at Perpignan is surrounded by superb hornbeams, to give shade—too hot to have it open to the sun.) A big willow had been uprooted further on—the wood looked stringy and strong. C. said that the willow trunk didn't want to split at all; exceptionally hard, it makes the best cricket-bats. News to me!

At the end of the summer term I regularly stayed on into vacation for a month or so, to *earn* some money by examining, instead of scrounging as in academic institutions, and throughout society, today. 'I have all this place to myself again now: term is over and everybody has gone away.' Indeed I always loved inhabiting it, like an empty palace, to myself alone. 'Richard has gone, it may be for eighteen months': he had a Rockefeller Fellowship to undertake researches into his chosen subject, Sugar and the West Indies, in the archives there and in the United States—a task to which he devoted himself with exemplary, inhuman thoroughness. Here I may take the opportunity to inform the scholarly world how he came by his subject. He hadn't an idea of his own for one: Kenneth Bell of Balliol suggested it to him. *Sugar!* Fancy anyone not having a subject of his own he wants to pursue—my mind was teeming with them, and always has been: all too many. For a work of scholarship, as with any other art or discipline, to be a creative work the idea behind it should be an inspiration of one's own, not a reach-me-down, like a commodity in a shop. Gibbon was not indebted to anyone else for the idea of *The Decline and Fall*, or Macaulay or Froude for their histories: they were part of their being, bone of their bone, flesh of their flesh. This is one of the differences between the work of a real writer, and even the best of academic work.

Penderel Moon had left college, on his way to a career more remarkable than any other of the Fellows—except Lawrence of Arabia—in India. 'And now Jimmy, who has forgiven me and stayed overnight, left before lunch.' I don't know now what Crowther had to forgive me for—perhaps for not being Marxist enough, or at any rate too independent-minded a Marxist. In the long run he did not forgive me for that. He may have thought of me as an apostate from the true faith, as Harold Laski did later—*he* described me as an apostate from my class. What about him? He was an apostate from his—well-to-do Manchester middle-class. Nor could that lot of the *New Statesman*—Kingsley Martin in particular—forgive me as a working-class product for not growing up the way *they* fancied: middle-class as they were. Imagine it: growing up in the image of second-rate publicists like Laski and Kingsley Martin! Indeed, the idea is unimaginable, it is so comic. As a Labour man, inside the Labour Movement, I always found myself in agreement with, and intellectually con-vinced by, another West-Country, working-class type: Ernest Bevin, for whom the *New Statesman* lot never had a good word, great man as he was, and little as they were. (That was why.)

I love the story of old Ernest, at the Victory Celebration after the election of 1945, greeting Kingsley Martin with ''Ullo, oogly! 'ow long before you'll be stabbin' us in the back?' It was just three weeks. What a hopeless lot they were, disastrous to the Labour Movement, always wrong, when what it most needed was serious-minded, responsible, intelligent leadership. This was precisely what Left Intellectuals are incapable of—I notice their successors just as bad, just as irresponsible and silly, malicious and malevolent, today. What accounts for it? Lack of any sense of political realism, for one thing; lack of any sense of responsibility, for another; *no* judgment, for a third. Perhaps that is enough to account for them.

Or Jimmy may have thought me becoming snobbish, my head turned by (the old) All Souls? Any reader of this book may judge of that for himself: it is pretty obvious that I thought myself the equal—and rather more than the equal—of any grandee going. It is just that interesting people are more interesting than uninteresting ones; it is also obvious that people are *not* equal in capacities, or talents, or interest, or looks, or muscles, or whatever. The very next sentence in the Diary makes my preference plain: 'So I have the place, as I wanted, to myself.'

'But not entirely to myself,' for there followed one of those odd experiences I sought.

As I came through the Radcliffe Square and into the front quad, by the iron gate, I found the Manciple and the Porter waiting in the lighted cloister, a light at the end, through the Chapel door. I thought of the Chancellor's procession through the quad today [evidently the Encaenia], which caught me between the two gates, so that I could neither go back nor forward out of the way. I said, 'What's doing tonight, Manciple? Is there a party?' The Porter stifled a guffaw. The Manciple replied to my further questioning as to what was afoot: 'It's Professor Davis being brought back tonight to rest in the College Chapel.' The Ante-chapel was lit up on both sides; when I came down again from my bedroom, the stained-glass windows were dark and no lights in the porch. But the place has its other inhabitant, and it is frightening. Is it Davis, or just the empty shell of the man? If one were to go into the Chapel now, there would be everything one recognised as him, except the man himself. Anyhow, I haven't the place to myself, when I look from my window to the darkened front that the Chapel windows present to the world.

I was alone with this *revenant*.

H. W. C. Davis had succeeded Sir Charles Firth as Regius Professor; but only for a couple of years: worn out with administrative work in the civil service during the war, he died in his early fifties, another war casualty. Before leaving for home, I spent one of the 'oddest of evenings' at the Firths'.

All day heavily engaged with examination papers, all the afternoon (drowsily), and all the evening with some revulsion. Then by bus (again—'The Evening Bus to Kidlington': will it ever be written?) up the Banbury Road to dine with the Firths. R. warned me that Lady Firth was a witch, and rather malicious. I found that that was what she was pretending, but beneath was an unhappy, nervous, overwrought woman. [She was in fact a little mad.] She told me a queer story of Robert Bridges's wickedness, as she called it, all irresponsibly: how Mrs Daniel had sent him on his birthday a rare book from her husband's old Press, and Bridges had sent her five pounds, just like that. It was true that she wanted it for a new winter coat, being poor; but it was carelessness in an old friend to hurt her feelings in that way.

Perhaps this was rather casual of the grand old man: he was in a way 'spoiled' by fortune and fame, his magnificent looks and female adulation, and he was never considerate: he had the ruthlessness (and integrity) of the pure aesthete.

In December I went up to tea with him, 'not really so satisfactory today as two or three weeks ago: no haul of phrases to come back with, but Chilswell as usual placid, and radiating a quiet ordered beauty. [That was Mrs Bridges's doing, a Waterhouse.] Old Robert more tousled and leonine than ever, but getting deaf. He's within sight of the end of his long poem: if his work goes well for the next three weeks, he says, it should be printing before Christmas.' This was, of course, *The Testament of Beauty*. It is difficult to convey the sense of rarefied, pinnacled respect with which Robert Bridges was regarded at the end of his long life, he is so absurdly disregarded today—partly because Hopkins, whom he gave to the world, is so highly regarded. It is probable that Bridges is underestimated today, as we overestimated him then, his was such a formidable, uncompromising personality. All the same, the message of *The Testament of Beauty*, that only aesthetic experience redeems life from the slime, was also Proust's, and Ruskin's, and Joyce's: as Bridges said to me, 'Joyce's aesthetics are my aesthetics'; and that his work was essentially rationalist, not religious, 'it goes against the clergy', (Hopkins for one). He told me, when the book came out, that he was sending copies to King George V—to whom it was dedicated—Maxim Gorki, and Joyce: a curious trinity, I reflected, but characteristic of him, like nobody else.

Lady Firth's reflection on Bridges had no effect on my opinion of him, any more than subsequent depreciation of him, by such as John Wain, for example—not to be compared with him as a poet. I found her more disturbing 'when she talked of my rooms and the man of upstairs. Do I see him, that handsome workman-like fellow in his late twenties, dark hair and violet eyes? That figure is a construction of the mind: I don't think I have ever seen the original of him anywhere, yet his image I see, in the dark blue overalls, sleeves rolled up above the muscular arm; but always in the boxroom, never in the bedroom. It can't be Birt, whom I never saw; which makes it the odder.'

We clearly stimulated each other; for 'a good deal more of this kind of thing she talked, to Firth's evident discomfort; he got up and walked about. Of the room in Pembroke where Chandler had poisoned himself; of their lunching there one day, and the depression the atmosphere gave her ("such terracotta wallpaper!"). Only a fortnight after, Mowat had come back with a rope in his portmanteau to hang himself on the peg behind the door.' Oman told me that there had been three suicides in a row in that room, both number 2 and number 3 averring that the association would not disturb them in the least; with the third the sequence ended. 'She told me of her queer experience going upstairs to her dressmaker's in a by street and, feeling the horror of the place, saying aloud: "And it was here she murdered the child: here in this fixture she placed the body." A servant-girl story, of course; and much else about willing the haunting presences of former occupants away.' She evidently lived on her nerves; it wasn't very good for mine.

Poor lady, she rather took to me—her own son, who came into Firth's library after dinner, was a mental case—and led me out into her private herb garden, which she tended 'with the same frustrated ferocity', and taught me the names of the herbs: tansy, bergamot and tarragon; Shakespeare's rue, fennel and hyssop and lemon verbena. 'I brought back a leaf of tansy, crushed and broken to bring out the rustic scent.'

And people?

On my way back into college that night I encountered a very different variation of the human comedy. In the Radcliffe Square, when I arrived at the Iron Gate, an exhibition of *l'homme moyen sensuel*:

A happy group of young men, some American, all drunk; and very affectionate—arms of one around the neck of another, around each other's waist, hands in each other's hair; the dark Square alive with voices, some soft and incantatory, some loud and strong: 'Fuck', 'you go and fuck', 'you'd do', 'bugger'. [Dear boys, they were only letting off steam.] Should I go and join them? But no: for me the inexorable gate and the lonely life of shadows. Later, I went out into the Square alone, for consolation. This time, against the wall under the chestnut in Exeter garden, a young man and a girl, small and in black, entwined. They loosened their grip as I and two quavering old women passed. In the streets towards the Broad and the Turl nothing and nobody, not a soul; even the wall under the chestnut was deserted when I came back. Once more, in at the strait gate and over the grass, which has in the drought become a Sahara, like my heart. Up to my room, where the examination papers lie in heaps upon the floor.

At one dinner party of young colonials I deliberately wrote down their names, 'out of curiosity to see what will become of them'. What did? Something came of Eugene Forsey, 'if that's how it is spelt: a quick, intelligent Canadian, of liberal, possibly Labour, sympathies.' I think he became something of a figure in Canadian politics, was it C.C.F. (Canadian Commonwealth Federation)? Forder, a rather impassive, charming South African, who didn't utter much, but gazed at one with large, serious blue eyes; Morgan, a clever, talkative Welsh South African, who had Lloyd George on the brain and recounted his oratorical exploits; Meadly, a handsome dark fellow, with grey eyes, dark skin and crisp curly hair. There was an awkward undercurrent to the talk,

about South African difficulties with the native races, which
Morgan wouldn't let drop. Meadly took no part, but settled
further and further back into his chair, getting more uneasy;
until he could stand it no longer, and got up to wait on us all
with whisky and soda. 'One's own nerves create subtleties, but
the gesture of serving looked like an instinctive reaction at that
juncture, himself probably unaware.' I wonder now what became
of them all?

Tea with the Kenneth Bells, I suppose in the Balliol region of
King's Mound—what became of him was as strange a story as
any.

Outside in the garden filled with autumn sunlight, I sat
on the steps and talked to Mrs Bell, resting on a couch,
not having recovered yet from a seventh child. Ugh! A
fine, long-suffering woman. One of the numerous family,
a boy of about eight, climbed dangerously down the
iron frame of a verandah from an upper window. Today
came a young fellow up for his Science Previous, having
already failed in Mechanics. Today he had been doing
Biology, an experiment he knew by heart yet made a
mess of it. He needed a small young rabbit, but had been
given a large one; he felt like writing at the bottom of
his paper, 'I hate this rabbit.' He was charming; under
eighteen, strongly built, broad shoulders and shapely
legs; a winning English face, fair and rosy, with a shock
of golden hair growing low down on his forehead; small
arched mouth made for love and taking little phrases such
as 'I hate this rabbit', blue eyes sparkling with mock
indignation.

I expect this attractive specimen of normal humanity made a
better success of practical biology later on.

A terrible French-Irish-American, brought in to lunch
today by Rudler, had a comic exchange with old Spenser
Wilkinson, who couldn't quite catch his English, spoken
in such a *mitrailleuse* fashion. He began effusively:

'I am very honoured to meet you, Dr Wilkinson.'
Uncle Spenny blinked like Edward Lear, in whose beard two

owls and a hen, four larks and a wren, had all made their nests:

'What d'you say?'

'It is a vur' great pleasure to meet you like this, Professor.'

'Why?'

'I have read many times your articles in the *English Historical Review* with much pleasure.'

'Never written anything in the *English Historical*. Still, that's neither here nor there. Go on!'

The visiting American found it difficult to go on from there.

A worse misunderstanding befell a complete foreigner, with a slighter hold on the language. Sir William Holdsworth—'with the learning of an elephant and the brain of a pea' (E.F.J.)—was at the head of the table; but shy, and with no social graces, said nothing to the foreigner, until the latter thought of the one peculiarity of All Souls, the former Bible Clerks, and asked: 'Have you any undergraduates here?' To which Holdsworth replied briefly, 'None', and relapsed into silence. This baffled the foreigner, who, after an interval, inquired politely: 'And how is she then?' To which Sir William replied, no less baffled: 'How is who?' The visitor, still more at a loss, said: 'The nun.' Sir William, becoming embarrassed, blushed scarlet: 'I never said anything about a nun.'

He was also getting rather cross at an improper insinuation, when the foreigner tried to explain that he had heard Sir William say something about a nun. This was more than the eminent historian of law could face. He got up and left. Someone else had to explain to the foreign visitor the vagaries of English speech, and the difference between 'None' and 'Nun'.

Staying on in Oxford for all that dreary examining, I was late home for vacation and it didn't last long. I resumed my ritual of walks and talks with my schoolfriends, or on my own. One evening there was

an interesting and rare enough conversation with Father, all about the Martins and Loverings, the china-clay families [to which we did not belong], the clay and tin. Evidently Father has an eye for character: he mimicked a man I had forgotten, blowing out his cheeks, sticking out his belly, putting one hand behind his rump and strutting in a portly, self-important way. All in a second or two. He sketched for me the character of old Cap'n Billy Martin, who made the fortunes of that family: terrible inquisitive, pryin' into everybody's business, wantin' to knaw the ins and outs of every mortal thing; shrewy, but talkative and would tell 'ee all about other people's affairs, an' sometimes about his own, when in a good temper. His son Hedley, very reserved, goes about his job without talkin' to the men or even to the shift bosses, except when he has got something to tell them; very pleasant usually, but liable to be sulky: once you're in his black books, look out—you may as well shift for yourself.

Father had a characteristic story of the clay works and Captain Billy's know-how. 'A Mr Phillips came to ask Cap'n Billy about the setts, and whether any of 'em would be any good. Cap'n Billy was wary, but couldn't keep him from suspecting a likely proposition at West Carclaze. Cap'n Phillips lets on that he thinks he'll take the sett, and will go and see Sidney Hancock, Rockingham Gill's agent, in the morning. But Cap'n Billy goes tonight, and the morning's too late for the sett when the other turns up at the office.'

Rockingham Gill was the London lawyer who had bought the great manor of Treverbyn from the Trevanions of Caerhays, the family from whom Byron was descended. I have told their story in a series of *Times* articles; Byron's cousin Trevanion, on the verge of bankruptcy, sold their estates, including this one, which turned out to be solid china-clay worth millions. The Rockingham Gill family lived off the royalties alone for three generations. Years later I met a daughter or granddaughter, who showed me early photographs of those works and told me a pretty story about it all.

Another of Father's stories was of 'old Cap'n Minnear striking tin at Buckey. He went over a hedge to ease himself, and while doing it noticed a stone in the field which promised a good-quality tin.' On his useful errand he had struck a rich lode, and working on the spot began soon after. I had forgotten this story. So that is how Minnear's Lane up there came by its name: I have often wondered, and I'll bet nobody at St Austell today knows how. As often happens, the original lode of tin is followed by china-clay (kaolin). 'Now there is a stream of clay at Buckey. Hedley Martin calls in there to see what the stream is coming from the works, and whether the quality is good or no. If it's small or poor, there's somebody shifted, or sacked, up in the Higher Quarters. I had not forgotten the noise of Buckey Stamps crushing tin, from my childhood: we heard the sound inter- mittently in the distance, something soothing in its regular rhythm and association, for we only heard it when the wind was in the south-east, and that meant fair weather, often a clear night of stars.'

Today one or two of 'Cap'n Billy's' descendants are among my oldest and dearest friends. Captain Billy had married a remarkable Carclaze woman, herself descended from Rebecca Pitt, way back, one of the Pitts of Boconnoc; whose story there in that splendid park and rambling great house, now reduced and shorn of much of its glory, I have written but not yet published.

What a happy harvest from one evening's talk with Father! Evidently living in a working-class home was not all loss—and I didn't need to cultivate the people, like Etonians such as George Orwell, with his *Road to Wigan Pier*, and the cult of squalor. (Fancy making a cult of him, and taking no notice of my evi- dence—the middle-class asses!) It was rarely that Father could be got to talk, he was so deaf; but he had a sly, Cornish sense of humour and an occasional 'h'; my mother had neither, though my character and traits, such as they are, come from her. He was a good man, decent and honest, hard-working and kind; she was a beautiful bitch, whom he—innocent that he was— adored. Poor souls, they had little in the way of education; he had gone for a year or two, at a penny or tuppence a week, to the first National School set up under the Act of 1870, and left at nine to begin work. My mother had even less schooling, but was a far more striking personality, a figure out of a D. H. Lawrence novel. I cannot write about her: it still upsets me too much.

Tonight, going to Carn Grey and Garker, a full-blown story

came into my head: 'Exile' or 'The Emigrant', all hanging upon the pathetic episode told us by a cousin in Father's family I met only once. When she arrived at the house of our old aunt in Michigan—Father's only sister—she stood outside the window looking into the lamp-lit room. When the old woman saw who it was, the tears streamed down her face, overjoyed to see somebody from home after all those years. This story I did write, but did not publish; I do not know what was the impediment: no encouragement I expect, and too easily discouraged—until I learned the hard way never to take notice of what fools think about anything. Birds are better—I watch the pretty things outside the window as I write.

And here was the life of the village, as I walked through it on a late night walk.

Nearly all the houses in darkness and, it being Sunday night, a good deal of copulating going on behind dark windows. Lights shone pathetically in the spinsters' windows: nothing doing behind their blinds, as if they hoped to attract some male moth to their bright patches. One at Miss Lewis's and Miss Parry's, for instance [two of my old schoolmistresses who lived together, or at least shared a house]; one high up in that angular cliff of cement wicked Uncle Bill had built. Miss Teague's bedroom also showed a rushlight glimmer: it popped out as I hove into view. She was a dedicated twitcher of curtains, and occasionally entertained Father; in return for what she received, she would send us cream, skimmed from the milk of the Boys' Scattered Home, of which she was in charge. She did not much like me; I fancy she thought I saw through her.

Across from it, with his back against the door of our old store, was Jimmy Champion, talking in the subdued confidential tone of the half-drunk to Tom Bazley, also well boozed. I thought of the times when I would find Jimmy out there o'nights, his dog standing by: we used to hear Clyma beating his wife across the alley, and try hopelessly to stop it, sometimes make a successful distraction, when he—a half-crazed former soldier—would rush out with his dog: we had scattered, but had stopped the fun.

So on, past the farm, looking blind and empty out over the undertown fields, beyond Lost Wood to the sea. But no Gwen there to talk to tonight, from high up over the wall, whence she would reach me down a camellia. She's married at last, leaving her mother with George and the hind to the memories of that house, where the father went mad, threatened and beat his wife, locked her up and had anyway ruined the farm. He spent most of his days at Bodmin, in the Lunatic Asylum, where he ended by cutting his throat. No loss.

George, a lanky, gawpy fellow with a kind smile, lived the rest of his days in that house—now obliterated by the extravagantly vast offices of E.C.L.P., the combine which has taken the place of the old St Austell china-clay families. George had the agreeable peculiarity of hiding away money in odd places, cups and jugs and mugs, boxes and drawers, holes and corners, cupboards and crevices. When he died a fine collection was made.

'On to my old school and the gateway—one of "Five Gates" as it was known to Father's generation—and the view up the slopes to the three trees on the brow, which I once wrote a little poem about. As far down as the stables of Hicks's Brewery—ominous place in old days, for at the corner there the girls coming home from shop used to be frightened by drunks, or else the noises of the horses kicking in their stalls behind the glazed windows. So back to New Road, and better-to-do middle-class houses.' Once one of these had a spot of romance for me: lived in by a retired non-commissioned officer of the Indian Army, with a good job in the town; his wife, picked up from behind the bar of a pub, with a corrected Cockney accent: she said 'dee' for 'day', for fear of saying 'die'. Compared with us, they lived in comfort. The secret of the attraction for me was the romance of India, the life of camps, bugles blowing, all the fellows about and the great heat over the plains. With her black beads of eyes, her kindly merry smile, she didn't know that; the joke was, she had a crush on the green youth.

At Porthpean one evening an exciting long ship lay in the bay, with funnel right at the stern: I couldn't make out what it was. 'Then I heard someone say it was an oil-tanker: what was it doing so close inshore? I turned round, and it was Connie Coode, who was so handsome and athletic a lad at school, famous for his strength and grip of hand. He was with his girl, of course, dark, liquid black eyes; Connie blue-eyed, curly gold hair. He had met a young man on the *Guildford Castle*, who knew me at Christ Church: it turned out to be Vaughan-Morgan, who lived in an expensive way on my old staircase in Meadows. He's going in for politics, like that charming nullity, Alec Dunglass: this was a preparatory voyage.'

I fear that these were the harsh judgments of a young man envious of the ease with which his affluent contemporaries could ease themselves into politics. Alec Dunglass, better known as Douglas-Home, the fourteenth Earl and all that, did better in politics than I evidently expected; he has won the respect of the historian for the honesty with which he has admitted how wrong he was, as a young man, to support Chamberlain's Appeasement. In those early days Dunglass was a friend of Roger Makins. Roger to me, years later, on Chamberlain: 'Poor Neville: he didn't know what he was doing.' Me to Roger: 'You didn't say that at the time, Roger: you left it to me to say.' Without intending it the Appeasers in the event ruined their country. Poor Connie was a victim. When Appeasement of Hitler brought the Second German War down on our heads in the worst possible conditions, a salvo of bombs upon Connie's ship struck, and left him paralysed all down one side and speechless for life.

My own approach to politics was not at all easy—as usual, the hard way, inconceivably hard; as it turned out, agonizing. Here was a foretaste that summer.

A dissatisfying experience on my way up to Carn Grey this evening: I fell into a meeting of the Workers' Union [to which Father belonged], with Will Adamson, M.P., addressing it. A tame but homely affair: all the people I knew from years of passing up and down that road— Tregonissey Lane End. Old Sam Kent, patriarchal, and half a dozen others leaning up against a half-finished gate outside the carpenter's shop; two sides of the square filled, and a half-circle in the road. George Carnsew was near me, handsome as ever, with those amazingly fierce blue eyes he gets from his mother, a well known street-walker in town in earlier days. On my other side, little Mr German, who bought our poor old piano [I had put some of my earnings into a splendid Ibach], and is devoted to music, which in his case means the cornet. Next him, fellows I was at the elementary school with, heavily set, hairy, unshaven. Any number of their dogs; black dogs, brown dogs, black and white dogs, black, white and brown dogs; an Alsatian crossed with a collie, a terrier or two. One dog was remarkable for the attention he fixed on the speaker, more intently —perhaps more intelligently—than the audience, though even he couldn't help dozing off at times.

What is wrong with these Labour speakers? Why can't they come to grips with the language? Anybody would think that language was their enemy, the way they hold it at arm's length, a trap into which they may fall at any minute. Adamson had no idea how to get across to the people, how to attract their interest. I notice an inability to say a simple thing simply with all these half-educated Labour speakers. Is it Ramsay MacDonald's influence? Or the influence of the House of Commons? The latter, more likely: they have dropped their local dialects, or tried to, on becoming M.P.s, and taken to what they consider Parliamentary English. In consequence, they have lost what natural force their native words may have had, without gaining anything. And the speech was pitched in a tone of indignant expostulation, as if we had been detected in dangerous error. So I went on as soon as I decently could, without uttering a word, though some people seemed to expect me to speak. One more opportunity lost, one more stone upon the grave of my political hopes.

Unfortunately, in the flatness of the surrounding country, with such competitors, such scarecrows, my hopes were encouraged. One could hardly do worse.

10

T. S. Eliot and Others

The year 1929 was decisive for me, both privately and publicly. In politics it really looked as if the rule 'of the hard-faced men who had done well out of the war' was at last coming to an end. Except for the brief nine-month spell of MacDonald's first government, brought to an end by the scare over the Red Letter —I was shocked when I had gone home to Cornwall to find how the credulous people had fallen for this rubbish—the Tories had ruled since they got rid of Lloyd George, the one man of genius on the scene in 1922. The return to the Gold Standard had forced deflation on the country, followed by General Strike and prolonged coal-strike, about which the indolent Baldwin, in the key position to do what was right and necessary, did nothing. What wonder that we young people then were sick of the old men? The men who should have taken their places were dead, except for a few survivors from the holocaust of the war.

In reading this personal account one must keep in mind the background of hope and expectation, the idealism and good will, the ambition to do our best, even a sense of duty. This sense— even if one disagreed with them—was the dominant characteristic among the public figures at All Souls: it certainly had its effect on me. Then, too, the distinguishing mark of college life and conversation was public affairs of every kind, not cricket scores or bumps on the river, or the small change of academic committees. This, too, had its effect: I don't think I should have been so much impelled into politics, if I hadn't become a Fellow of All Souls. I should have been dominantly literary in my external life—as the Diary shows over and over I was in my innermost nature. I was by nature a writer; the Diary itself is evidence of how long and hard the apprenticeship was. But I was also something of a politician, a fanatic and an intriguer, and a far better speaker than a Will Adamson was—which is not saying much. Had I the patience? I can only say that in this year I became a Labour candidate, and remained one for twelve years. As the result of my labours, my home constituency became a Labour seat, the first in Cornwall, in 1945. It was bad enough to be a political candidate, but to be an M.P.!—the life would have killed me. After a severe haemorrhage during the Second War, my doctors *made* me drop it; perhaps nothing else would have done, such was the obstinacy of the brute.

Anyway, here was the background—Hope! We shall see what a false dawn it proved to be: far worse than the deception the generation of 1789 experienced—Wordsworth, Coleridge, Southey—with the way the French Revolution turned sour on them. To us there happened the evil fraud of the election of 1931; Hitler's conquest of Germany in 1933; the Spanish Civil War; the renewal of Germany's bid for *Weltmacht*, the Second War, with its consequences all over the world, the ruin of civilization.

As an historian I put a large part of the blame down to 1931. The panic the Tories engineered against the Labour Movement—over a mere Budget deficit of £75 millions, and going off the Gold Standard, when we should never have returned to it at dollar parity in 1926—produced an overwhelming majority in Parliament and practically wiped out the Labour Party there: 55 M.P.s in a House of Commons of 615! The 'unspeakable assembly', I have called it; for this immense majority proceeded on its way—with another fraudulent election in 1935 (as Amery admitted to me)—all the way along, backing Baldwin, backing Chamberlain, letting down our friends, appeasing our enemies, undermining the Spanish Republic, sapping French will-power, selling out on German rearmament, Austria, Czechoslovakia—until the bemused country woke up and found itself in mortal danger in 1939. In all those years this country was still the foremost European country, with a certain primacy to exert; all that time the Tories had an absolute, overwhelming majority to lead this country and Europe on the right lines. No pacifist lunatic fringe on the Left could have stopped them from the necessary and right policy towards Germany—keeping our

friends together, the alliance firm; the most powerful opponent
of rearmament was Chamberlain himself—in the interest of good
Budgets for his class.

Oh, what a good old time they had of it in the 'thirties! How
well off they were; what a grand time for them, while we saw
every good cause betrayed and sold, our hearts ached with
anxiety, in my case anguished by what I clearly foresaw would be
the end of it all—at any rate, *after* 1931. One could then only
keep in the dreadful business out of apprehension, indignation,
anxiety, fear. When I look round on the ruins of *their* society
today, I hope they like what they so richly deserved.

If I live, I will certainly give my evidence as to what it was
like to put up with it, tell the story of my own candidature down
here in Cornwall—not the stupidest or most gullible of areas:
we didn't have such a bad record against those bloody old men
of the sea. All the same, the Tories down here had not only their
Appeasers, but some ardent pro-Hitlerites—the idiots: as if
playing Hitler's game was going to do them any good!

For the Labour Party the panic put across the country in 1931
was disastrous. A mere rump of 55 M.P.s—all the experienced
Labour leaders out of Parliament, its leader become the old
pacifist sheep, George Lansbury, with the unknown Attlee as
deputy. MacDonald and Snowden had been seduced into the
arms of the enemy—MacDonald had been idolized by simple
Labour folk: in my constituency I have seen a working-class
family in tears at his defection. More important, the whole
balance and working of Parliament was disastrously affected:
a handful of 55 M.P.s couldn't effectively oppose anything;
after the subsequent fraud of 1935 there were still only 155
Labour M.P.s: they couldn't stop Baldwin and Chamberlain.
The so-called 'National' Government could get away with
anything; they proceeded to sell out the vital interests of the
nation, in the interests of their class: they thought Hitler was
anti-Red. This is, quite simply, what was at the bottom of
the ruin of Britain: it enabled Germany to make her second
attempt in immeasurably more favourable conditions than in
1914.

I hope those people responsible, those of them who remain and
are capable of reflecting on the long-term consequences, like

what they see of them. Those of us who went through the 'thirties on the other side didn't much enjoy the experience. I haven't forgotten or forgiven a moment of it—and I have kept the evidence. On the morrow of the unspeakable election—my first experience of these delights—one of the most distinguished men in the country, Gilbert Murray, wrote to *The Times* (in those days it mattered): 'I, in common with millions of my fellow-citizens, voted for the National Government—and regard the result with the deepest dismay.' His dismay was far more justified in the upshot than he can have imagined; it only shows how silly the most distinguished of men can be, over politics. But the theme of this book is Swift's: the universal idiocy of humans in politics.

So much then for the background of the hopes of 1929 to 1931.

I sacrificed literature to politics; but, thank heaven, not wholly. I continued to write—poems, stories, Diary, Notes—mostly for my own private consumption. Even here, it will be seen that the encouragement I received so generously from Eliot was almost entirely of my political writing. It will be seen that he constantly pressed me to contribute articles on these themes, Communism, Marxism, Shaw, to the *Criterion*. Fortunately I seem to have preserved his letters from the first, and in these years they were quite frequent, occasionally two or three in one week. Altogether I must have a *cache* of at least eighty of his letters, besides all the presentation copies of his poems and books he sent me.

There are even more of the letters of Adam von Trott, a famous figure of the German Resistance now. When Christopher Sykes was writing his admirable biography—a remarkable work of reconstruction, considering that he never knew Adam—I made a search for these letters for him, but could not find them among the masses of paper here, my *Nachlass*. It is only in the course of the thorough routing out I have had for this book—as bad as historical research—that I have come upon them at the bottom of a box of my own letters home to the family. My letters to him disappeared in Germany; I have always been sorry for that, for they were among the best I ever wrote: they would have made a symptomatic part of the history of our time, the relations between an Englishman and a German. Moreover, they were a moving record of a despairing love; however, it is all there in the Diary and the poems.

So, in my personal life too, 1929 was decisive.

My first contact with Eliot, I find, was as early as 1927 over a letter I had written to the *Criterion*, which was critical of a piece I did not think much of, by his American friend J. Gould Fletcher. Eliot wrote to me at 'St Austells' (*sic*, he had evidently never heard of the place): 'I will print your interesting letter with pleasure ... I expect to spend a night at All Souls with Geoffrey Faber during this month and hope to have the pleasure of meeting you.' I had evidently answered Fletcher's reply, for in January 1928: 'I should like very much indeed to print your letter ... I should like very much to see you again, and incidentally to hear your opinions on [Henri] Massis and Gide.' Very much interested in André Gide, all of whose books I read and whom I kept up with in the *Nouvelle Revue Française*, I was not a bit interested in Massis, as Eliot was; he was, I think, rather a Catholic reactionary, of no importance anyway.

Meanwhile, there was doubt whether the *Criterion* could continue, because the Lady Rothermere of the day suddenly withdrew her subsidy. 'I shall be all the more sorry if we cannot go on with it, because I had hoped to entice you as a contributor in more ways than merely as a correspondent.' He wanted 'to widen its scope a little and tackle more seriously the kind of problems in which you are particularly interested. And I want to get more men of about your own age whatever their views ... In any event do not fail to let me know whenever you are in London.' There followed a long letter from Faber all about the problem of financing the *Criterion*; his firm in its early stages was pretty hard up.

Eliot in May, sending me a book to review: 'but I am writing primarily to tell you that the *Criterion* intends to survive as a quarterly ... I should very much like to have you as a more frequent contributor. If there is any essay you have written, or want to write for such a periodical, and whenever there is any book you care to review, I hope you will let me know. I wish

that you would occasionally come to London during the vacation.' Next week, 'I have received [Roy] Campbell's poem and
Massis' book ... I am very glad that you agree with me about
Campbell; I shall try to get him to contribute to the *Criterion*.'
Roy Campbell's poem 'Tristan da Cunha' had greatly impressed
me, and I think it was I who pressed Eliot to get Faber's to publish his work, which they did with *Adamastor*. 'About Massis,
well, I had rather wait for an opportunity to talk to you ... About
your other suggestion concerning myself. It is extremely flattering
and kind of you. I am not able to consider it seriously at present,
because the possibility seems to me so remote. But we can talk
of this later.' I wanted him for Professor of Poetry at Oxford.
"Meanwhile and more urgent, you have not answered my suggestion that you should write an article for the *Criterion*. I shall
not be satisfied with little reviews. Apart from the immediate
political questions of the day, is there not some more general
problem on which you would like to write? May I add, as it is
a great compliment to yourself, that my friend Fletcher has
much admiration for you?'

How nice of them, and how friendly they were—far friendlier
than I was, hag-ridden by illness. This was one of the reasons why
I wouldn't go up to London; I preferred to entertain people at All
Souls. Still I can't quite think why I held off so much; I didn't
want to go up to London to hobnob with Eliot—absolutely
charming as he was—still less to meet Fletcher, whom I never did
meet. In June it is: 'What you suggest writing is exactly what I
wanted from you ... Meanwhile please try to find time to
meditate such an article for the December *Criterion* ... I still hope
that you may come to London. Fletcher in particular is most
anxious to meet you.'

To this I did not reply, and was apparently reluctant to write;
for next month,

> I have not heard from you ... but I should be very glad
> if you could let me know whether you think you can do
> such an article as we discussed ... It would fit in very well,
> because we have in view a series of investigations of con-
> temporary creeds as a study of contemporary Socialism and
> Communism. I have thought of dealing myself with the

question of Fascism, and have recently worked through four or five books on the subject. The more I read about it the more uninteresting it seems, but it might be worth while to say even that. What I am trying to do is to find out whether there is any idea in Fascism at all; if not it might be at least worth while to say so. The books on the subject seem to be of two types. Those written by people who wish to prove either how virtuous or how wicked the régime has been; and those who wish to prove that Fascism is the realisation of a magnificent political ideal. The former have a certain scandalous interest, the latter are extremely dull. I only chatter about this in order to give you some notion of the possible series. The question is not to examine particular facts of government, but the importance of certain political ideas.

A week later: 'Go ahead with your article in your own way, and don't worry about fitting it into anything else. I shall be very glad of any reviews also ... I am wondering if you might possibly be in London about the 25th of July. There will be a small *Criterion* dinner on that date, and I should be very happy if you would come as my guest.' What a dear he was, and how anxious to get me up to London; but I hardly ever went there and, though I did go on contributing to the *Criterion*—under constant urging, as one can see—I never went to any *Criterion* dinner to meet anybody. 'P.S. I should like to see anything you write. I have got the *New Statesman*, but have not yet read Connolly's article.' I suppose I was suggesting Cyril to him.

I was still holding back, for in August: 'I will let you off your Communism article until the next number if (1) I can arrange a symposium on Shaw's *Intelligent Woman's Guide* (2) and you would contribute to it about 1000 words' opinion. Have you read the book? I thought of asking Laski, Belloc and Fr D'Arcy among other representative views. But if you are not agreeable, or if I can't work it, I shall try to hold you to your engagement for the December number!' Only three days later, 'I am delighted to have you contribute to the symposium ... but I shall hold you to the "Communism" sooner or later, as there is no one whose opinions on the subject would interest me more. What about a

Note on the *Liberal Industrial Report*, if it can be done from a non-party point of view?' I had evidently suggested that he comment on Julien Benda's *La Trahison des clercs*, making a sensation among intellectuals at the time; Eliot was doubtful, for 'we are sometimes accused of devoting too much attention to ephemeral French bickerings ... The book is slight, and he does not make the best of his thesis.'

As to meeting people, Eliot himself at this time was very selective about the people he would meet. Shaw, for example, was not to his taste. When Lady Astor impulsively rang him up to come and meet Shaw at dinner, Eliot replied, 'Lady Astor, I am afraid I do not have the pleasure of your acquaintance.' So Nancy told me years later, without resentment or malice—after all, she was a Christian if not a Scientist.

In October Eliot makes his first appearance in the Diary.

> I have been in suspense for the last two or three days as to Eliot's taking my Shaw article, and what he will think of the poems. The article is quite aggressive, and makes one or two shots at his own beliefs. But I depend on him to learn if my poems can possibly be thought any good by the outside world. I also wrote to tell Graham Pollard[1] that I found his youthful poems in a drawer at home. Yesterday when I opened the typed letter, half sleeping and half waking, thinking it might be Eliot's, I read with consternation: 'You had better put those poems in the dustbin. I had rather that you did this than keep them, as then I should be relieved of any fear of blackmail.' It was a shock in my state of drowsiness, until I woke up to the fact that it was only Graham Pollard, in the old perverse mood.

Actually Eliot did publish my poems in the end, went through them with his sharp long pencil, threw out one or two, and wrote the blurbs for the first three volumes. So if my poems were good enough for him, they are certainly good enough for his inferior successors in the firm, or the *T.L.S.* which publishes so much journalistic rubbish masquerading as poetry.

Next month he was writing: 'That's satisfactory about Eden; but when I send you a book you must remember that I not only

[1] The eminent bibliographer, son of A. F. Pollard of All Souls.

leave the length of the review to your judgment, but also whether it is worth reviewing *at all*. About the other thing: make it as long as you can: for I told you that I wanted an article and not a review.' I remember now that I felt timid about writing an article—hence all this persuasion, and how patient and courteous Eliot was! He evidently had confidence in my judgment, more than I had—or rather, in other people's.

So if you can write an article on Communism, you needn't bother about more than a reference to the books. In the December *Criterion* you will see a very superficial article by me called 'The Literature of Fascism'; what I want is something of at least the same length by you to succeed (and eclipse) mine, on the Literature of Communism, though you need not call it that.

About the Professorship of Poetry, may I say that Faber has already talked to me about it. I merely don't want you to waste time. The point is that it is an appointment only for a period, so would leave me at the end looking for another job; also that I should have to take an M.A., and I have no time for such kickshaws unless they were pressed into my hand; and I am too disreputable a figure anyhow; and in short I don't want my friends to take that trouble for nothing, as it would be.

He was perfectly right. I longed to have him as Professor of Poetry—the perfect successor to Matthew Arnold long before, by whom he had been much influenced. He once told me that, younger, he could recite whole paragraphs of Arnold's prose; his own was very like, cool, reasoned, lucid, a trifle supercilious. But the second rate academics of the Eng. Lit. establishment wouldn't hear of it: at that time they depreciated his work, as their successors have done mine on Shakespeare. They at last caught up with Eliot: apparently it takes these people about twenty-five years, a generation, to do so. Why don't they know their own rating? I suppose it is a pretty good index to what it is that they can't tell. At any rate the Merton group forked in one of their own as Professor—Garrod—and Oxford had very little opportunity of hearing Eliot, any more than they had of hearing me. I do not repine: their loss.

It was still some months before I could prevail on myself to produce that article on Communism; when I did, Eliot's reaction was interesting.

> It is a satisfaction to know that my article [on the Literature of Fascism] passed your approval; I felt that I had ventured on something beyond my competence. I am also glad to know how you feel about your own; because I had meant to write and suggest that you should follow it up with something which should express your personal views. I found it very profitable reading; but it did lose in vigour from the fact (or as it struck me) that you were merely asking for a fair hearing for something which is maligned but which you cannot support wholly. I liked the tone, but it will be much more interesting to have your own beliefs. So may we say December for your next essay?

I cannot think now why he was so anxious for me to express my own beliefs any further than I had done in the article. I have looked at it again, for the first time since it was written, forty-five years ago—in some trepidation lest it appear nonsense; instead of that the tone is judicious, the argument sensible. The gist of it is the distinction between the great importance of Marxism intellectually—as a social historian I have been influenced by it all my life—and Communism in practice, which does not necessarily follow. Here is the summing up of Marx's *Communist Manifesto*: 'One can agree with a good deal of its diagnosis, without accepting its remedies.' And my conclusion from the whole argument was that it 'makes the arrival of the Labour movement to power almost a certainty, rather than that of a revolutionary proletariat.'

The fact was that working-class horse-sense—like Ernest Bevin's or Herbert Morrison's—saved me from swallowing Communism whole, in the way my middle-class friends did in the 'thirties: Stalin's purges, Communist collaboration with the Nazis against the Social Democrats in the Berlin tram-strike of 1931, the insane Communist strategy that the first priority was to destroy Social Democracy, the Molotov–Ribbentrop Pact, and all. They swallowed everything, those who remained alive to swallow: fools (weren't they?) like Ralph Fox and Maurice Dobb

and Crowther; Spender and Middleton Murry and John Mac-
murray for a time; Christopher Hill for a much longer time. I
wasn't being taken in; I profited greatly from my wide reading
in Marxism, but I never committed myself to Communism. I
was just a Labour man.

On the last day of 1928 Eliot wrote:

> Faber has shown me an essay on the Pitcairn Islanders
> which amused me very much. I understand that your
> object in sending it was to get it published as a book ...
> I should like to use it in the *Criterion*, if there is no great
> hurry. On the other hand, if you really prefer to get it done
> separately, I would gladly urge it on the Woolfs for a
> Hogarth Pamphlet ... Incidentally, you spoke vaguely of
> getting at a certain piece of work that I suggested to you for
> the *Criterion*, during the vacation. I don't want to hustle
> you, but I should like to know whether it will be ready
> soon ...

The booklet on the Pitcairn Islanders had been sent on to me
by Keith Hancock, of whom I was fond. When he went back to
Australia I promised that I would look after his literary interests
as best I could and try and get his articles published over here;
with the result that several of his pieces appeared in the *New
Statesman*. Now I was doing my best for his Pitcairn essay, which
was, I think, ultimately published by Faber—the Woolfs didn't
want it. When Ernest Jacob—whom I also tried to get published
in the *Criterion*—and I both stood for the Chichele Chair of Modern History, Hancock was very keen on Jacob's election. Quite
all right: no expectations from humans.

At New Year 1929: 'I should particularly like to have your
article for the March number ... I look forward to reading it,
but would much more like to have a talk with you. Some day I
hope to get you and Smyth in the ring together.' This was the
Reverend Charles Smyth, a Tory Anglican don at Cambridge I
did not think highly of—Eliot had a *penchant* for him because they
had similar views. 'I am rather puzzled by what you say about
Lancelot Andrewes, as there is so little matter in the book which
could be called political.' I fancy I must have thought Eliot's
declaration of his position in politics as 'royalist'—it reminded

one of the deplorable *Action française* of Charles Maurras—as rather silly, at best irrelevant.

That same month I had promised an essay—'I am counting upon it and looking forward to it.' I was now pressing David Cecil upon him as a contributor: 'I do wish that I had had the suggestion of David Cecil before. I have met him, some years ago, and had kept him in mind as a possible writer; but his name never occurred to me in connexion with Strachey's book, though he should have been an obvious choice ... Will you tell him that I should be very glad if he would suggest something else—or you might be able to suggest for him something suitable for him to do? ever cordially ...'

Next he was returning to me a manuscript of Jimmy Crowther's—'a little thin for our purposes'. In June: 'I am very glad to hear from you and I quite understand as I knew that you were very busy during the Election.' That was in May; for the first time the Labour Party—without a scare or a fraud, unlike 1924, 1931, and 1935—was returned the largest party in the Commons, and formed a government, though dependent for a majority on the divided Liberals. This proved fatal—ludicrous as it was for the Liberals to continue as a party at all: it served no rational purpose; in English conditions one was either a Labour man or a Conservative.

'By all means let us have a review of Pollard's *Wolsey*, as you say it is a really important book.' It was. 'The other review I should like also ... I enclose a page proof of my Note on Barnes and yourself; you will probably think it very silly and amateurish, and if you care to show me up I will reserve three or four pages for you in the September number for that purpose.' What charming modesty he had, even if self-deprecation was partly a game. The horrid schizophrenic Wyndham Lewis, who did the famous early portrait of him, once said to me, 'Eliot's so sly —he's so *sly*!' This only meant that he was a clever man and a great gentleman, who was anxious to avoid unnecessary offence, and enjoyed a rather devious practical joke. (He played one successfully on me, which we shall come to in time.) I do not remember now about Barnes, or who he was; I suppose he had been speaking up for Fascism, to my disapproval.

In October, 'Your letter, and the enclosed review, gave me a great deal of pleasure. It is more satisfactory to have you like this essay than to have you like the *Andrewes*, because it is nearer to the sort of thing that I am qualified to do. And I am glad that you like the poem, though I have rather a low opinion of it myself. I have always abstained from having my own work reviewed in the *Criterion*, and I don't think I should depart from it; certainly not unless the critic found every flaw in the texture—and you have been very lenient.' I do not know now which poem we were referring to, probably one of his 'Ariel' poems, each one of which he used to send me.[1] I have never kept copies of my letters, never having had a secretary—as he had; but Faber's probably have a file of the other side of the correspondence, for any literary historian who wants to look it up.

He went on to talk about Value—a concept which obsessed my mind at the time, along with the Non-Productive versus the Productive in economics. 'I quite agree with you about Value. It is the subject to which all others lead, and which one always has to tackle, usually amateurishly, if one tries to follow any subject out to the end. The people who write about it are very dull, very long-winded, and very unconvincing.' He may have been thinking of the Harvard Professor Perry's laborious and unreadable book on the subject. 'It would certainly be a subject worth taking up in the *Criterion* ... The contributors ought, I think, to be people who have had to try to think it out for themselves and have come upon it from quite different starting points: art, literature, economics, etc. Would you take a hand? ... I must tell you again how much pleasure your commendations have given me. I wish that we might meet sometimes.'

What a pity it was that I held off as usual—as always, as I have done all my life. Most of all in later years, when he became so famous and life was a burden to him, I deliberately kept out of the way, and would not impose the further burden of my society upon him—though the very last time I saw him, how pleased he was. (I nearly left the party without speaking.) Valerie, his second wife, has told me, after his death, how much more closely he kept in touch with news of me, and knew about me,

[1] 'A Song for Simeon' was published in 1928, 'Animula' in 1929. It could be either of these.

than I ever knew. I keep in touch with his spirit. I often dream of him, sometimes with tears. When the news of his death reached me in California, I went up into the mountains above Pasadena to think of him—ridge beyond ridge of those bare heights and canyons, empty and desolate under a Sunday silence —if only there had been the sound of English church bells! Later, in Somerset, I had one of those curious coincidental experiences: driving out in the evening from Sherborne, with no particular idea where I was going, I found myself at last in East Coker. (Years before he had sent me the poem in proof, and much appreciated the notice I wrote of it.) There in the church, whence his branch of the family left for America in the early seventeenth century, were his ashes.

I do not propose to go beyond this year 1929, the bulk of his letters is yet to come: they continued fully into the 1930s, then came the Second War, everybody scattered, and the years of international *réclame* Eliot himself never expected: the G.O.M. of English letters. In those earlier modest days, though I hadn't much cash, I was rather better off than Eliot—he had to be careful about money. When I did go up to London, at long intervals, I entertained him once and again to lunch. The only club I had was the English Speaking Union, far more congenial in those days; he had to explain that he couldn't lunch with me there, for his wife Vivien frequented it—they were now separated and she would make a scene. Anyone who has had to live with a schizophrenic female will know what hell it is; I will not go into what he had to put up with, scenes at the office, lying in wait for him when he should come out, holding on to his books, keeping his name in the telephone book at her address so that his calls came through to her—all the usual tricks one knows so sickeningly: just what Geoffrey Hudson had to endure twice over. (*Why* did they let themselves in for it?)

Anyway Eliot's favourite restaurant at this time was 'L'Étoile' in Soho ('my tastes are simple but expensive') and there we lunched—never in his grand days at the Athenaeum. Once, when he was slumped into his chair, depressed with what he had to endure, I chivvied him out of it with 'Look at you now, doubled up as you are …'; with charming smile he bucked up—he had a sweet disposition, 'gentle' as Edith Sitwell always described him;

though he could be firm—Valerie has seen him take an importunate fellow to the door and show him out. (I have never done that, or laid hand on anybody: my aggressiveness is purely verbal.)

As the 'thirties went on Eliot proposed that we set up house together: he really needed someone to look after him; but so did I. By the mid-'thirties I was living in London part-time, with a temporary lectureship at the London School of Economics, God help me! I got so far as to scout round for a possible neighbourhood for a flat, and found a charming square in an inexpensive area, I think Finsbury, with an improbable name: Lloyd Baker Square, I suppose obliterated now. By then I was beyond undertaking it: I went back to All Souls to write up my researches in the Public Record Office, in *Sir Richard Grenville of the 'Revenge'*, and for the operations that made life possible for me. Eliot found a literary lady to look after him, and subsequently John Hayward for companion; and together then they were able to afford a housekeeper.

I have sometimes wondered, if *per impossibile* Eliot's proposal had come off, how it would have worked out. From the literary point of view, much better for me; from Eliot's, John Hayward was a better grammarian than I. From the historical point of view I could have been useful—as I was over *Murder in the Cathedral*. Eliot asked me to suggest some reading on the subject of Thomas Becket; among two or three suggestions was Dean Stanley's admirable *Historical Memorials of Canterbury*, and that is where the historical material comes from. After that I suggested Thomas More for subject; Eliot said that he couldn't write two successive plays on two Thomases. Years later Bolt wrote his fine play on the subject, *A Man for All Seasons*: one could wish for no better.

Back at Oxford the now familiar routine of a don's life took up my time; there is evidence that it took up too much of it. In February, 'a day's deliverance from pupils and the constant pressure of something to be done. No speech, no lecture, no article to prepare; no anything but a little work for myself. So the whole day has a savour for me.' One day I registered 'a guilty morning, reading Rebecca West's book of essays, when I should have been preparing my lectures.' One brief entry in my Calendar tells its tale: 'Five b——y tutorials in one day.' It was too much. One day, one of my naughtier pupils, son of a rich Tory M.P., asked me to tea 'in his luxurious rooms in Longwall [where Ronald Firbank had had his when living in Oxford], wine-coloured velvet curtains drawn, a shaded lamp, subdued richness. We were joined by another exotic, his friend: a handsome dark type, sinuous and supple, rather childlike and feminine. He lay on the floor, moving limbs beautifully, to pore over photos of phallic-looking temples in a luxurious German book on Islamic art.'

The conversation took rather a Firbank turn: the two naughty boys were out to *épater* the young tutor, who was determined not to be shocked, and also to give nothing away.

I don't remember any such impression of voluptuousness before—the expensive books, the talk about art, the casual way they talked about a friend of theirs who has 'clap'. Horrifying in a way; one would say, 'Except for that, he seems quite well. But he's given up doing anything about it.' My conversation was usually intended to be improving—no hope of that with these young reprobates: I let them talk. The more feminine of the two was excited by the idea of crucifixion, and had a theory that it meant impaling by a stake, driven up from behind. The other: if that's true, nobody could last three days as the crucified often did. His friend: 'Oh, but there's apparently a way of putting it up so nicely that at first you didn't feel it.' They're both wild, what with nerves, and affectation, and being so stupid. Mais quelle sensation de volupté, tout le même!

I suppose that this was a pass at the innocent tutor. They were both wasters. I wonder what happened to them?

Normal life proceeded on its course. Noreen was in Oxford;

This morning, going to call on her in Beaumont Street, I found myself in a stream of people all moving together making for one point: the memorial cross at St Giles's, flags beneath it, flowers piled on the steps, the people silent, men took off their hats. [Would they today? That was an older

society, more given to respect and more worthy of it.]
I stood behind a young man wheeling an invalid on an
open bed: I could see only the white sheet and a white
arm upon it. After the bugles sounded, there was a complete and deathly stillness. I looked up at the houses around,
people in the windows motionless and without a word.
The place itself, the tall houses with their balconies, the
stripped trees and church in the background, all gave me
that odd sensation of having been through it before.

Afterwards I wondered what it meant to those hundreds
of people: they seemed pleased by the excitement and to
have enjoyed a semi-religious experience. I suppose they
are prepared to sacrifice themselves, and others, as cheerfully
now as before. In front of Balliol a fat old man said, 'They're
coming away already, Mother!'—he felt late for the fun.
Ever since I have been back in my room, after the muffled
peals of bells, there have been buglers and drummers
going up and down the High; and a military band playing
marches and tunes of merriment. What an attractive thing
war is to *them*, and how much more enjoyable Armistice
Sunday than other Sundays!

These were my sentiments then; I observe some consistency
with my attitude throughout my life—also our closeness at the
time to the First German War, and the large part it played in
our minds.

Life in term-time was pretty hectic. Entries in my Calendar
speak for themselves: Jan. 14th, 1929: 'Call at Transport House,
Smith Square, 8 p.m.' Was this to inquire about a possible
candidature for a constituency? Nothing about it in the Diary—
merely my external life: it shows where my heart really was.
'Jan. 15th: In Town. Jan. 16th: Ill at night. Jan. 17th: Ill at night;
up late. Jan. 18th: Term begins (*leider, leider!*).' That term I was
speaking not only to the University Labour Club as usual but to
the City Labour Party. And I had E. F. Wise to stay: he had been
an able civil servant during the war and was thus a valuable
recruit to the Labour Party, a competent fellow capable of
administering something; where most of the faithful were, as
Churchill said all too truthfully, not capable of running a whelk-

stall. (Old-fashioned image: there used to be whelk-stalls in the Market House at St Austell, where the young Winston had spoken in the glad days of 1906.) E. F. Wise died young: another loss.

Among my pupils was a rich young American of charm, Martin Philipsborn, whom I have kept in touch with all my life. He had a gallant record in the Second German War, and was one of the first people to break into Belsen and witness its unforgivable horrors. He proudly brought three American Generals to visit me at All Souls after the unspeakable Germans had got what they so richly asked for. In the intervals of tutorials there were walks with Bowra—always *walks* with him—who introduced to me his handsome blue-eyed Nordic, Hans von Seebach. (What happened to him?) Humphry Sumner invited me for the first time to dine at Balliol for a Sunday evening concert—contact with him was always a rather bleak affair: such frightful self-control, such inhuman discipline. Once, when he was a boy, his sister told me, their father gave him a beating. Humphry can never have done anything wrong: all he said was, 'Thank you, Father'! As David Cecil would complain, 'Why can't he say, "Damn, I've dropped my cigarette!"?' Why, indeed, couldn't he let himself go?—Well, I suppose I know why. As Warden of All Souls later, he died of duodenal ulcer.

I continued to dine out. One evening with the Beazleys at the exquisite Judge's Lodgings in St Giles's, built as a town house for the Marlboroughs. Marie came down to dinner in a black velvet frock, extremely *décolletée*, with a yard of wonderful old lace below. Her schoolgirl daughter gave the game away with 'Oh, mummy: you told us not to change!' After dinner there turned up one of Jacky's pre-marital friends; there ensued an embarrassing sulky silence: he evidently couldn't bear Marie. (Few could.) There is a fascinating untold story behind the known life of this greatest of Oxford scholars, a man of genius. Very beautiful when young, the poet Flecker had been in love with him and written him poems; Jacky, too, had written poetry, every scrap of which he had destroyed when he settled, with Marie, what his life was to be. Nothing remained. But he always retained his liking for erotic French novels, and when a Spanish artist turned up during the Second War—to draw a characteristic portrait of Gerald

Berners cherishing a lobster (lobster for lunch every day)—the artist penetrated the mask of the scholar and equipped him with a beautiful Grecian youth.

A naïf entry complains that social life was becoming too much for me.

> I must for some reason have sprung into prominence in the university: all the last week I have been waited on in my rooms by the most conspicuous of the younger dons (Maurice B. came three times in succession to take me for a walk), and there's been a flood of invitations to dine out. One of them I compromised by inviting the inviter to dine with me instead; another I accepted; one more and one to lunch I haven't replied to, and I have just been caught in the street by Michael Holroyd, and said I was hung up for ten days. As if I want to go out of my room to see anybody, except Ernest or David or Bruce! I'm not likely to be entangled in their bloody social round if I can help it.

There follows a whole sequence of dreams, which interested me more than any social life. I have said that I was curiously passive about personal relations: I never went out of my way to know anyone. Even my closest friends—Richard, David, Bruce, Charles Henderson—had all taken the initiative; obviously Eliot had too. The truth was, I found dining out rather a nervous strain, not a pleasure.

However, with my literary interests, I went dutifully up Boar's Hill to tea with the Masefields and Bridgeses, and up the opposite hill to Elsfield to dine with the Buchans. John Buchan was away all day in London; he caught the early morning train from Oxford, with a compartment to himself in which he wrote, worked all day at his publishing, Reuters, or Parliament, then back in the evenings to Elsfield. Here was a Sunday night on which John Foster drove me up in his car—today he has ceased to drive, and I have become the driver. Rather attached to him as I have always been, then we seem to have been closer; I lent him my French novels. When I went to collect him, I was startled by a beautiful apparition in those bachelor rooms: a girl 'stunning in black velvet with a gold sash, hair too the colour of gold: so striking an appearance that I was confused and never said a word to her. John has greatly improved his dark panelled room: it now gives a rich impression of luxury, thick brocade curtains red and gold, chairs a dusky gold, fawn-coloured carpets, calf-bound books bought by the dozen for decoration. The lady of the sofa went well with the furniture.'

The impersonal spoke more intimately to me. 'We arrived with amazing moonlight, half as bright as day, over the village. We stood in the porch; a glance back over the orchards and houses opposite showed them silvered or blackened by white light or shadow. The yard must have been originally a farmyard, when Dr Johnson used to come up here to drink tea with his crony;[1] outbuildings around. I watched the steep-roofed house shouldering its chimneys against the moon: a Gothic cliff, sharp in the brilliant night, splintering the cold wind.'

I had not been to tea with the Masefields for a couple of years.

The family completely unchanged since then: everything is as it was, except Mrs Masefield a little more dilapidated, Judith older in face, Masefield fatter, healthier, balder. It's an odd menage: Judith shows signs of discouragement, probably owing to the proximity of a powerful mother: at times she seemed quite extinguished. Tea-time was charming today, such nice scones and cake and talk. About Cornwall, and the village of Mawnan and the rectory, 'Sanctuary', which they take in summer.

Charles Henderson used to have stories of the eccentric Rector, Father Leverton: 'I cannot go out because of the rooks [the populous rookery bespattered him], and I cannot swim because of the serpents.' Apparently snakes do swim in those streams. He insisted that monkeys got into his bedroom; the parish thought him dotty. But here too the old boy was justified. A neighbour over the wall did keep monkeys as pets; whenever they could get away, they made straight for the Rectory, climbed up into his bedroom, and grinned at him in bed from the top of his four-poster. The Rector was not seeing visions after all.

Mrs Masefield, in her Pre-Raphaelite attitude as wife of a famous poet, was unaware of the figure she cut. Penderel Moon

[1] Cf. *Oxford in the History of the Nation.*

had hilarious memories of her in the Lollingdon days, lecturing away in an August garden about the causes of the war to Penderel aged eight or nine, Judith and one or two other children rather younger. It began with the Roman Emperors, but got no further than Attila the Hun. The little son Lewis used to be propelled forward to say how d'you do, while his hat was lifted from behind by his mother, with irresistibly comic effect.

At home in college were more memorable spectacles. I could look down from my window that winter to see Warden Pember and his old friend, Sir Edward Grey, going by over the snow: 'the Warden resplendent in top hat and handsomely agitated with buttoning his gloves; Grey, simple and undemonstrative, with soft black hat and shaded glasses over his eyes. I thought, there goes a man more bound up with the war than almost any other man in Europe. It was curious to watch him, keeping carefully to the narrow path in the snow, and with that tremendous background behind him.' It might have been taken to be emblematic: Grey had kept to the narrow path, doing all in all to avoid the war the Germans were bent on; but, as re-insurance in case of failure, he saw to it that when war came, Britain went into it, the centre of a Grand Alliance, her only security against an over-mighty Germany. After twenty years of Tory rule, in 1940 Britain had to fight on alone: the historian can never forgive it.

A little later I had the privilege of seeing Baldwin, the most powerful politician in the most responsible position in all those years, being conducted through the Codrington Library by his friend the Warden, self-consciously proud of his charge. There strode the benevolent figure of the ironmaster, heavy and paunchy, watch-chain across stomach, hair with a glint of copper in the brown, with leathery chaps. I was working away at the table in the alcove. Baldwin had reason to learn of my obscure existence later, when I brought home the loose indolent way this sly politician had sat towards the safety of his country. He excused himself to his old Harrovian friend with 'I was holding down a job I was no longer physically capable of.' Then why not have given it up to one of those who were—above all, to one of the *younger* men, Eden or Macmillan, Amery or Churchill? Every one of these was on right lines—and kept out. The noises of the Oxford streets brought back echoes of my times abroad, as Oxford made David think of Venice, 'a place to come back to; if one lives there all the time one takes its beauty for granted.' 'Just now I heard the nostalgic horn of my Munich taxi; it never fails to bring back the lovely squares on my route from the Theatinerkirche to the Deutsche Bank, past the Hofmaxburg and the nice bookshops where they have a lot of French books. The more distant motor horns remind me of the streets of Paris.' On a walk to Iffley with David, he was reminded of Venice as 'we watched, standing by the lock, the double light of day and reflected water; the light-ripples repeated themselves along the stone. He said that was like Venice, a ceaseless motion of watery light upon the buildings.'

Here is a corroborative letter of his, from St Fagan's Castle, Cardiff, where he was staying with the Plymouths: he was to dedicate his Cowper biography to the Countess.

You never write to me—but as I have never written to you who am I to complain? Have you had a nice vac? I have, except that Cowper haunts my most light-hearted moments, moaning 'I am not finished—I am not finished', with dreadful depressing persistence in my ear. However, he is getting on a bit—but I wish I was more prolific like you. And I get slower, not faster. I have such an unwieldy mind—it takes hours being cranked up into motion—and when it is going at last, it will not stop when I have to stop but goes on wasting its energy, when I am supposed to be at a meal or packing or doing something or other which stops me writing. I have not much news. I have read very little except a German book, which no doubt you know, by Thomas Mann, called *The Magic Mountain*. I cannot make up my mind if it's a fake or an absolute masterpiece. But I think it's a masterpiece on the whole, with the German faults, heaviness and morbidity and slight turgidity—but with real imagination and spontaneity and emotion. I cried over it— but I find that that's no test of merit, as I do it more and more easily.

The young David was too kind to the portentous Mann, who certainly thought *Der Zauberberg* a masterpiece, as he did everything he wrote. He thought himself Goethe and Faust and God in one—not the slightest sense of humour about himself. 'Spontaneity'? Certainly not: *everything* in Mann is pondered (ponderous too) and contrived. And the hullaballoo in Britain and America about *Death in Venice* à propos of Britten's opera—ludicrous! A not particularly distinguished short story hipped up into philosophical dimensions, the subject sentimental beyond belief, really rather pathetic, and totally humourless. Read Mann —and then compare him with Proust! One is on a different level of imagination, clarity, and intelligence.

David continues:

> Politics, too, are dreadfully dreary, don't you think? There is nothing that sounds more admirable as an idea than the League of Nations—but the reality fills me with a sort of melancholy nausea. It has an indefinable touch of North Oxford and the Liberal Summer School—and its only policy seems to be that all the nations that want to make peace shall unite to have a war with all the ones who want war. However, all this will strike you only as a sign of my invincible and wicked Toryism ... Where are you? How are you? What are you doing? Are you happy? or sad? coming back to Oxford? or burying yourself in a foreign capital? I do hope not the latter. I am so looking forward to seeing you next term. Anyway you must come up to add to the number of All the Souls on All Souls' Day. So I shall see you. I go to the Dolomites Saturday with my brother for 10 days walking tour. Then Venice till the end of June. Write to me at 21 Arlington Street and it will get forwarded.

This was the London house of the family, where the great Lord Salisbury lived even as Prime Minister. David's brother was then Lord Cranborne, who was one of the war-generation who had survived—to take absolutely the right line about Appeasing Germany, and to be excluded by Chamberlain *because he was right*. David's little *boutade* about the League of Nations is not to be taken seriously; his uncle, Lord Robert, sacrificed his political career to devote himself to the League, which was largely his brain-child. The family joke was that he thought the League of Nations existed to support the League of Nations Union. North

Oxford was always a bit of a joke to David: I remember the witches in *Macbeth* being described as North Oxford witches. But they were not three—far more numerous.

David finished his biography of Cowper, *The Stricken Deer*, as sensitive and perceptive a book as one could wish, all the more remarkable from so young a writer—two or three years my senior, he was still under thirty. It was deservedly awarded the Hawthornden Prize, and he was promptly taken up by Blooms-bury. As for my being 'prolific', there was little enough to show for my efforts. A batch of my poems had been published by an American literary paper, *The Forum*, with a rather sentimental portrait. Another American literary journal, produced in Paris, *This Quarter*, published several poems of mine. I have kept the numbers, and am surprised to find my young self appearing alongside Mayakovsky, Pasternak, Remisov, Ilya Ehrenburg; Herman Hesse, Stefan George, Samuel Beckett, Paul Valéry; e. e. Cummings, Allen Tate (to become a friend much later); here too appear H. E. Bates (whom I met when we collaborated on the *New Leader*), the young Louis MacNeice, and the inevitable Montgomery Belgion, mystery man—who on earth was he? Though I met him several times over years, I never succeeded in making him out. Occasional poems of mine appeared too in the *New Statesman*, and prose pieces in the *Adelphi*.

Altogether it didn't amount to much. And I was being steadily pushed more and more into political thinking and politics. Even Eliot's influence, as can be seen from his letters, was all in this direction. When at length I produced the political book towards which my thoughts were working, *Politics and the Younger Generation*, he was keen to publish it and took great pains with it. It came out in the worst possible circumstances, just before the catastrophe of 1931; it represented the hopes of 1929. It was just in time for some of its 'advanced' sentiments on religion and morals to be made use of against me in the election. Day by day the week before, the *Western Morning News*, read all over the West Country, came out with juicy extracts, suitably flavoured, to do harm among Nonconformist voters. In the event it made not much difference; the Labour Party met with disaster all over the country, I kept the Labour vote in Penryn-Falmouth steady, at about 10,000.

It all gave me acute anxiety, and added fuel to my Swiftian complex about humans. I was powerless, faced with a combination of all the powers that be. When I rang up this paper—respectful enough after the Second War, with its laying waste of Plymouth (the Astors there had strongly supported Appeasement)—and reminded them not to infringe my copyright, I was told, 'The legal department has taken good care of that.' Oh, the Tories made hay of us in 1931 and right through the 'thirties; did they feel so happy in 1939? Or do they today? My friend Keith Hancock was not impressed by my book, and no doubt it was the work of a mixed-up young man, trying ardently to think out what he thought for himself. R. C. K. Ensor said it was not so good as G. D. H. Cole's *World of Labour*. It was intended to be a totally different book—and who remembers dear Douglas's works today?—not a factual and descriptive survey. Though I buy up and suppress any copies I find today, I suspect that here and there it has some original thinking in it. I might not even disagree with it all if I were ever to read it again; and *pace* my friend Hancock, I am hardened enough to quote what a young Cambridge man, who subsequently became Vice-Chancellor at Oxford, had the goodness to say: 'We would have followed him anywhere.'

1931 put paid to all hopes of that; henceforth we ploughed the sands along the track that led to 1939. I hope they liked what they got when they came to it. If they had listened to me they would never have got there.

11

Adam von Trott

Adam von Trott is now an historic figure of the German Resistance, with memorials to him in Germany; and Christopher Sykes has written his biography.[1] It is not my business to write or rewrite it; this is my autobiography, and I should concentrate here on the effect that this intense relationship had on my life. It had a certain symbolic significance as it developed, illustrating something of the difficulties in the relations between Britain and Germany. For me it gave, so close and intimate was the relationship, a window into the German mind such as few Englishmen possessed.

It will make a complex and difficult, in the upshot an agonizing, subject easier if I make it clear that this was an ideal love-affair, platonic in the philosophic sense: we never exchanged a kiss, let alone an embrace. We were both extremely high-minded, perhaps too much so—Wystan Auden would not have expended pains on such an arduous and, in one sense, unremunerative relationship; he would have been more cut-and-dried about it, and cut his losses much earlier than I did.

It must be remembered too that, though Adam was five and a half years my junior—Shakespeare's Southampton was nine and a half years his junior—I was much more unsophisticated, as this book shows. In affairs of the heart I was less mature than Adam, who had already had an affair of two years' standing with a girl. For, though there was something feminine in his wonderful looks, and he had entertained an adolescent *Schwärmerei* for his boy-scout leader of the Nibelungenbund and could easily develop a sort of hero-worship for an older man, like Visser't Hooft— celebrated in Christian Student movements of the time—he was

[1] *Troubled Loyalty.*

fundamentally heterosexual. That was to be expected, and accepted; from that point of view I was always a defeatist, perhaps too much so.

Another conditioning circumstance that must be taken into account is that Adam was an aristocrat—I suppose he rated as a Baron. (Humphry Sumner always addressed him as such: he would.) Adam never mentioned it or used it; but socially all doors were open to him. Here, too, how much more mature and sophisticated he was than I, liable to a sense of *social* inferiority and always on the edge of nervous strain.

Adam came from a family of distinguished public servants. His father had been *Kultusminister* to the Kaiser—a kind of Minister of Education. One of Adam's earliest memories was of the daily drill on the great dusty barrack-square before their official residence at Potsdam. It is characteristic of the Germans, though he never told me this, that when his father resigned during the war, Adam had been ridiculed and humiliated at school as the son of a fallen Minister. So like them. On his mother's side, the von Schweinitzes were a diplomatic family: Adam's grandfather had been Bismarck's ambassador to the Court of St Petersburg.

This contrast in social class made little difference between us, for—though I was conscious of it—he set no store by it, or hardly any. (Still, there it was in the background. This made things easier, later on, between him and David Astor.) With a great gift for establishing personal relations, Adam's manners were not in the least stiff, in the German way; they were rather English, and 'democratic'. He had an American grandmother, and was descended from the statesman John Jay: that helped. For another thing, his difficult elder brother was a Communist and had gone over to the people, living with the people (another George Orwell case), for what that was worth. For all the brother's Communism, he objected to Adam's 'cosmopolitanism', his crush on England: there was a tension between the two brothers.

And there was tension within the family. Relations between the father, much older, and the mother were not easy. She was a remarkable woman in her own right, a noble character, but severe, with an element of New England Puritanism and strong convictions. There was a strain of 'going to the good' in the family: Adam's elder sister dedicated herself to good works, and today—in the ruin of our time—the family home is some kind of institution, which she runs, for children. In the background was a large family estate with a fine eighteenth-century country house. The family were very hospitable; though Germans, they were of the salt of the earth.

Adam once and again asked me to stay there; needless to say, I never would. At Oxford, with All Souls behind me, I remained top-dog.

Though Anglo-American in his manners, contacts and aspirations, Adam was intellectually deeply German. This was reinforced by his hopeless addiction to Hegelianism. Christopher Sykes is mistaken in saying that I regarded Hegelianism as an 'imposture'; I regard it as a *disaster*, both for Germany and for Europe. (As a Latin like Santayana did.) Sykes makes perceptive allowance for the disturbed state of mind of so many intellectuals under the Weimar Republic, with old landmarks removed, old values questioned (rightly), and the general uncertainty with regard to Germany's future.

Precisely. What Adam—and German intellectuals generally— most needed was a sense of concrete reality, of the external universe, of definite plastic form; either Anglo-Saxon practical empiricism, or the Latin realism. In any case, common sense, sense of humour; add poetry, or music, or art, according to taste. Adam had little enough of these last, and Hegelianism encouraged, corroborated, justified his eternal self-questioning, his constant doubting of everything, the endless *Verwirrung* and *Verzweiflung*. In the long run I could not stand it. As I have said, with Hegel black was never black, nor white white, each was for ever engaged in the process of becoming the other. It was the intellectual disease of the German nation. Christopher Sykes regards Adam's as a 'violent passion' for it; it certainly ran through and through all Adam's letters to me. He thought once that, of all Englishmen, I was the one sensitive enough to appreciate its beauty! This throws some light on Adam's typically German failure to understand another person. I *detested* Hegelianism, and the perpetual, fruitless self-analysis, and analysis of everything it led Adam into—until it seemed there was no solid ground for existence whatever. All this is expressed in his Letters —of which I am now the chief repository.

No doubt Adam was attracted by the opposite to all this in me—the mutual attraction of opposites was in itself an Hegelian theme: thesis—antithesis—synthesis, of which we heard *ad nauseam* from Marxists in those days. I thought, and still think, that what we stood for—common sense, realism, poetry—would have been far better for him. Perhaps this was what he meant by admiring the 'unity' of my outlook: we should say 'integration', which I had certainly striven hard to achieve, as the Note-Books testify—with what success the reader is in a better position to judge than I. The German in him resisted; and, as time went on, it became something of a tug-of-war, like that of Germany against Britain. He wanted to assert his value for me, intellectually, evidence of his importance for me—just like Germany. His importance for me was personal: I could not conceive of taking his lead with regard to any matters of the mind. Any more than Britain, with her greater knowledge and experience of the external world, her sounder political tradition and *savoir faire*—apart from anything else—could conceive of taking Germany's lead in regard to Europe and world affairs. Germany's whole record in the twentieth century shows how ludicrous such an idea was. Germany would have done much better to have fallen in with British ideas, more sensible and moderate, more practical and humane. Other people could live with them; no one could live with Germany's, not even Germany.

This was Adam's case when he met me; he confessed that he had been reduced to despair. According to his letters, I gave him some sense of concrete purpose, a sense of security and confidence. One must make some allowance for youth, and characteristic German sentimentality and exaggeration; but this was what he said, and why, I suppose, he fell for me—at the beginning. As time went on, he found that what he *thought* made no impression —how could it? It didn't make sense. Even Sykes, more sympathetic to Hegelianism than I could ever be, allows that Adam could make simple things excessively obscure. His sister allowed that he had a faculty for making himself and others unhappy. His lifelong friend, von Kessel, said that he was 'a genius, difficult to live with'. Adam was not a genius, and I never found him difficult to be with; difficult to put up with, perhaps—like Germany Moeller van den Bruck wrote that 'we Germans are a problematic

people, born to create trouble for ourselves and others.'
'Problematic'—there is significantly no precise English equivalent,
the German means more like 'troublesome'—occurs frequently
enough in Adam's letters: he certainly made great trouble of
heart and mind for me, as for others. I would have preferred him
to go the way of literature and art—he had a feeling for literature,
but again for the extreme, the mad, or the strange: Hölderlin,
Novalis, Kleist, E. T. A. Hoffmann. When Hitler achieved power
in 1933, I knew it was the end, and said to Adam, 'Roll up the
map of Europe. There is no more to be done. Why don't you
give yourself for the next ten years to a great work of scholarship?
Burckhardt's *Civilisation of the Renaissance in Italy* needs its
complement for Germany and Northern Europe. There's a
magnificent subject waiting to be done.'

Adam said that he couldn't do it, and went along his own path
to his death—as Germany went along hers to her destruction.

It has been necessary to say as much to give the background to
one of the most significant relationships in my life. But I must
turn to the personal, my own story, back to the beginning—I
have not space for more in this volume. How much it meant to
me I can see from turning to the Diary, where the visiting card he
left on me is pasted in. I had forgotten it: 'Adam v. Trott zu
Solz, Stud. Jur.', and in his hand, bold, masculine, clear—unlike
his personality or his thought—his address for me to write to him,
'Imshausen bei Bebra, Germany'. I had come upon it by surprise,
in the 'sixties, thirty years after, and had written on it: 'O God!',
and on the back: 'This dropped unexpectedly out, 16 April 1963.
Impulsively I kissed it in memory of my dead friend.' Then,
later, 'And kissed it again 12 Feb. 1975.'

Christopher Sykes will see that I have been true to the friendship, after my fashion. It did not end 'catastrophically', as he says,
though he allows that every one of Adam's friendships—Adam
was a great virtuoso of friendship, I in some sense a victim—was
at some time or other 'endangered'. Our friendship was, rather,
suspended; though I am proud to say, as I once told David Cecil,
who knew all about it, that we never had a cross word—too
considerate of each other. David had the generosity to say how
right that was for such a relationship between two remarkable men.

It was not Adam's looks that I fell for, when I first met him, though they were stunning. Everybody testifies to that: Claire Siegfried said that his was the most beautiful head she had ever seen. There was a grave nobility about it: long head with a magnificent domed forehead, sculpturesque, hair early withdrawing; then those wonderfully expressive violet eyes, with long golden eyelashes; a sweetness of expression, with a slight downward curl of the lip and a duelling scar to testify to his masculinity. He was six feet five tall. Well aware of his shattering beauty, he told me that at sixteen he would put on a deliberately haughty expression. Of course there was an element of narcissism, of which he was also conscious; on others his charm had an irresistible effect. Yet, there was more to it than that: I found that his intuitive responses and sympathies were so subtle and fine that he could tell what I was thinking, or feeling, more immediately than anyone I had ever known. This kind of telepathy I had never met before. Was this love? I had never really been in love. Was I prepared to commit myself? Was I ready to take the plunge at last?

On my side, it must be remembered that poets are sometimes in love with the idea of being in love. Here was a new experience to explore; on my side there was a certain self-consciousness, an awareness, though very different in kind from Adam's. His was analytical, perpetually analysing everything away. This is the very antithesis of poetry: it kills it, as second-rate literary critics never realize. Thomas Hardy knew better; so does Philip Larkin; so did I. Hardy quoted Leslie Stephen: 'The ultimate aim of the poet should be to touch our hearts by showing his own.' Larkin comments, 'That is really all anyone needs to know about writing poetry.' John Betjeman would subscribe. Instinctively this was the course I followed with Adam. I wrote him the best I had it in me to write—which is why I regret the destruction of my letters, however humiliatingly they might read. What they were like the historian can tell from a few pencilled notes I find on an envelope of one of his: I was in Dublin, pursuing Swift: 'the daffodils and wind blowing over the grey water. Your last letters attain the level which I would. A homeliness emancipated from conditions. Self-surrender.' He once objected to my *penchant* for description; I might well have objected to his for perpetual fruitless analysis—it didn't get one any further; or, rather, it further unsettled him. I thought to remedy this. But Britain could never cure Germany's morbid condition.

There is a literary element in falling in love, for an intellectual— as another Oxford intellectual well saw; Aldous Huxley: 'If it were not for literature, how many people would fall in love?' The Diary has plenty of description, both of him and of my own state, morbid or not. I had not been knocked out by my first view of him—it was not 'love at first sight', as with Lionel Curtis and Lionel Hitchens. Adam was first brought over from Mansfield College—where he was outside real university life—by General Swinton, the inventor of tanks, who knew people in the German Army. It was Penderel Moon who first noticed Adam's extraordinary eyes.

> Moon is very good at constructing character from faces, though with him it is a sharp intellectual process, and with Adam purely one of immediate intuition. Moon could tell that he wasn't the ordinary intelligent young student [he was then nineteen], but above all things reflecting. They are a rare violet colour, but of a liquid softness I have never seen before. When he came up my stairs as I was going up to dress —David had been with me all the evening and only then gone—I looked over the rail into his eyes, looking up at me brimming with light. I remember their gleam too, less attractive and a little uncanny in the darkness of our walk together to Beaumont Street.

What I did not then diagnose was that Adam's were inward-looking, there was an *Innerlichkeit* about them. He had not found Mansfield very inspiring, or been inspired by 'the inspired Mouse', Dr Selbie, whom all Oxford crowded to hear. (I went once; once was enough.) Adam was delighted to penetrate All Souls, and I asked him to tea twice, once with David and Eugene Forsey, again with Richard Hare and Richard Best (a good friend of mine, well-off and hospitable, son of a Lord Chancellor of Northern Ireland). Not unnaturally, Adam fell for All Souls. Later, he cherished the illusion of standing for a Fellowship; with his Second in the Schools he would have stood no chance at all: another example of a German's precarious hold on the reality of the external universe. No wonder Hegel expresses their soul!

It was bitterly disappointing that his acquaintance with All Souls had come only at the end of his term at Mansfield, and he was highly delighted when I asked him to dine on his last night before leaving. 'It was only then that I got to know him. He told me how glad he was to get my note, for he thought I had been disappointed by him, and that he had made no impression on me.' That was pretty revealing: he was out to make an impression on me: he sure did!

The strangest evening I ever spent, just in talking quite ordinarily, one each side of the fireplace. I had thought of him as a youth, charming and sensitive, intelligent, radiant with his beauty and inevitable happiness. But no: he was anything but this last, and to an extraordinary degree. He has based his whole outlook on life upon his acute and even morbid sensibility, upon his own feelings and the intuition of others, personal relations have become the stuff of his mental universe—which seems incredible to me. It made me go back a long way in my own emotional history to achieve a state which was in sympathy and in tune with his. His feeling of defeatism for one so young was so difficult to comprehend, it took constant intellectual effort to follow him. I made it, for tonight I fell in love with him. I felt here is the one I have always hoped to find; someone beautiful in all ways, mind and body, and who could go along with me the way I want to go. No woman or man had I ever come across was this that I longed for.

For me it meant release from my own cage. It is well known that love is blind, and some corroboration that this was love is that my usually sharp vision was somewhat blurred—everything about a Hegelian is somewhat blurred. I did not notice the absorbed egoism—of a very German character; or that I was being seduced emotionally—Adam was already a practised hand: anyway I was willing to be.

At the moment I had a feverish cold, which helped to send up my temperature and exalt my imagination. I went to see him off before midnight,

in the wind with a racking cough and a light feverish head
... A.v.T., his initials and his name I shall always remember.
He didn't want me to write mine: he said he couldn't forget
it, or All Souls. Perhaps he won't forget All Souls; for the
rest I have no illusions, even though I love him. I know well
enough by now that I have the will not to expect, nor to
encourage, a dream ... I am quite prepared to get a card from
him and hear no more. It is a sort of fatalism which I expressed to him; I called it cynicism, which he did not
accept. But it is better to have no illusions.

This represented my long-term view, a reinsurance which has
stood me in good stead. I was a defeatist about love and had only
contingent, not ultimate, expectations. I held a Manichee view
that it was enough to desire anyone to elicit no response; conversely, for any to show desire for me—there had been several
such—was enough to put one off. I think I must have been not
so much difficult as impossible. I prided myself upon walking
along a razor edge, never having what I wished to have, without toppling over. It was an act, a precarious act for health and
sanity, but it kept things under one's own control. I doubt if
Adam had met with that in relation to him. It was another
challenge: things were too easy for him with the girls. In his
relation with me there was from the first the possibility that I
might close down on him, beyond a certain point, however
much I might suffer in doing so—I was humble enough to
assume that he would not suffer so much. Nor did he—though
I am consoled that his experience with me was one of the most
disturbing in his life, unforgettable and never forgotten.
  In that evening of revelation I told him how 'the irrevocability
of things put an inestimable price upon them: that our talk would
have greater value to look back upon, a creation of memory.
[Here was something of the immense influence that Proust, not
Thomas Mann, had on my mind.] Adam spoke of a life based on
memory and desire—as if I did not know these twin chords, and
all that they spoke to the heart, how they echo through all the
misery and glory of my life alone.' At the end of my life I can
say that these have been the motifs running all through it. But
the phrase was his.

When I came back to my solitary room, in which life was lived so intensely, everything bore the impress of his personality. 'My top row of German books knocked a little askew where he had picked out Rilke's *Stundenbuch* to read while I dressed for dinner. The cigarettes open on the chimneypiece, the blue ashtray by his chair; the cushion which had fallen back while he talked with such earnestness; the reading lamp on the chair where I placed it to read a sonnet of Shakespeare's by ... Then there is his card he has left. Shall I ever hear of him again?'

So far from not hearing, with his infallible intuition in the realm of the emotions, he sent me from London a telegram with the two words, offering a code: 'Memory and Desire'. This was encouraging: it completed his conquest. For the next few days I lived in a dream, recording everything he had told me about himself, trying to shore up these fragments against what ruin time might bring. In the intensity of the experience I practically dreamed the lines which became the nucleus of a poem describing him:

> Summer will come, and make you brave to war
> And harden you ...
>
> And Autumn will lay a still cold finger
> On your beauty, and dim your liquid eyes
> And suck the juices of your lips.
> This living dream you are shall see eclipse,
> And I'll not mourn you in my waking state,
> Wide eyed and in my frozen heart secure.

Here was the ambivalence in my attitude, seeing through the fever of the present to an inevitable future, willing to suffer: prophetic in a way.

I registered every moment of the brief time we had had together: 'the way he bent his head because of his great height as he talked to Richard Hare, who was dazzled by him and anxious to meet him again, either here or in Germany.' He had been a bit stranded in the smoking-room with elderly Swinton.

People talked to him about his grandfather, ambassador to Russia in the 'eighties, but Moon couldn't think of anything to talk to him about, though he was the first to notice, what didn't at first dawn on me, how extraordinarily beautiful he was. When I talked to him about Thomas Mann and Franz Werfel, his eyes lit up. He was much against the domination of contemporary German literature by the Jews: I was surprised to hear that Mann was a Jew, though I know Werfel, the Zweigs and Wassermann are. They didn't really represent the German tradition, though there hadn't appeared any alternative.

I should interpolate that this was just German commonplace at the time; Adam was in no sense anti-Jewish, in fact his English girl-friend was partly Jewish. His enthusiasm was all for Dostoievsky, and above all Hölderlin: 'I can see that that would be so with his fascination for madness.' He said once or twice that fatal evening that we belonged to a generation that was mad. I did not share this view at all—I had strong hopes of the younger generation, of whom I made a cult as against the Old Men—but no doubt there was a good deal of madness about in his Weimar generation, beginning with his brother. An aristocrat a Communist, going slumming with the people! 'He told me of all the hesitation and doubt of himself, the lack of any purpose he has in living, or even any interest in what he does: he said he couldn't stand life much longer like that.' I was astounded, from so young, so beautiful a being: I had no lack of purpose in living, and was intensely interested in everything I was doing every moment of the day. The days were simply not long enough to get everything in (I still find that). He must have found this exhilarating.

Conscious of his appearance, he said that no one would suspect all this, to judge from it.

One certainly would not. I thought of him those first three times as a typical young German, sanguine, enthusiastic, vaguely idealistic about social service and Student Christian Movement objectives (like Wadleigh),[1] with a jejune taste for the romantic and exotic in literature. But I've never been so mistaken in external appearance. He looks healthy and, like a child, pleased to open his eyes upon the delightful world. And yet, there he is, a young man out of

[1] Cf. *A Cornishman at Oxford*.

Dostoievsky; I shouldn't have thought such a one existed outside of Russia and the books. He asked me if I had read *The Idiot*, with which he was possessed, and wanted to tell me all about it. Why he should be fascinated by madness I can't think: one would never imagine it of such beauty and such innocence.

But he was less innocent than I was. I don't know if I let on that I disapproved of Dostoievsky. I do not wish to appear as a moralist, but I have always thought that there was a deep immoralism in him, no clear recognition of any boundary between right and wrong, a characteristic Slav irresponsibility about doing the most awful things, a formless chaotic boundlessness of mind. Genius certainly—but I prefer the civilized Turgeniev, whom Dostoievsky detested. And now I wonder if my own youthful intuition at this point was not unexpectedly penetrating. Might there not have been a Slav element in Adam through the Schweinitzes? No one has suggested it; but they were Prussians, and there is a Slav ring to me about the name. Adam had the irresistible charm the Slavs have—and no German has—but also their chaotic formlessness of mind, no bounds to it and no boundaries; within, an endless *Verwirrung der Gefühle*. No wonder Adam fell for Hegel; Anglo-American pragmatism would have been better, the aesthetic naturalism of a Santayana too much to hope for.

At the time I put it down to family conflict and lack of sympathy—which he yearned for and could never get enough of.

His father is an old man, and there has always been a strain between his father and his mother, which accounts for his *Nervosität*. He has little feeling for his home, has lived away from it a good deal, and regards going back with fear rather than any pleasure. While he was at Mansfield he became fond of 'a little German girl' whom he had met here; but what was so painful was that he could not hold to his affection for her, he had not got the stability. It began by being a dream like every other of his loves for girls, and then he found that he couldn't hold to it. So he had parted from her; it was always like that, he no longer had any confidence in himself.

(What I was abounding in, with no confidence in other people: they never came up to one's expectations. He didn't, this great love of my life. They always fall down—my expectations too high. But I expect *everything* of myself, and now can make myself do whatever I will myself to do.)

He believed that the only solution for his 'problem' was desire: he had only to remain true to that, and love would follow. I said that that was all very well for him, he had nothing to complain about: with his looks, women would always fall in love with him. That made him impatient: plenty of women fell for his looks, he never knew anyone to love him for what he was, when once the other really saw. I was bound to be happier, he said: there could not but be women attracted by my mind, and what I thought and wrote. I said that that wasn't what I wanted: I longed for comradeship in mind as well as personality, and that I had never found the two united in any woman; nor perhaps would he. But this was not what he wanted; he wanted to solve the problem of his own personality. To hold fast to desire was the only way for him; desire and memory were the pillars of life, and if they failed him there would be no further purpose in living.

I was astonished, overwhelmed by this outpouring, and wrote,

What it meant I couldn't make out, nor can I now … Perhaps he was treating me as the elder brother whom he is accustomed to rely on as philosopher and friend; anyway I took up the rôle with some success, though my heart wasn't in it.

He said he had at least that night found someone to whom he could look up as teacher, when usually it was he who stood in that relation towards others. I asked how he could recommend to others the course to follow, if he was so uncertain of his own. He wanted to know from me what were the secrets of writing, and whether salvation for him lay that way. I didn't tell him about my long and arduous apprenticeship through the Diary—no one knew about that; I said that, from what I knew of writing, one had to grip the vision one saw in one's mind, and express it as simply and directly as one could. And that this took time.

It surprised me that for one with any power of visual conception he should not have been attempting it for years, as I had from schoolboyhood. He had never tried to write— perhaps the family tradition or his school was against it; he felt the mental picture melting away from him as he tried to put it into words, even to me at that moment. Standing up to go that night he said something that shocked me, with my conviction of the absolute value of art; that a poem after all was a dead thing: what was alive was the experience that moved in the mind.

There's German philosophic idealism for you: the real thing is the idea, internal to oneself alone, not its objective expression in the form of art, externalized and universal, having a real existence as such. This reduction of the external world to the inner idea, then reinforced by maniac will-power, is precisely what I mean by Hegelianism having been such a disaster. When he came to write, one could see this running all through his letters—I shall quote some; he would never have made a writer.

'What should he do? He wondered if there wasn't a way of coming here for a full three years at a college, or of getting into English life for a time. I suggested the diplomatic service, or to go on the staff of a big German newspaper. He had tried the London correspondent of the *Frankfurter Zeitung*, but had failed to interest him.' In the end it was I who made the suggestion that he should come to Oxford as a Rhodes Scholar and backed him with my recommendation—but this was some way ahead. It was a vain courtesy, if nothing else, that led him to ask when I was coming to Germany. Late that night I escorted him along to Beaumont Street, where he was to take leave of a friend. 'He strode along in the obscure lamplight, the skirt of his full coat swinging under the belt, the gleam of his eye now like steel in the darkness. I noticed his set profile, an effect of fanaticism when his lip drew back from his teeth, and I saw them squarely clenched. There was a light in his friend's window; he went up to it and— more Dostoievsky than ever—peered in: his great height was just above the window level. I held out my hand to say goodbye, and shook his, which returned a limp unresponsive warmth.'

Stunned by this experience, I spent the next few days in a

dream—at the same time, not so much stunned as not to be watching myself as usual.

I have watched the progress of this love day by day, as if it were a disease. And now there is an odd phenomenon to record. I have lived these last three days with the illusion of his presence, the image of his face and look and gesture always with me—and today I can't recall the illusion or the vision of his face, however much I try. I know exactly what he looked like: haven't I got him pinned down all right in words? There isn't anything about him which I couldn't describe, yet when I try to imagine him, another face comes in the way. A pupil of mine at St Edmund Hall is the only other man I know of the same physical type: very tall and slender, with full lips and long hands, a beautiful fair head poised exquisitely above throat and shoulders. The other one, though of fine and delicate features, has nothing of Adam's subtlety and variety of expression: something rigid in the fixity of his features, his eyes cold and as much grey as blue. However, this is the face that comes stealing in and blurring the picture whenever I try to re-create the image of Adam. Last night I thought of their resemblance and wondered if this would happen: and behold it has.

I suppose I had exhausted the image, and myself, thinking so intensely about him. Who the handsome pupil was, I have totally forgotten: no doubt the usual type of fine young Englishman, conventional, who went on to a conventional unmemorable life, without imagination and quite without the exquisite responsiveness of the other which had so disturbed me.

However, I had my own therapy. I wrote a longish poem describing it all: 'The Progress of Love'. I have looked it up with some trepidation. I was bound for Dublin in pursuit of Swift; when I got there, A.E. (George Russell) published it in his *Irish Statesman*. I find, to my surprise, that it is all right: only the third stanza, which strikes me as sentimental, shall I omit when I publish my Collected Poems. 'Writing that poem has put an end to the acutest part of my unhappiness: perhaps it deflected it into the strenuous path of getting over technical difficulties. The fifth stanza was given to me, the rest has formed itself upon that model.' Such would be my message to Adam still: if only you could *externalize*, get out of the never-never land of inward self-analysis, create something—like Robert Bridges's:

> I too will something make,
>   And joy in the making,
> Although to-morrow it seem
> Like the empty words of a dream
>   Remembered on waking.

Surely this was the healthier way, instead of sterile and endless self-questioning? One took oneself for granted, chipped away here and there, shaped oneself up—and went forward to do something, or at least create something. My poem ended with the lines:

> Nor can you altogether die, as long
> As I shall live you will go on in me.

True enough—and how strange that it should have been so: we both of us thought that there was a kind of fate in our meeting, though I could not have imagined the fate that would be his: the butcher's hook in Plötzensee prison.

Curiously enough, I did not dream of him at night: it was my waking state that was a dream. Instead, I had a dream of Virginia Woolf, whom I had not met, but who was a prime influence on my writing. Very visual, as always: 'a concert of chamber music in a Lincolnshire garden; I was immensely struck by a beautiful one-movement piece by her. I was to lunch with her, and going down through the fruit garden, I told her what had impressed me so much—the effect of a dying cadence the piece had achieved, descending half-note by half-note through a constant transposition of keys.' Actually there was a phrase of music which I always associated with Adam: the lovely curve of tune with which the Rondo begins in Beethoven's Sonata, Opus 22.

We went in through the back door (my mother was there too) into the kitchen, where lunch was laid: a certain affected slovenliness gave the house distinction, though the lunch was well laid out with linen, plate, flowers. Leonard

Woolf was hovering about as if this was his handiwork.
Virginia and I went to the front to look at the view: a low
greystone William-and-Mary house, level lawns coming up
to it; beyond, the gentle pastures and long views of Lincolnshire—which I had also never seen. We went to the end of
the garden, Virginia not at all interested in the effect of her
music on me; in the ploughed field at the bottom she
plunged her hand into the upturned soil, and behold it ,was
covered with *merde*. It was disgusting, but she insisted on my
looking at her hand, stained and brown, and that she was
suffering. I looked—the hand was covered with boils, little
heads amid the brown ooze. I must have lost all appetite for
her lunch; for indeed we never came to it.

What on earth did this dream mean? I leave it to the psychologists; I have no qualification to be the Simon Forman *de nos jours*.

Meanwhile, I had received a letter from Adam, the first of a long
series which it defeats me to put in order, for he rarely dated a
letter—another feature of the vague inner world he inhabited.
I cannot always read the blurred dates of postmarks; but there
they are, the stamps with Hindenburg's square visage, 'der Alte
Herr', and sometimes those of Friedrich Ebert, the decent
working-class Socialist who had been the first President of the
Weimar Republic. It wasn't a bad thing in the earlier years that
Hindenburg should have succeeded Ebert: it helped to reconcile
a lot of people to the Republic who would otherwise have
sabotaged it. In the end, the reactionary camarilla around him
did sabotage it and let in Hitler—thinking to call the tune!—but
that was when Hindenburg was nearing ninety and quite senile.
The Old Men, whom I loathed, again! But the Younger Generation in Germany did not mean Adam—as he and I hoped—but
Hitler!
    The editing of these Letters would need a full-time American
research student, with all the conscientious patience of the tribe,
or possibly—with all the rest of my *Nachlass*—the resources of
Mr W. S. Lewis's Horace Walpole factory at Farmington, Conn.
For Adam's unhoped-for response to me was such that he wanted
our correspondence to be a continuous conversation, like that we

had begun on that fateful evening at All Souls. I could not but respond, but it was very absorbing of time; Richard Pares wrote me from America and the West Indies, full of reproaches for not writing to him. I did my best, though I couldn't rival Bruce, who wrote to a graceless (actually, rather graceful) boy-friend of his every day for years: think of it, he gave to this unremunerative object what should have been devoted to the fifteenth century! As Shakespeare wrote to his friend, Southampton: 'So great a fool is love ...' Even I cannot but regret that the effort I put into writing the best that was in me should have gone up in smoke in Berlin—if it did when Adam's flat was damaged in a British air-raid; just as the early portrait William Coldstream painted of me was destroyed in London in one of those cultural exchanges with Germany.

Adam's letter, and the tone of it, fixed him on me. He had written immediately from London, saying that 'our souls loved each other that evening.' Virtuoso as he was, he was sincere; later evidence from others makes it clear how much this meeting and the friendship that developed from it meant to him. Poor boy, he did his best; and so did I—but always with a weather eye open as to what could possibly come of it. He wasn't to blame for the fact that, in a certain sense, he was impossible; others might think, as I have said myself, that I was impossible too. In the end we were very different persons, set on different courses, pulled apart by the course of events in Germany. In the shorter term Adam adopted my hopes of Social Democracy, based on the promise of 1929—to be falsified by 1931, when my book came out. He arranged for a German translation of *Politics and the Younger Generation*, which was coming out in *Neue Blätter für den Sozialismus*, published by the group he had joined, when Hitler came in.

In the not so short term, too, I was able to bring Adam back to Oxford for three years as a Rhodes Scholar—his letters show that he was anxious not to let go his hold on me—and that played its part in his eventual formation and *Zustand*. When he was executed, I used to blame myself for his fate, or at least wonder what part I had in it. But it really followed from Adam's own volition in joining the particular Resistance circle of Stauffenberg and Bernstorff, who had great influence with him. What an ineffective lot of conspirators they were! Hitler should have been bumped off years before. As for the idiot Communists, talking violence and doing nothing—with their leader Thälmann got up to *look like* Lenin, beard and all—and then suffering passively, they should have done the job, and saved millions of men's lives. Instead of that, they joined with him in 1939: Britain's ultimate resistance to him, far too late, was described during 1939–41, until he attacked the sacred soil of Russia, as an 'imperialist' war. What lunacy it all was!

We must keep to 1929, with its innocent youthful hopes.

March 20th. Near midnight. Today there came a letter from him; and, what I had scarcely dared hope, it seems he has been filled with thoughts of me all these last days, as I of him. An extraordinary providence that led to that crossing of our paths: could I have ever known, or he, that we should make that impression on each other? It seems incredible that it should ever have happened; it might so easily have not, and my life would have been infinitely the poorer. At the moment it gives me great happiness to have my love for him returned in that undreamed-of way. When he wrote, it was for the same reason that haunted my mind: he could not hold on to what he called the 'adventure' of the soul that night, and I the 'experience'; he feared he might forget it and me, and asked for my picture to remember me by ... I can't think what we did to each other that night. We dined in perfect sobriety; we came up and sat all the evening on each side of the fire, I a little feverish with my cold, and he through that crisis of the emotions he was going through. It's a distressing experience, but one which I am prepared to go through with, though it can bring only unhappiness in the end. He can never hold to his love for me: we can ultimately make nothing of it. So I have given him perfect freedom: he can always rest assured of my devotion to his memory.

So that volume of my Diary ends. It was not a bad forecast in the long run. In the shorter term we jogged along rather better than might have been expected. Adam had need of me, and was not letting go; I was going to remain true to myself in not letting him down: this was what love demanded.

Adam usually wrote to me in his very German English; though he spoke English fluently, with very little of an accent—for he had had an English nurse, whom he adored, more than his formidable mother—it shows how German he really was that his English never grew idiomatic: it was always German translated. On his way back through Holland he wrote, in German, of the anxiety with which he had waited to hear from me—the over-strained language of the German soul:

die entsetzlichen Ängste die eine solche Pause mit sich bringt ... Ich musste erkennen dass unsere Freundschaft, die für mich eine so endgültige Bedeutung hat ... durch unsere Trennung ein neues und unheimliches Schicksal begonnen hatte ... Wirst Du warten können auf mich und die Besinnung, nach der ich mich sehne und vertrauen, dass unsere Beziehung so tief in meinem Herzen liegt, dass von ihr das, was wir Glück nennen, allein abhängen wird! ... O wie dankbar bin ich Dir, dass Du mich nicht aufgeben willst, denn dann brauch ich es nicht zu tun.

Und so weiter: there was a great deal more of this sort, and how his eyes had looked clearly into the fire of Eros, and of the *cri de coeur* —it sounds so much better in French—he had uttered to me, his friend. Then the return: 'O mein lieber Freund, dass Du mich so wenig nur kennst, um meiner Verzweiflung zu kennen, die mir sagt, dass ich nicht aus der Ferne zu Deinem Herzen durchdringen kann ohne jenes Bild zu zerstören, dass Du von meiner Nähe hattest' ...

Always this concern with himself going on and on: dear Adam, egoistic as I was myself, you were a *kolossal* one. I wonder we got on as well as we did; well, we had a great deal of patience with each other. He had need of me; for me, this was love—and I suppose, at least good for my German. From Amsterdam he wrote again, in English: there was so much reality for him in our relation that it had given him a new confidence in life; he felt 'the wonderful power' of my 'tenderness, and was proud to be the object of my thought.' That was all very well; 'both of us should try and learn how beautiful life can be after that experience of meeting each other ... I shall promise to hold fast by the desire of being your true and thankful friend.' We did hold fast, after our fashion.

Arrived at his home, Imshausen in his native Hesse, he wrote in April, 'Oh that we could speak together, that you see how I am and how I think of you.' It had filled his 'heart with unspeakable joy that you reacted like this to my last letter', in which he had tried to master his 'desperate unrest'. Our meeting had had for him too 'a sense of fate' about it; during the time we had together he felt a 'harmony' in his 'problematic', which had nearly torn him in two by its conflicts. So I had incurred 'a fatal obligation', even if mysterious, to provide a home for his 'mental homelessness'. Alien as all this may seem to English experience, and unattractive to an English ear, it must have spoken for many others of his generation in Germany, uprooted, restless, without a goal and nowhere to look. Sykes thinks that, as a patriot, Adam had been deeply wounded by Germany's defeat. I don't believe it—at any rate he never spoke of it to me; the only thing he mentioned was the demoralizing effect the pride of English prisoners had had on the Germans: not at all downcast, they took things as they came and never imagined ultimate defeat. John Buxton told me that the same was true in the Second War: long before the war was over the British prisoners in his camp were running it—and the Germans too! I always believed that it would have been better for Adam if I had run him—a worse mess of it could hardly have been made as things were.

He went on about 'the unity of thought and feeling which had so much impressed him, and 'which speaks out of all your letters as something—even if I had it when together with you—now quite unattainable for me.' There we were, back on the old treadmill: doubt, inner uncertainty, insecurity, instability of feeling; nothing concrete, steady, or stable. One of these letters struck me as absolutely Hegelian: 'I see and feel so much about the world in me and around me but *am* just nothing. But perhaps I am altogether only becoming ...' There you have the Hegelian cliché, the evil of Hegel, deep in the German soul: nothing ever *is*, simply, concretely, definitely, but is always in process of *becoming* something else, usually its opposite. One can see how this could lead, in more positive and effective minds, to the absolute immoralism of German politics—in its crudest and most effective expression, in keeping with the mass-standards of today, to a Hitler.

Adam qualified this by saying that he feared I might think him 'a Narcissus'—which, of course, he was, and what wonder with those unparalleled looks?

He wanted to tell me about his affair with his girl-friend, who didn't like the name Adam. (I loved it.) 'You ought to know that I love her lips, her eyes, her skin passionately and—now I am away—she really loves me too; and that I can't think of you when I think of her, and conversely; and that she will come and see me in Berlin ... but that embracing her means forgetting, and being with you meant understanding.' He added a note in German that if I wanted him to leave his girl to save our friendship, he would do so: 'Ich beschloss Dir dies zu sagen: Wenn Du glaubst, dass ich um unsere Freundschaft zu retten das Mädchen verlassen soll, das mich liebt, werde ich es tun.'

What an extraordinary thing to say! I wouldn't have dreamed of his leaving his girl for my sake—far too high-minded and too much respect for him to trench on these private preserves. By his next letter he had parted from her. He had come to think that the affair was simply sensual, that the girl didn't care for him as he really was, etc. 'A woman's real love is something which disarms me entirely. But it is a hell to think that you are just a plaything' and sensuality just covered up the conflict of feeling. (Hegelian conflict, no doubt. Why not take it for just what it was?) 'I had the feeling that Alice liked my pretty face and found me "complicated".' Nothing of what there was between us two existed with her: nothing of 'the great experience in coming to me at just that moment to share what I really cared for with somebody else.' The poor girl just wasn't up to it. The contrast between the letter he had received from her and that from me, 'arrived at the same time this morning, was too much for my courtesy'. Well, not much of a compliment in that, the sort of effusion to be expected from some ordinary little German female!

So he had got back from her the wonderful silhouette portrait of himself, on which his father had written his name, Adam, and sent it to me—to complete his conquest. 'Oh, es ist eine Qual sein Glück und sein Leben auf die Liebe zu bauen'—yes, indeed. In English, he wrote that love had little to do with pity or patience. Here was something quite un-English, and I suppose deeply German. For alongside of this exquisite sensitiveness, an intuitiveness paralleled only once again later in life (with another, very different, love), there went the brutal German strain. There was the duelling scar on that beautifully formed lip. And I was told later that he turned an English girl-friend out of his flat in Berlin one night in the snow, with nowhere to go. 'Love has nothing to do with pity or patience'; it may be a German view, but it shocked me. On the other hand, I am bound to own that no unkind word breached our friendship; too much respect for each other's extreme sensitiveness, we left disagreements unspoken.

'Ich will diese vielen Worte nun abschliessen und Dir nur sagen, dass alle diese Tage mit Gedanken an unsere Freundschaft ausgefüllt waren, die so tief symbolisch mit meinem augenblicklichen inneren Zustand verknüpft scheint.' To this there is a pencilled note: 'I still find it heart-breaking, and weep for him. 1975.'

Those last letters were forwarded to me in Dublin. Before I crossed the Channel, 'yesterday and today I went into Mansfield. The whole place spoke to me of Adam: it could not but catch something of his personality in the two months of his life there: lived, yet I saw nothing of it. Once only did I see him near the place: that raw day when I went to put him off dining, I was so unwell with my cold. I met him coming along the road and we went back together along Holywell to Blackwell's, where we parted. I remember looking after him, so tall and erect, and a little self-conscious as he walked.'

Yesterday Bruce and I got into Mansfield by the charming lane that follows the boundary of Wadham Garden. A spring day, very clear and blue, with white clouds billowing across the wide spaces. The afternoon was quiet and deserted [not ruined, as today, with the mammoth Science complex]; Bruce and I loitered, though he didn't know what so absorbed me in thought; a gardener at work on the lawn, an aeroplane overhead with its drone dulled in all that quiet. How empty the place was! I felt acutely the sense of his being absent from it.

Today too Stonier said, 'Let's go down by Mansfield.' At the gate we went in; I wandered inside the entrance hall, hoping there might be a list of those in residence this last term. No: not the name I hoped for, nowhere at all. We went out; from the steps I noticed one can see the twin towers of All Souls, as he must have seen them. I wonder how much, if anything, they meant to him?

We have seen that they did come to mean something.

From Dublin I wrote to him, for a scrap of unfinished letter to him—all I have—begins: 'I have just time to begin my reply to your last two letters, before rushing off by car to lunch at a place, Powerscourt, some way out of Dublin.' The car must have arrived to take me to this palace of a place, with its falling terraces and fountains, the Sugar Loaf in view as if it were part of the immense park; within, lunch in stately grandeur, waited upon by liveried flunkeys in red plush, wigs, white silk stockings. The whole place now a burned-out ruin.

Absorbed by Adam, and his demands upon me for letters to keep the illusion of conversation going, I was neglecting to write to my college friends. Richard was touring the archives in Philadelphia and New York, and wrote me an immensely long report on Jamaica, to heap coals of fire on my head, beginning, 'My good Sir, You are an idle hog.' Here is some of it, to provide an English contrast to so much German inwardness.

This is a lovely island, but a dim town for its capital. It's the tropics without everything which makes life tropical. Meagre Scotch boarding houses (I am staying in one), peopled by decayed frumps, sub-prosperous retired publicans and seedy American commercial travellers, do not make up a tropical scene. The commercial travellers ought to be better; I came out with a whole squad of the unofficial army of American imperialism, and some of them rather good fun ... It's evident the army of American imperialism is very like that of British imperialism; but how much more effectively managed.

The smells are ordinary smells of a tropical town: bad drainage and primitive cooking and sweat, maturing in the heat to a very pleasing compound which I have met before in Turkey and recognised at once ... The Chief Justice is a stock tropical product of the British Empire. When not engaged in fighting the Boers or the Germans with a perverse and intoxicated loyalty to the King and Country, which I suspect owes something to Kipling, to Holdsworth and to the polo-ground, he has spent his life repressing vice in one tropical dependency after another. He ... has a semi-public feud with the Governor. It's my opinion that a West Indian island wouldn't be a West Indian island without a feud between the Governor and either the Chief Justice or the officer commanding the detachment of the army or the navy stationed there. I never read of a time or an island in which there wasn't one, and even though these officials can't interfere with each other as they formerly could, it's proper that the tradition should be kept up.

The negroes are jolly and comic. I can never get used to seeing those clumsy wooden heads, that look as if they were made by a child learning sculpture, on the subtle and well proportioned bodies ... I don't know if there is much colour feeling; I think probably not, for there are so few poor whites in Jamaica. The Chief Justice said that the few whites who married half-castes were ostracised; but I suppose there comes a point where the coloured people 'pass'. An especial irritant here is a fat old American who has the idea that I am the British lion and persists in twisting my tail about the general inefficiency, poverty, dirt and backwardness of the British and the inevitable and proximate breaking up of the British Empire. It has raised an emulous old gentleman from Montreal, who was quiet before, to great ingenuity in thinking up everything he knows and some things he doesn't against the United States.

Though I really think life in the United States is exhilarating and admirable, I was horrified to find how glad I was to get away from it. I felt as if a loud, aggressive and tiresome noise had suddenly died away, or as if I had taken off a tight uncomfortable new shoe and put on an old one. Indeed in a way I shall always be sorry I ever went to America, and feel as if I should never be comfortable again for feeling the presence of this portentous shadow. The country is so vast, so formidable, and the people so brisk and confident and triumphant ...

But this was America in early 1929, before the Stock Exchange crash and the World Economic Depression; and certainly not the United States after Vietnam.

Richard had had a terrible time of it with the archives in the West Indies; some of them fell to pieces at his touch, after two hundred years in that climate, and ill kept.

The Records are—some of them—in an incredibly disgusting state, foul-smelling, dusty, disordered, disintegrated and eaten by juicy and obscene white ants. I can't speak of them with patience. In one room the filth is so positively sinister that I continually expect to see, perched on a moulding bundle at the top, an obscene bird oozing with some loathsome rottenness awaiting to catch my eye before it flaps out at me. (Birds that whirr out of the grass from beneath my feet are physically shocking, but the birds of my nightmares are always birds that sit immovable for hours, waiting to catch my eye. I suppose the Jamaica Chancery records would be the right kind of habitat for the Maitland—do you remember the Maitland?)

Of course I did: it was a terrifying bird of a dream of Richard's. He had a bird-complex; I have never met it in anyone else, but he was really frightened of birds (he made an exception for adorable ducks). Once when we were walking in the gardens of exotic Sezincote in the Cotswolds—that exquisite Regency creation touched by the Indian idiom of the Brighton Pavilion—a big bird suddenly flew up out of the bushes. I saw that Richard's complex was genuine: he was almost hysterical.

Coming nearer home:

I am sorry to have missed Cruttwell on Waugh and my 'little friends' generally; they seem to have had a busy season publishing indecent novels and inaccurate histories and puffing each other in the papers. I should have liked to read Cruttwell on Evelyn's last performance in the evening papers in which he puffed Acton, Hollis, Robert Byron, Quennell and Stokes as the world's five bright young men. [They were indeed very good at writing each other up; Richard and I, as dons, were outside the *claque*.] Since I have the *New Statesman* sent to me every week, I find my tastes in literature weekly and obscurely dictated to me by Connolly and Quennell, a position in which I never expected to find myself. If I am to be further imposed upon by one A.L.R. in the same paper I shall begin to think I am indeed the Man in the Street, while everybody else I know is inside the Office.

In fact I never became a regular contributor to the *New Statesman*, though it published an occasional poem or article. I simply could not bear the factious irresponsibility of its outlook under the egregious Kingsley Martin. That exemplar of Christian charity, Malcolm Muggeridge, ex-Trotskyist friend of A. J. P. Taylor, has confessed that he couldn't stand the physical proximity of Kingsley Martin. I couldn't stand his intellectual odour. He was not a bad man, but he was inside out and upside down; whatever responsible people in the Labour Movement were or thought or did, they were always wrong. During the whole period of the Labour Government of 1945–51 there was hardly ever a decent word for it in this organ of the Left Intellectuals. No wonder Ernest Bevin—indeed all responsible Labour people —have such contempt for them. *They were useless*—and worse, malicious and venomous. (They are still at it today.) What an immature Labour Movement needed above all was responsible, sane leadership from its educated element; *then*, when there was something that needed criticism, the criticism could be taken seriously and taken notice of. Instead of that, the Labour Party got—Kingsley Martin and the fatuities of the *New Statesman*. They are no better today. Quite a number of my friends, reliable Labour men, ceased to take it or read it.

So, good Party man as I was, I was never a *New Statesman* type; from early days I reviewed fairly regularly in the *Spectator*.

Richard concluded, 'I think the best thing you can do for Woodward from me this time is to ask how his research is getting on.' This was naughty, for in fact it was not very advanced and not very profound: he was engaged in writing *Three Studies in European Conservatism*, and lightweight pieces like another notorious historical essayist at Oxford today. However, in his case, the heavyweight research was eventually achieved—unlike the other case that comes readily to mind, who should be setting a better example. Here was Richard, turning his back on youthful frivolities, beginning on the tremendous labours that made him the best authority on the eighteenth century in England. And after the horror of the election of 1931, I was to follow him in the treadmill of the public records—P.R.O. and B.M.—for years.

He reproached me for my silence: 'Do you feel no shame that I am reduced to hearing snatches of Common Room conversation through Pares [a brother] and Lady P. [his mother]. She is my Invisible Eye; sends me all the inept cuttings and University news, and even your own table talk.'

Of course I should have written to dear Richard—it was very remiss of me; but it is fairly obvious that I could not keep pace with it all. His letter serves to illustrate the interests of mind—and the manner of writing—of the clever young Fellows of All Souls of the time. Here was another, perhaps the most remarkable of them all and, like Richard, another Wykehamist: Penderel Moon. (In those inter-war years the Wykehamists formed the largest element in college, as before the 1914 war the Etonians had done.) Here was Moon writing to me at this time from India.

Out here there is nothing to mark the passage of time. Even the landscape seems unchanged with the changing of the seasons. As I look out from my window [in Jullundur City, Punjab], the same prospect greets me as did three months ago—cactuses, old bricks, a few vultures and some hesitant and brownish grass ... I have an uneasy suspicion that this famous heat may prove a bit of a frost. I notice however a curious stillness and even a sombreness stealing over the world at about 3.30 p.m., as if everyone was sleeping the sleep of imperfect digestion—as, I fear, many are. I still retain a respectable exuberance of spirits. But who knows what transformation three years in this country may effect.

He was to spend the greater part of his working life dedicated to the interests of the Indian people, increasingly in sympathy with their aspirations, and all the while living the life of absolute service to the country, in accordance with the high moral ideal he had always possessed, fortified by his discipleship of that absolute moralist, the celebrated Joseph of New College (whom I didn't much hold with). Joseph was of a bleak austerity; but one notices young Moon's exuberant spirits, which he always retained undaunted, his good humour, and—not to mark too much of a contrast with the very German Adam—Moon's humour. Richard possessed it, too.

Here was Moon at work: having to do part of the work of Deputy Commissioner not yet arrived, take his qualifying examination,

> and above all there has been this really remarkable plague of locusts. I've been directing operations throughout the whole district and have been enjoying it. In the midst of all this political turmoil which bulks so large in our thoughts, it has been pleasant to escape every morning and evening into the villages, where the services of the British officers are still appreciated, and the people so obviously grateful for one's efforts. But it has all been very tiring physically, riding very often 6 or 7 hours a day often amid great heat, besides keeping my other work going.

One observes the climatic amenities of Empire—white ants in Jamaica for Richard, locusts in India for Moon. There follows in more detail than I can quote this young man's estimate of the political situation from ground level. He was coming to the view that 'all this unrest is not the mere froth of an idle and insignificant intelligentsia; what we are up against is *essentially a mass movement*. I can't help thinking that Irwin [later Lord Halifax], or his advisers, failed to recognize this, and seriously underestimated the strength of the Congress Party.' Moon goes on to depict the situation in his district, from which he was being moved to the crisis centre of ill-omened Amritsar. He arrived there

> to find a complete 'hartal' (strike) in progress and no conveyance of any kind to be had at the station. So I was perforce obliged to walk to the Deputy Commissioner's house with such air of dignity and unconcern as I could

command. As I stalked solitarily and somewhat ridiculously
up the road, to the evident satisfaction of the bystanders, I
felt the position to be one to which you would have been
admirably adapted. I can picture you beneath that broad-
brimmed hat of yours, 'pallidus et ferus', taking your con-
temptuous way along the street.

It seems that, as for Keith Hancock so for Moon, I had entered
into negotiations with the *New Statesman* for occasional articles
from the latter on the Indian situation; but there were difficulties—
an official would have to have what he wrote censored. I am
surprised to find what an operator I was—almost a contacts
man: Lionel Curtis was a genius at that, and that was what
Adam's real gift was too.

Moon was as avid for college news—that fascinating society
for young men—as Richard was. 'I see that Archie has left us;
does he however still drop in and face Cruttwell at lunch?' This
was Archie Campbell, one of Auden's lifelong friends, who had
crossed the High—now one of the most perilous journeys in the
world—to become a law don at University College. 'How queer
about Hudson'—I forget what amiable eccentricity of Geoffrey's
this referred to. 'I have met several Bohemian and volatile friends
of his since leaving England.' These would be Archie Lyell,
Denis Kincaid and Robert Byron. 'I had a fine ride with the
GURU [the local holy man] on an elephant the other day. The
Guru's supposed mother has presented me with a photo of it all;
there we are in the midst of a sort of royal procession, I myself
looking about 15.' This was about what he did look like for many
years, extraordinarily spare and lithe and young.

'Are you devoting July to your constituency? Sir John Maynard,
your erstwhile rival, was a great man out here.' I had forgotten
that he was my competitor as Labour candidate for Penryn and
Falmouth that summer, and that I had defeated him, though sent
down to us by the Party Headquarters. Perhaps this was a mistake.
'I can't tell you how I miss you. My barren mind is, left to itself,
becoming a terrible scene of desolation.'

Such were, and such were the interests of mind of, my 'Younger
Generation' on the threshold of the deplorable, the disgraceful
1930s that ruined our hopes and, in the event, ruined Britain.

Index

313